Printing in Plastic

Build Your Own 3D Printer

Patrick Hood-Daniel

James Floyd Kelly

Apress®

Printing in Plastic: Build Your Own 3D Printer

ISBN-13 (pbk): 978-1-4302-3443-2

ISBN-13 (electronic): 978-1-4302-3444-9

President and Publisher: Paul Manning
Lead Editor: Jonathan Gennick
Technical Reviewer: Tony Buser, Darrell Kelly
Editorial Board: Steve Anglin, Mark Beckner, Ewan Buckingham, Gary Cornell, Jonathan Gennick, Jonathan Hassell, Michelle Lowman, James Markham, Matthew Moodie, Jeff Olson, Jeffrey Pepper, Frank Pohlmann, Douglas Pundick, Ben Renow-Clarke, Dominic Shakeshaft, Matt Wade, Tom Welsh
Coordinating Editor: Kelly Moritz
Copy Editor: Mary Behr
Production Support: Patrick Cunningham
Indexer: BIM Indexing & Proofreading Services
Cover Designer: Anna Ishchenko

Distributed to the book trade worldwide by Springer Science+Business Media, LLC., 233 Spring Street, 6th Floor, New York, NY 10013. Phone 1-800-SPRINGER, fax (201) 348-4505, e-mail orders-ny@springer-sbm.com, or visit www.springeronline.com.

For information on translations, please e-mail rights@apress.com, or visit www.apress.com.

Apress and friends of ED books may be purchased in bulk for academic, corporate, or promotional use. eBook versions and licenses are also available for most titles. For more information, reference our Special Bulk Sales–eBook Licensing web page at www.apress.com/bulk-sales.

JFK: For Decker and Sawyer—we're gonna have some fun!

PHD: I would like to thank my family, especially Ana, my wife, for enduring my insanity during the development of this 3D printer project.

Contents at a Glance

Contents

About the Authors

Patrick Hood-Daniel's interest in technology started in 1979 at the age of 11 when his father bought him his first computer, the TRS-80 Model 1 Level 1. Patrick's first program was a 3D CAD program written for the Model 4, a more advanced computer featuring much better graphics capability. Patrick continued to develop this and many programs for the IBM XT and 286 computers; he started programming professionally after graduating high school. Knowing that he needed some formal education to continue designing and developing visually stimulating subject matter, Patrick began his university career at a community college in Tampa, Florida, graduating with honors; he immediately transferred to the University of Miami to study Architecture and Urban Design under the great minds of New Urbanism, graduating again with honors and receiving the Henry Adams Medal for excellence. Patrick then focused on assisting the development of the many buildings being built in the Miami area with the City of Miami Planning Department. He also pursued a Master's degree from the University of California; upon graduation, he began work with Downtown Houston as the Director of Planning, Urban Design and Development. Patrick also developed embedded systems for robotics plus linear motion mechanics and control systems for CNC and related developments. Patrick has a strong desire to disseminate this information, so he created buildyourcnc.com and newbiehack.com; he shares ideas with others at buildyourtools.com. Patrick has interests in personal fabrication with CNC, 3D printing, laser cutting and engraving, PCB manufacturing, and various other forms of robotics. With a desire to continue his knowledge of computer programming, Patrick is still learning and providing solutions under C# and WPF to clients.

James Floyd Kelly is a writer from Atlanta, Georgia. He has written books on a wide variety of subjects, including Open Source software, LEGO robotics, and various tablet devices, as well as a book detailing how to build a CNC machine (with Patrick Hood-Daniel). James has an English degree from The University of West Florida and an Industrial Engineering degree from Florida State University. He has an extremely patient and understanding wife who is concerned that their two sons will also develop a strong interest in tools and tinkering.

About the Technical Reviewers

Tony Buser began his technology career in 1995 by writing HTML code. From there, he moved into web site and intranet application development and now works as a web developer for MakerBot Industries in Brooklyn, NY. Tony loves turning virtual digital information into physical reality, and he believes that the affordable and easy-to-use 3D printing and personal fabrication technology might very well be the most significant new technology since the World Wide Web. He is excited to be a part of its development at such an early stage and can typically be found spending untold hours in his basement workshop in Reading, PA with his four 3D printers: two Makerbots, a RepRap, and a whiteAnt. And he's always building more.

Dr. Darrell A. Kelly, (PhD, Chemistry) is an avid tinkerer and DIYer. A retired chemist with over 30 years at Monsanto/Solutia, he now divides his time between teaching chemistry part time at Pensacola State College and tinkering in his workshop building toy trains, 3D printers, CNC machines, and other "special projects" that his son, co-author James Floyd, somehow manages to talk him into joining.

Acknowledgments

Writing a book isn't easy. Writing a book that require readers to cut wood, drill holes, wire up electronics, and install software? If you listen carefully, you can almost hear the Mission Impossible theme song. What would have been (should have been) an impossible task was made possible thanks to a large collection of folks that, fortunately, lent their time and talents to make this book a reality.

First and foremost is the Apress staff. Like an acceptance speech, we worry we'll overlook someone, so we'll start by thanking Apress as a whole for giving this book the green light. There are dozens of folks at Apress who work behind the scenes to publish great books and you can read a complete list of their names a few pages earlier.

But we want to offer up special thanks to the following individuals who have simply gone above and beyond what was expected.

Thank you, Jonathan Gennick, for your excitement and interest when we pitched the idea. You stuck with us, asked the right questions, and pushed for the right content.

Thank you, Kelly Moritz! Kelly should get hazard pay for this book; long days, long nights, hundreds of e-mails, many phone calls, and two authors to deal with as well as two technical editors. Kelly, you are awesome.

Thanks you, Dominic Shakeshaft. Somehow you developed amnesia about the *Build Your Own CNC Machine* book and allowed us to pitch the *Build Your Own 3D Printer* book. Dominic, we have this idea for a third book…

We had two technical editors for this book and this, although not typical, made our jobs easier by having two pairs of eyes checking and re-checking our work: Darrell Kelly (James Floyd's dad) and Tony Buser. We've not been given enough pages to properly thank these two for building their own 3D printers and providing essential feeback about the process. We'd just like the two of them to know that their hard work is appreciated and their offered help is more than we can ever repay. (And Tony's been making quite a name for himself in the 3D printing community, so be sure to follow him on Twitter or check out his blog at tonybuser.com where he posts all sorts of stuff (videos, photos, commentary) related to 3D printing.)

Introduction

The book you're holding in your hands is going to show you how to build your very own 3D Printer. It's not science fiction. It's a device that will allow you to print out (in plastic) whatever you can imagine. (Okay, that's a bit of a stretch – there are size limitations when using this machine.)

Read the book – build the machine – print stuff that you can actually hold in your hands, use for prototyping your own inventions and replacing worn out parts, and basically taking something in your mind (or at least on a computer screen) and make it real. Congratulations – you've got a little bit of science fiction sitting on your desk.

What Exactly Do I Get?

You've obviously picked the book up and we can only hope you've read the cover – "Printing in Plastic: Build Your Own 3D Printer." It's not too difficult to guess what the book is about, is it? Well, if you're still a bit confused, let's clear it up right here by giving you the most basic explanation of what this book is going to teach you… and here it is:

You are going to be provided with the building plans, a list of required supplies and tools, and step-by-step instructions to cut, drill, assemble, and wire-up your very own machine that prints in plastic. But wait! There's more!

You are also going to be provided with instructions on how to connect your new machine to a computer so that you can print out (in plastic) things you design using freely available software. But if you act now, we'll also throw in a few bonus items!

We'll not only cover the software and how to use it in the book, we'll also provide you with some sample items to print with your machine so that you can test it and show off your 3D objects to your friends and family.

As a Thank You Bonus for purchasing the book, we'll also be providing you with a great website and forum where you can post questions, share pictures, and learn how to push your machine's capabilities even further.

Does that sound good? Do you want one? Are you ready to start?

Welcome to the Future!

Take a look at Figure I-1. If you've got the time, some patience, and, let's face it, some spending money, that little bit of the future can be yours. Your very own three-dimensional printer!

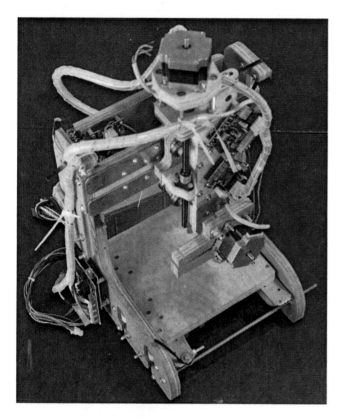

Figure I-1. *Your very own 3D Printer.*

If you take this book and follow its instructions, you'll end up with your very own three-dimensional printer, sitting on your desk or worktable, connected to a computer, and capable of printing (again, in plastic) whatever you can come up with and design (using some specialized software).

What kind of stuff might you want to print? Well, the first thing you need to know is that whatever you print, it isn't going to be very large. Look back at Figure I-1 and you'll notice that the device isn't that large to begin with – so you won't be printing dining room chairs or the world's first all-plastic Zamboni. Nope – think smaller. Keychain dongles. Coat hooks. A replacement side mirror for your child's horribly damaged remote control car. A bobble-head figurine of your spouse. A small 3x5 picture frame. Drink coasters customized with your family crest. Small stuff, okay?

Not feeling creative? That's okay – you can also print out designs from others. If someone has created the perfect little plastic army man figure and shared it on the Internet with the world, go ahead and download it and print it. Print sixteen and have your own little platoon on your bookshelf! Or modify the design a bit if you're feeling experimental. You really can't go wrong here.

No, you can't use it to make coffee. No, it won't print a medium-rare steak. And, no… it won't fabricate a solid-metal replacement gear for your fishing rod. 3D printers like this one are machines in their infancy, with the same expectations a parent might have for a child – in time, it'll grow up, be able to perform more advanced tasks, and, attend a good college (okay, maybe not that last part, but we promise you'll definitely be seeing these on campuses in the future).

Good science fiction always feels plausible – as if the future is just around the corner. We may not have all the Wonder Devices from books, TV, and movies, but we're on our way. In the future, people will tell a computer what they want and a magical machine will provide it. But getting to the future seems to always take small steps. And that's exactly what this book is about – small steps. Building your own 3D Printer is your first step (later steps include having your printer print out its own replacement parts or even upgraded parts to turn it into a more capable 3D printer) to having a bit of the future in your own home or office – a machine that prints what you request from it.

Welcome to the future – we hope you like it.

Patrick Hood-Daniel
James Floyd Kelly

CHAPTER 1

Before You Begin

Look at the cover of this book again. What is that unusual looking device pictured there? Yes, it's a 3D printer, but what exactly does that mean?

This chapter will tell you. We're not going to bore you with a lot of techno mumbo-jumbo or a complete machine-by-machine history of how we got here; you can find all that on `Wikipedia.com` or another web site. Instead, this chapter will provide a simple (and short) discussion on what this device is, what it does best, how it works (again, in simple terminology), and how to proceed through the following chapters to begin building your own 3D printer.

What is a 3D Printer?

Let's start with the easiest part first: the word "printer." For most people, the term *printer* is fairly obvious. It's a small, medium, or large device that folks use to create a hard copy (i.e. paper) of their digital files (Word documents, photos, brochures, PDF files, Internet receipts for online purchases, web articles, and more). Printers come in a variety of shapes and sizes; there are several methods of putting ink to paper.

The two most common printer technologies used today are referred to as ink jet and laser. An ink jet sprays a bit of ink (black or color) on the paper, and after a few seconds, spits out the latest chapter of your novel, the report your boss wanted ten minutes ago, or directions to the nearest computer repair shop. Laser printers use a different, more complicated method of applying an electric charge to a round drum that picks up toner (a laser printer's "ink") and then applies that toner to a page.

Ink jet and laser printers print on flat paper. The output of these devices is two-dimensional. Paper has a length and a width. A standard paper size in the U.S. is referred to as 8.5" x 11"; this means the paper is 8.5 inches wide and 11 inches long. Technically, paper does have a third dimension, thickness (or height), but we're not going to worry about that right now; paper is thin enough that we'll be safe referring to it as a 2D. Figure 1-1 shows a piece of 8.5 x 11 paper. We are limited to applying ink on this paper in four directions: left, right, towards the top, and towards the bottom.

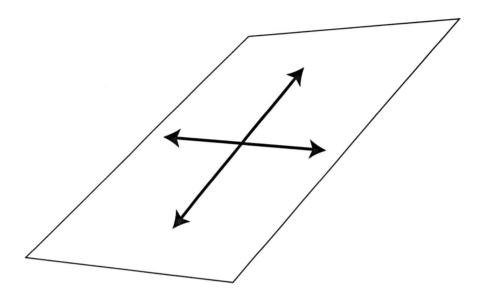

Figure 1-1. *Ink and paper allow for only two-dimensional printing.*

So, knowing that an ink jet or laser printer creates 2D output, we can hazard a guess that a 3D printer would print in that third dimension: up off the paper!

But ink doesn't stack well. Yes, ink can build up (you can run your fingers over some types of paper and feel the ink), but it doesn't come up and off the piece of paper high enough to be noticeable. If 3D printing is to be truly possible, it needs to substitute ink for some other material that will *stack* or *build up* in layers.

One of the materials that can be printed in the third dimension is plastic. The term "plastic" covers a wide variety of materials and is considered to be a generic term, so we'll get a bit more specific a little later in book. For now, let's define the 3D printer as a device that can apply melted plastic (that cools down and hardens) in all three dimensions on a flat surface: left and right on the surface, up and down on the surface, and vertically going upwards away from the surface. (Yes, down should be allowable, but since we're dealing with a device that applies melted plastic to a work surface, the only direction we can really go is up, away from the surface.)

Take a look at Figure 1-2. Instead of ink, plastic would allow us to print up from a flat surface, creating three-dimensional output. The 3D printer applies the plastic in layers that build up, creating the 3D effect. Layering is the method used by a 3D printer to turn a two-dimensional object into a three-dimensional one.

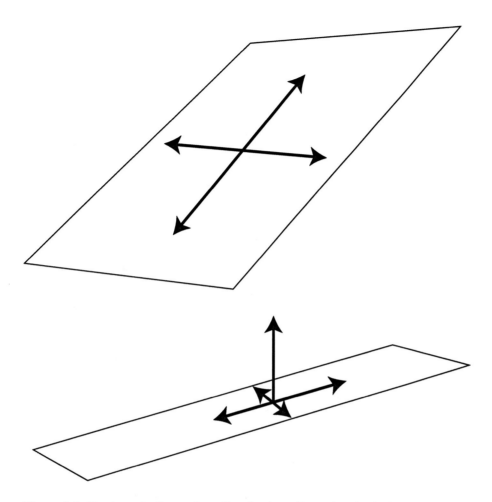

Figure 1-2. Plastic and a flat surface allow for three dimensional printing.

Are you starting to understand what a 3D printer can do? Sure, you can use it to print TOP SECRET in two inch tall letters on a piece of paper, but let's move away from the idea of printing words in 3D and consider other options. Printing in plastic will allow you to print all sorts of things in 3D that would otherwise have to be represented in a 2D drawing. You could print a replacement gear for the one that cracked in that little wind-up robot toy. Or how about a set of buttons (using colored plastic that is readily available) to give your favorite jacket a new look? And yes, you could even print yourself a plastic mug or teacup. The possibilities are exciting.

There are some advanced uses for a 3D printer as well. A jeweler could print some small medallions (in plastic) to use as molds for custom silver jewelry. An inventor might use a 3D printer to create an inexpensive prototype of a handle for a new screwdriver, testing it in plastic first to make certain the design feels comfortable. A robotics hobbyist would find a 3D printer useful for printing out small gears or wheels that are unique in size or shape and can't be purchased in stores. The list doesn't end, and it's likely you have your own ideas for how you might use a 3D printer.

But simply having this device on your desk isn't enough. It's not going to magically read your mind and print out the plastic object you need. A 3D printer is a computer-controlled device and therefore must be connected to your computer to do its job. And in order to actually get the 3D printer to print something, you'll need to install some special software on that computer, which will be covered later in the book.

Questions and Build Help

We have tried to include everything that you will need to know and buy to build your own 3D printer in the pages of this book. But we can't predict every question that a reader might have. And, to be honest, it's not unknown for technical errors to creep into a book of this nature. We've done our best to have multiple sets of eyes go over the material. We've also had multiple editors build the machine—more than 4 in all! (Patrick Hood-Daniel has built several machines, James Floyd Kelly built one, and Darrell Kelly and Tony Buser (the book's tech editors) have also each built their own machine.)

Even knowing that the machine works properly if assembled correctly, you may still have questions. That's okay. There is a web site managed by Patrick that hosts a variety of videos and files plus a discussion forum. Readers can log in to the forum, post questions (or read other questions), and find answers. We encourage readers to not only post questions but to submit pictures and notes about their own experiences building the machine (and maybe even modifying it).

You can find everything related to the 3D printer in this book at `www.buildyourtools.com`. Post your questions there and you'll likely receive some fast responses from the growing 3D printer community.

The 3D Printer is Evolving

This book took over five months to complete; late into the book's progress an occasional change was made to the machine, requiring some of the chapters to be updated. For example, we discovered that some of the electronics used were going to be retired. We were able to update previous chapters with the new information.

But as a book gets closer to the final deadline, it becomes difficult to go back and retro-fit changes or update information. There were some discoveries that we couldn't add to the appropriate chapters, so we're including an Addendum chapter at the end of the book; this chapter will contain the latest comments and notes regarding the build. For instance, late in the project, we found that shaving a small notch off of a key part would allow the Plastic Extruder (the piece of the machine that does the plastic printing) to be held more firmly in place; this information has been added to the Addendum because, although it's not required, it adds an improvement to this machine that we would otherwise not have been able to offer to you so late into the book's writing.

We recommend that you read the entire book front-to-back before beginning the project. We especially recommend that you review the Addendum.

Videos, Building Instructions, and Parts

Again, we'd like to direct your attention to the book's web site at `www.buildyourtools.com` where you'll find the building instructions (as PDF files) that you will use to cut and drill all the plywood pieces that make up the 3D printer.

You'll also find videos that Patrick has filmed to show how to assemble the 3D printer, mount all the electronics, and install and configure the software used to print out 3D models. These videos don't go into the level of detail found in the book, but they offer Patrick's helpful commentary; also, seeing the construction can assist you during your own machine's assembly.

You'll also be able to purchase pre-cut and pre-drilled components for the machine should you decide not to tackle cutting and drilling your own plywood pieces. The parts sold on the web site are cut and drilled using a CNC machine, reducing human error when it comes to measuring, cutting, and drilling. The web site will also sell most, if not all, of the electronics components. Right now, most of the electronics must be bought from third party sources such as Makerbot.com or other electronics suppliers; that will change (or may have changed by the time you read this), making www.buildyourtools.com your one-stop source for everything you need to build a 3D printer.

We Want to Hear from You

We love to get feedback (we like the praise better, but we understand that there are occasional gripes). Visit the book's web site at www.buildyourtools.com and let us know what you think of the book, of the 3D printer (Patrick's name for it is WhiteAnt; he gives all the machines he develops names), and of your results.

3D printers are a new game for DIYers; these machines are still in their infancy, so keep that in mind as you use your device. Your 3D Printer is designed to allow for upgrades (to the motors, circuit boards, and more) as you'll likely find yourself wanting to make changes over time if you really get into the 3D printing hobby. You'll find a strong community of hobbyists and companies (such as Makerbot) sharing what they know, creating new products, and just pushing the 3D printing hobby further.

We wish you luck as you start down the path to building your own 3D printer!

CHAPTER 2

■ ■ ■

Hardware and Tools

Unlike a lot of DIY projects, the 3D Printer you're going to build isn't going to require a large number of tools, just those that can cut the structure of the machine from plywood and drill the holes for bolting parts together. (The electronics portion of the build will be covered in later chapters, along with any specialized tools that you may need.)

Caution As with any project that requires tools, we want to issue the standard warnings and recommendations: read the manuals, handle all tools with care and respect, and never rush things.

If you're unfamiliar with the proper usage of a power tool, find the manual and read it, or ask someone knowledgeable for assistance. Also remember that the Internet is your friend. If you've lost a manual, you can probably find it on the manufacturer's web site as a downloadable PDF file. There are also videos galore (on sites like www.YouTube.com) that provide tutorials on how to use tools properly—maybe even the exact tool you're using.

Tools are dangerous if you don't respect them. With parts that move at hundreds or thousands of RPMs (revolutions per minute), your eyes and fingers and other body parts are no match for power tools. Wear goggles (get in the habit of putting them on anytime you enter your work area) and always be aware of where your hands and fingers are with respect to the business ends of power tools.

And finally, this isn't a race. Yes, we know you're anxious to build and finish your 3D Printer. But take your time. Working with a table saw, for example, is much faster than using a handsaw. But table saws are hundreds of times more likely to remove a finger than a handsaw (where you're holding the tool in one hand and the part to be cut with the other). The benefits of power tools are, of course, power and speed and accuracy, so balance these out with a good bit of patience and awareness of what you're doing and, most importantly, where your fingers are located.

Respect the tools you're using, and you won't be one of the over 175,000 people who end up in the Emergency Room each year from improper power tool usage. We're not trying to scare you away from building a 3D Printer, but we hope we've convinced you to spend some time learning how to properly use the required tools.

And what tools are those? Glad you asked.

The Power Tools

We're going to list the tools you need for this project, but keep in mind that when it comes to tools, there seems to always be something better in someone else's garage. If you've got a handsaw, your best friend probably has a circular saw. And his neighbor probably has table saw. The grass is always greener, right?

As you review the list of tools, keep in mind the following things:

- *It's often not wise to purchase a tool for just one project.* Purchase a tool if you believe it will benefit you with the 3D Printer project plus future projects down the road. (That said, your authors tend to follow the motto of *You can never have too many tools.*)

- *Consider tool rental.* Given that a good table saw can run $300 to $2000, depending on features and name brand, you may want to consider one of the many tool rental companies. For instance, you can rent a table saw for $50 to $75 per day (or less). The only caveat is you'll need to go pick it up and bring it back, so bring a buddy as they tend to be heavy. (And don't forget to ask for the operations manual. If they don't provide one, find another rental company.)

- *There's nothing wrong with asking to borrow a tool.* We all have friends who have a nice assortment of power and hand tools in their workshop or garage. Invite the tool owner over and show them what you're building; you may find they'd like to build one, too, so your tools borrowing is no longer an issue!

- *But don't be offended if the answer is no.* One of the authors (JFK) is very resistant to loaning out his tools after a bad experience a few years back when a semi-expensive hand sander was dropped by a borrower. Many tool owners are just as protective of their investments.

- Always clean a borrowed tool before returning it. It's just good manners.

So, with all that said, here are the tools that will be beneficial to your project. Some are absolutely required, others are recommended, and others are not necessary except for possibly adding some finesse or flair to the final look of your 3D Printer (also referred to as 3DP).

Table Saw

Can you cut out the 3D Printer parts from plywood with a handsaw? Sure you can. But the real question is should you use a handsaw? Probably not. The 3DP has some wood parts that require some fairly accurate cuts in order for parts to either match up or mate properly with other parts.

Using a handsaw inevitably leaves an uneven cut line. You could use something like a belt sander to smooth down the cut line, but you also risk taking away too much of the wood and reducing a measurement (such as a width or length).

We recommend using a table saw, as seen in Figure 2-1. Table saws come in a variety of designs with names like Contractor Saw, Benchtop, Cabinet, and Hybrid. (If you want to learn more, visit `http://en.wikipedia.org/wiki/Table_saw` for a breakdown of features as well as pros and cons.)

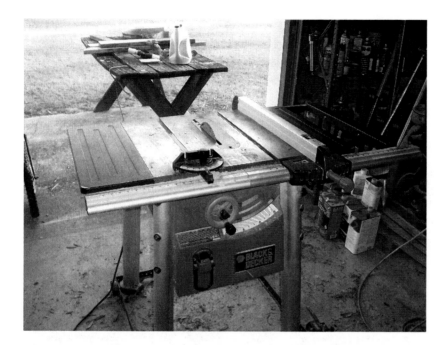

Figure 2-1. *A table saw will make the accurate cuts needed for the 3DP.*

A table saw will allow you to cut some of the longer edges needed with more accuracy and a smoother cut surface. Make certain when you're using the saw fence that your cut will be square.

░ **Note** A good way to ensure that a cut part will be square is to simply measure before cutting. Measure the distance from the front of the saw blade to the fence. Then measure from the back of the saw blade to the fence. Check to be sure that both measurements are the same. If they are, then your fence is square. If not, then at least you know about the problem before making a cut.

Some of the parts used in the 3DP have a matching component (such as a left side and a right side piece), and a table saw with a cutting fence will allow you to cut duplicate parts with matching dimensions easily. Once you set the distance between the fence and the blade, you can be reasonably confident that a second piece will match the first piece in at least one dimension (length or width).

Are there options if you don't have access to a table saw? Yes. You can use a circular saw with the proper type of cutting blade (for plywood) like the one in Figure 2-2. Make certain that you clamp a level or other straight edge to the piece that you plan to cut to guide the circular saw. And if you're not completely familiar with circular saws, you should know that the best way to cut with them is to use a pair of saw horses, otherwise you cut into any material beneath the piece you're cutting.

■ **Note** You can also lay a sheet of foam insulation underneath a piece that you plan to cut using a circular saw. You can read more about this method at `www.woodworkingtips.com/etips/etip010810sn.html`.

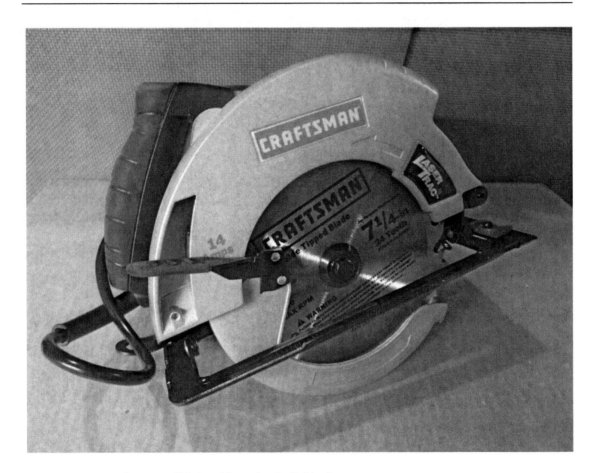

Figure 2-2. A circular saw will help with cutting individual parts.

Keep in mind, however, that a circular saw or table saw won't be helpful with cutting some of the smaller, more detailed parts like the indentations seen on the building plan sheet in Figure 2-3. For the notches that are cut into a piece, you'll need a different tool.

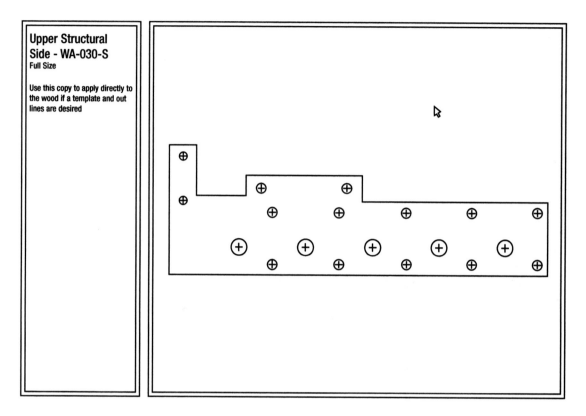

Figure 2-3. Some parts have cuts that can't be made by table saws or circular saws.

Bandsaw or Scroll saw

A bandsaw or scroll saw (see Figure 2-4) can be useful tools to have but are by no means required. They are helpful in making intricate cuts such as inside corners. They are also helpful in cutting notches because bandsaws and scroll saws give the straight up and down cuts that you need for that purpose.

Figure 2-4. A bandsaw or scroll saw can be useful for cutting ninety degree corners.

If you examine the building plans, you'll notice that parts cut do not have curves and angles; all cuts are right angle cuts. Some of those cuts (like the one seen in Figure 2-3) can be a bit tricky, and that's where a bandsaw comes in. Its small blade can get into corners and handle notches. But even a bandsaw or scroll saw has limits: because of the way the blade cuts and how you feed the piece into the blade, you'll be forced to curve the piece as the blade moves toward a corner. This will result in a small curve instead of a sharp ninety degree corner. If you look at the building plans in Figure 2-5, you can see that the notch has a crisp ninety degree corner.

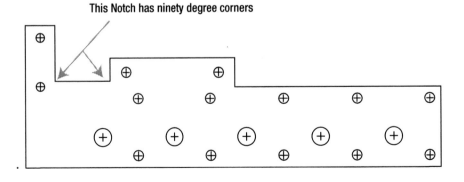

Figure 2-5. The building plan shows notches with crisp ninety degree corners.

But take a look at the actual notch made with a bandsaw in Figure 2-6. See how the corner has a slight curve to it? In order to remove that curve and get a tight ninety-degree corner, you'll have to make many cuts (passes) to carve out the waste material until you achieve the ninety-degree corner.

Figure 2-6. A bandsaw can cut ninety degree corners after multiple passes.

So if a bandsaw or scroll saw can't cut a sharp ninety degree corner in one pass, how do you fix this issue? There are a few options. The first is that for some of the notches, having a perfect ninety degree corner simply doesn't matter. When it does matter, you can use something like a scroll saw (also known as a sabre saw or jigsaw), as seen in Figure 2-7.

Figure 2-7. A jigsaw can help remove material in corners.

A jigsaw is useful for cutting into a corner and removing wood a bit at a time. Scroll saws typically run between $50 and $200 and rental companies tend to rent them out at $25 per day. This is one of those tools where buying may be better than renting, however, especially if you plan on taking more than one day to cut out all the parts.

If you don't have access to a scroll saw, there is another option we can recommend, but it can be tedious. A coping saw (Figure 2-8) will allow you to make ninety degree cuts over multiple passes, but it is time-consuming and tiring.

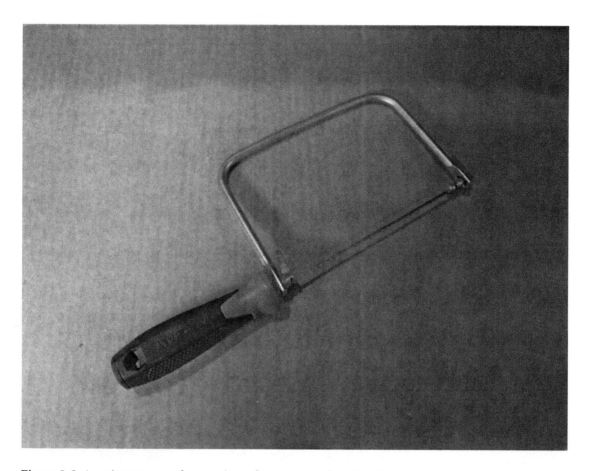

Figure 2-8. A coping saw can also cut ninety degree corners but it's a slow process.

You'll be cutting a total of seventeen wood pieces to build your 3D printer. In addition to cutting these pieces, you'll also be drilling holes in them for mating with other wood parts or to bolt on other objects (such as motors or rail). For the drilling, you'll need a combination of tools and specialty bits.

■ **Note** There are many cuts shown in the plans that don't have to be perfect ninety degree cuts. We'll do our best to point out what cuts require precision and when it's not as important. Take care to read over the building plans as well. You'll see that there are many opportunities to apply curved cuts in corners (and on edges) to make the parts more aesthetically pleasing. The building plans often show a version of a part with some curves applied to it. Rest assured, we'll let you know when you can apply a little artistic flair to a part and when you need to be precise when making a cut.

Drill Press

Hands down, one of the most useful tools for building your 3D printer will be the drill press (Figure 2-9). There are a lot of holes to drill into the plywood parts, and a drill press can help you drill these holes accurately.

Figure 2-9. *A drill press will be an extremely useful tool for the 3D printer project.*

You can find inexpensive drill presses for around $80 to $100; the more expensive versions can run up to $400 or more. If you're considering renting, look to pay around $50 to $75 per day.

You may be wondering whether you can drill these holes with your typical electric hand drill (or battery powered drill) like the one in Figure 2-10.

Figure 2-10. *Using an electric or battery powered drill is possible but not recommended.*

Yes, you can drill the holes, but we don't recommend it. The holes you will drill need to be perpendicular to the surface of the parts. Using a hand drill can be tricky when it comes to making certain the holes are drilled straight down into the plywood material.

If your only option is a hand drill, you might consider purchasing (or renting, if you can find one) a portable drill press like the one in Figure 2-11.

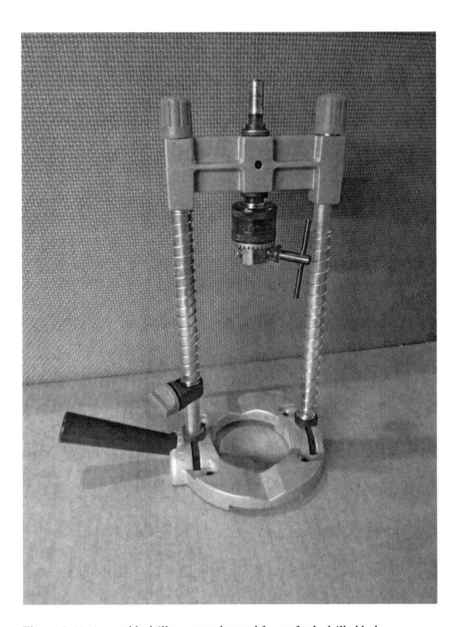

Figure 2-11. *A portable drill press can be used for perfectly drilled holes.*

The portable drill press will at least allow you to drill perfectly straight holes into the plywood. It can be a bit finicky if it's not clamped down properly to a work surface, but using one is much better than trying to drill all these holes by hand.

Some Hand Tools

We've just provided you with the list of power tools that you'll need to get the parts cut and drilled for the 3D printer. There are also some hand tools that you'll need or that can make your job a little easier.

Rulers

For measuring out the cuts and drill points you'll be making, a basic ruler and tape measure will be handy. But there are some cuts and drill points that require more accuracy than a standard ruler with 1/16" increments can provide. If you can find a special carpentry ruler with 1/32" increments, your cutting and drilling will be much more accurate and the machine's overall assembly will go more smoothly.

Figure 2-12 shows a special Incra ruler that allows you to insert a pencil point and mark the wood in 1/64th of an inch. You'll need 0.5mm pencils for the small holes, so buy a bunch. The metal block on the end also allows for extremely straight lines to be drawn along the edges of the ruler. And if you insert the fine pencil point in the various holes on the ruler, you can slide the ruler along an edge of a work piece and the pencil point will draw a line the distance you've selected from the edge.

Figure 2-12. Rulers like this Incra ruler are indispensable for fine measurements.

Whatever tool you choose for measuring and marking, pick one that gives you the best chance at marking cuts and drill points as accurately as possible.

Clamps

Ask most woodworkers and they'll tell you the same thing: you can never have too many clamps. And since clamps come in every shape, size, name, and price, the best recommendation we can make to you is to purchase them when you need them based on the job at hand.

For the 3D printer project, there are matched parts that are mirror images of one another. In these instances, it's often easier to clamp the two pieces together and drill them at the same time, ensuring that the drill holes will line up when the machine is assembled. (Many of these pieces also contain counterbores, however, so make sure when you choose to drill two pieces at a time that you drill the counterbores separately and on the proper sides specified in the plans.)

Squares

If you intend to check the straightness of the cuts on the plywood pieces, you'll definitely find a small engineer's square useful. (A larger carpenter's square will work, but since most of the parts for the 3D printer are less than 12" in length, a smaller square should be enough.)

Use a square to make certain all your parts have right angles. This will become important later in the project when you begin assembling all the plywood parts and want to ensure that the machine will operate properly and that no moving parts will rub or interfere with other components.

Screwdrivers and Wrenches

Screwdrivers and wrenches (and sockets) will be required during assembly. You'll need Slot and Philips head screwdrivers; having electric or battery operated versions of these tools will save time and require less energy on your part.

Drill Bits and Counterbore Holes

We talked about drills earlier in the chapter; now we want to explain that there are two types of hole that you will be drilling on this project. The first type of hole is a straight-through hole. You'll select the proper bit for the drill and drill a hole completely through the plywood. Straight-through holes are easy; they are the sort you've been drilling since you first learned to drill.

▨ **Note** For best results when drilling completely through a piece of plywood, we recommend placing a bit of waste wood underneath the piece you are drilling into. This waste piece will prevent splintering of the wood (forcing you to recut the piece) when the drill bit breaks through the piece you are drilling.

The second type of hole is a counterbore hole. A counterbore hole will use a larger bit (more on what kinds of bits to use in a moment) to drill a hole into the plywood a certain depth without going all the way through the plywood. You can see an example of a counterbore hole in Figure 2-13.

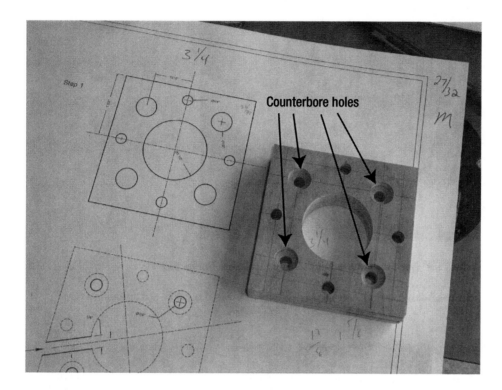

Figure 2-13. A counterbore hole does not go all the way through the plywood.

A counterbore hole is useful when you wish to bolt two pieces together without the head of the bolt sticking up. Instead, the bolt head will dip below the surface of the work piece (also known as *flush to the surface*), providing a smooth flat surface, as seen in Figure 2-14.

Figure 2-14. A bolt head inside a counterbore hole, sitting just below the surface.

Now, to drill all these holes, you can use spade drill bits or twisted bits like the ones shown in Figure 2-15.

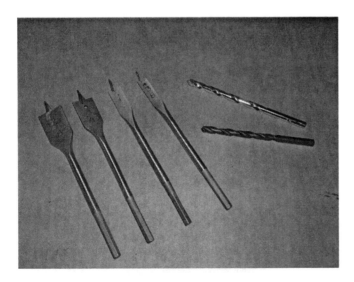

Figure 2-15. Spade drill bits (on left) and twisted bits (on right) will work for drilling straight-through and counterbore holes.

Spade and twisted drill bits will do the job, but for better results, you might consider using brad point bits (also called spur bits) for straight-through holes. Brad point bits, like the ones seen in Figure 2-16, have a sharp point on the end.

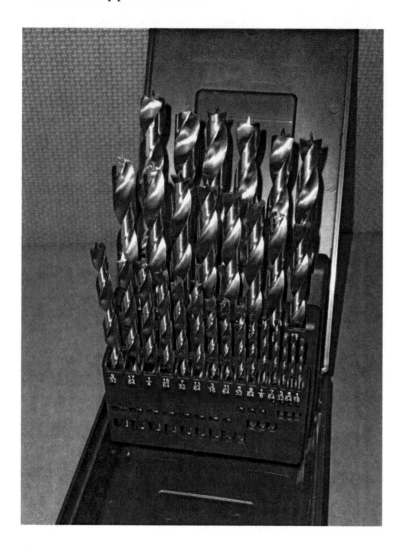

Figure 2-16. Brad point bits provide better results than space and twisted drill bits.

When you are marking your plywood pieces for drilling, we recommend using a sharp transfer punch like the ones shown in Figure 2-17 to create a small dimple to mark the centerpoint of the hole to be drilled. These transfer punches come in various diameters for inserting into previously drilled holes (match the diameter of the hole to the punch). If the fit is good, the punch will mark a dimple in the center of the hole.

Figure 2-17. A transfer punch is helpful for marking centerpoints of drill holes.

Once you've marked the centerpoints using the transfer punch, the brad point bits (with their sharp tip) will make it easier to drill on the exact centerpoint. Again, the punch and brad point bits are just a recommendation; they're not required. But we think you'll find it easier to drill accurate holes with brad point bits than standard spade or twist drill bits.

As for counterbores, you can also use standard drill bits. But we recommend the use of Forstner bits shown in Figure 2-18.

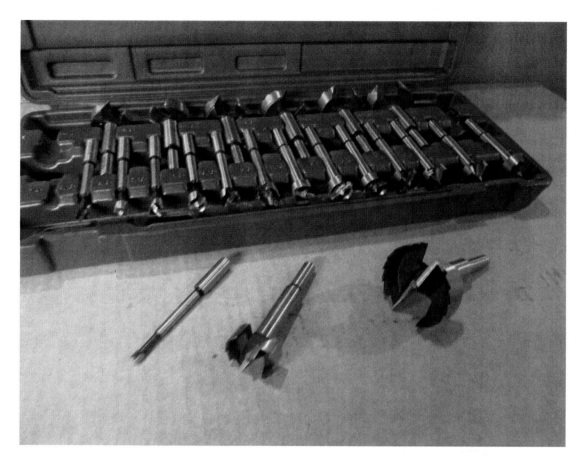

Figure 2-18. Forstner bits drill cleaner, sharper counterbore holes than standard drill bits.

Forstner bits drill extremely clean and sharp holes. You can use them for straight-through holes, as well, but the benefits of Forstner bits is that they come in much larger drilling diameters than you'll typically find with other types of bits while still fitting in a drill press or electric drill.

Whatever bits you choose to use for your drilling, keep in mind that drilled holes cannot be un-drilled. It's often easier to cut a new plywood part if you make a mistake drilling than it is to try and fix a drilling mistake. That's why we'll remind you here to always double-check with the building plans to make certain you've marked the drill points correctly. Use a transfer punch tool (if you have one) to mark a starting point for your drill bits. And always verify the diameter of the hole being drilled and select the correct diameter bit before drilling.

Summary

The list of tools you will need isn't long, but what we've listed in this chapter as the best choices will certainly make your job a little easier if you have access to them or can rent them. If you're a bit concerned because you lack access to some or all of the recommended tools, rest assured that you can cut and drill the parts needed for the 3D printer with the basic tools (such as a circular saw and jigsaw). The key is to measure and mark accurately and to take your time with the cuts and drilling.

In the upcoming chapters, we'll walk you through the cutting of each part and explain where you need to be cautious. We'll point out the key measurements and try to make it as easy as possible to duplicate our work.

Our intent with this book is to provide you with as much detail as we can on every step of the process. Cutting and drilling the parts will take some time, so *don't rush it.* Take your time. Check the building instructions often. And, if you have any questions, don't hesitate to consult the book's forum discussion and post a question (or read what others have posted—you may find your question already answered). You can find the book's forum at `www.buildyourtools.com.` Register, log in, and look for the "Build Your Own 3D Printer" discussion section.

CHAPTER 3

■ ■ ■

Tips and Advice

With any DIY project, it's always a nice bonus if you have some hints about what to expect, what kinds of bumps in the road might be ahead, and how others before you have tackled the job. We'll keep this chapter short as we know you're anxious to get to work on your 3D printer, but we don't want to get started without sharing some tips and advice we've discovered during the cutting, drilling, and other tasks required for this project.

As with any advice, you're free to ignore it. We'll tell you throughout the book how we perform certain tasks, but if you've found a better way to do something, feel free to do so—but please consider logging into the book's forum and sharing your own tips and tricks with other readers. Just as there are many tools that can be used to cut and drill the 3D printer parts, there are many methods for cutting, drilling, and wiring up your machine.

That said, we do want you to know that we did encounter the occasional roadblock, requiring us to take a step back, figure out where we wanted to be, and then find a detour to get there. We'll document as many of those throughout the book as we can, but there are some standard recommendations we can make that will hold true for the entire project that we'll point out here.

Read the Entire Book First

Yes, we know how difficult it is to slow down and read all the instructions first. We, too, always want to jump into the deep end of the pool without knowing the exact depth. But projects like this have the tendency to throw a curve ball at you here and there. (You can always just read the assembly chapters and then build the 3D printer frame, followed by the electronics chapters, and so on. But a thorough read of the entire book will help you understand the scope of the whole project.) We've tried to make the steps in this book as easy to follow and as non-technical as possible, but we cannot emphasize enough the benefits of reading through the entire book before starting on this project.

If you can take the time to read every chapter first, you'll gain a better understanding of how the machine works. You'll know which parts require more exacting cuts and which ones have some wiggle room. You'll know how the parts fit together. You'll read about options regarding the building of the machine and have time to think about those options, ask some questions, and maybe check some prices before committing.

But you'll also find one more benefit from reading the entire book before starting—you'll be less anxious about the work to come because you'll have read our experiences and looked at our results. Nothing beats having a detailed map from Point A to Point Z. (Well, that's not entirely true—many folks like the unknowns of a trip, but since you're going to be spending money, and plywood isn't very forgiving when cut or drilled improperly, you might prefer to know what's coming, right?)

It's your call, but we hope you'll keep reading. We're confident that having a solid understanding of the entire process before a single piece of wood is cut or drilled will pay off later when you're covered in sawdust.

Examine the Plans

Before you do any cutting, drilling, or assembly work, you really should invest some time in sitting down with the building instructions and examining all the parts that you'll be cutting and drilling.

There are a total of 17 parts to cut from plywood, and many of them have strange names (located in the upper-left corner of the page). If the names don't make sense, that's okay. Each part has a special function and some of those functions aren't readily apparent until you see how the machine operates as a whole.

One very important item that we wish to point out with the plans is the inclusion of a full-size template for every part. We've done our best to make certain that every part is well-documented when it comes to measurements, but if you should find a missing measurement on a sheet or suspect a measurement we've included is in error, all you need to do is grab a ruler and perform your own measurements on the full-size template. If the sheet with dimensions lists the width of a part as 9-3/4" and your measurement of the full-size template is 9-1/4", the good bet is to go with the template. (But we also suggest you visit the book's discussion forum to verify the error; more on that in a bit.)

■ **Note** If you haven't already downloaded the 3D printer building plans, point your web browser to www.buildyourtools.com and grab the zip file containing all the PDFs. After downloading the PDFs, be sure to look through the files and make certain you have all of them.

The full-size template sheets are easy to identify because they have no measurement values on them. It is even possible to secure the full-size template sheets to the plywood and use the lines and center points for all cuts and drilling of holes. We did not use this method; we chose instead to use an accurate ruler and pencil to mark out the cuts and drill holes. After a part was cut and drilled, we placed it over the full-size template image and verified that all the cuts and drill holes were accurate. Choose the method that works best for you.

Just so you have a better understanding of the difference between a sheet that provides a part's measurements and the full-size template sheet for that part, take a look at Figures 3-1 and 3-2. Figure 3-1 shows a close-up of the measurement sheet for Part K or the Z Axis Rail Support. (Figure 3-1 does not show the full PDF sheet, just a portion of it; refer to the actual sheet for more details.)

Z-Axis Rail Support - WA-070-S

Steps 1 and 2

Drill two (2) 7/16" holes at the top of the part. To permit screws to reach the cross dowels, drill two (2) crossing holes centered along the thickness of the material.

Note: No dimension is given for the edge holes as material thickness will vary.

Drill four (4) 5/16" holes on the left side of the part. Use the Strong-Tie part to mark the holes. The Strong-Tie part will be aligned along the center of the part, so use both Strong-Tie and abut them along the center.

Drill seven (7) 5/32" holes for the abutting rail to the right side. Both rails will receive #8 screws.

Drill 4 counterbores to flush the head of the screws as the rail will be mounted on the same face as the screw heads.

In Step 2, simply drill at the center of the counterbores at 1/4" diameter.

The top two holes are used for fastening the top bearing support array of 5/32" holes on the right are used to fasten the StrongTie are used for another StrongTie rail but are adjustable to press firm mounting the extruder or CNC spindle.

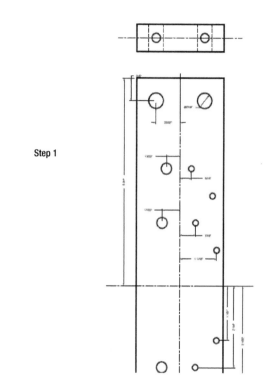

Step 1

Figure 3-1. *The measurement sheet for the Z Axis Rail Support (or Part K)*

Figure 3-2 shows the full-size template PDF file for the Z Axis Rail Support (Part K) at 50% size. When printed at full size, you can easily tape down the template to the plywood and cut and drill the part. You can also place the finished part on top of the full-size template to verify all your cuts and drill holes were made properly.

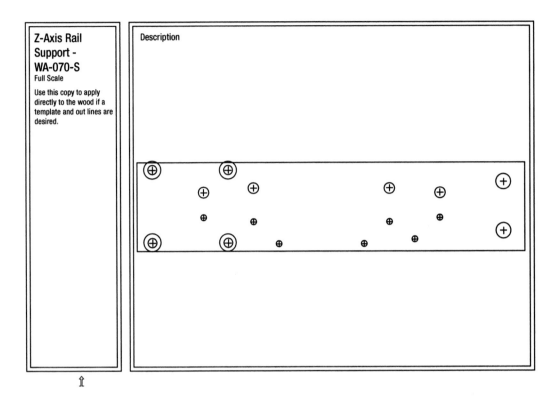

Figure 3-2. *The full-size template sheet for the Z Axis Rail Support (or Part K)*

Print the Plans at Actual Size

It is possible to reference the PDF files on your laptop to obtain all the measurements for drilling and cutting. But be kind to your eyes and make it easier on yourself by having the PDF sheets printed on 11"x17" sheets (also called tabloid). We suggest that you have them printed at a print shop like FedEx Office. Be sure to specify that the sheets are to be printed actual size with no reductions.

As stated earlier, once you have all the sheets printed out at actual size, the template sheets can be compared to the actual parts you cut and drill. This will only be successful if the PDF sheets are printed on 11"x17" paper with no reduction in size.

▪ **Note** If your printer supports printing on 11"x17" paper, printing the plans yourself is easy. Open the PDF plans in Adobe Reader and click the Print button. The print dialog box will appear (the window that allows you to choose the printer and printer options). Make sure the Page Scaling selection is set to None.

Verify All Measurements

But how can you know for certain that the sheets have printed at actual size? The easiest way is to take the measurement sheet for a part (Part K, for example, seen in Figure 3-1) and verify that two or three of the measurements printed on the measurement sheet match the measurements you obtain by placing a ruler to the full-size template sheet. If the measurement sheet says the length of Part K is 11.5", then the measurement you take with the ruler on the long edge of Part K should equal 11.5". If not, something's wrong. Either you measured incorrectly (so check again) or the template sheet is not printed at actual size.

▓ **Note** Always be consistent in how you measure. For example, if you measure from the inside of the sharp black line representing the contour of one part, measure from the inside of all the lines for other parts. Some folks will measure outside-to-outside, some inside-to-inside, and others will split the difference (which is quite hard with such a thin line on a set of building plans). Just be consistent and never be afraid to double-check a measurement.

Even if you trust that your sheets have been printed at actual size, we recommend that you verify the dimensions provided on a measurement sheet against the full-size template sheet before performing any cut or drilling operation.

Figure 3-3 shows us using our Incra rulers to verify that a dimension taken from a measurement sheet matches the actual dimension measured on the full-size template. It takes just seconds to do but can save you a lot of time by reducing the chance you'll cut a piece incorrectly and have to go back later and re-cut.

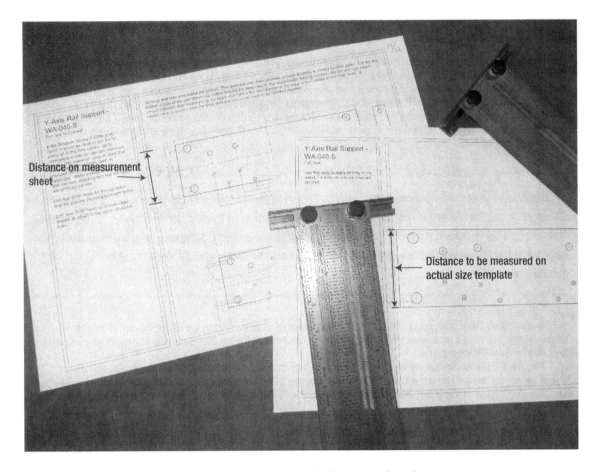

Figure 3-3. *Use a ruler to compare measurements to the full-size template sheet.*

What do you do if you find that the measurements don't match? If a measurement sheet tells you the diameter of a drilled hole is ¼" but you took a ruler to the full-size template sheet and measured the diameter of the hole at 3/8", then something's amiss. Double-check your measurement again and, if the discrepancy is real, it's time to get an official answer before actually drilling the part.

Point your web browser to www.buildyourtools.com and post the discrepancy under the Measurement Verification section. Likewise, the page for this book on the Apress web site has an Errata page where readers can post errors they find. We will do our best to quickly check the discrepancy and, if the error is real, provide a correct measurement as well as updated building plans. For a complete list of any errors found, visit www.buildyourtools.com.

Label the Parts

Most of the parts you'll be cutting are fairly unique in shape and will be easy to figure out using the building plans. If you examine the plans, you'll notice that every part also has a unique name; Z Axis Rail Support, X Axis Motor Mount, and Lower Structural Side are just a few examples.

It can get a bit tedious to write out the full name of every part, so throughout the book we'll be using letters of the alphabet to reference the parts. You've already seen one example earlier where we refer to the Z Axis Rail Support as Part K. There are 17 parts in all, so we'll be using letters A through Q when referring to specific parts. (There may be the occasional exceptions when we use part names during the assembly process to make it easier to understand how multiple parts work together.)

After cutting out a part, we suggest writing (in pencil) the part letter on the actual plywood. Write it on the back and front. We also use sticky notes with a part's letter written on them to make finding the parts easier and reduce squinting. Figure 3-4 shows a photo taken after all the basic parts were cut out and labeled. (Cuts are just along the width and length of the parts; more detailed cuts and drilling will be covered in later chapters.)

Figure 3-4. All the parts are cut out and labeled.

Do you have to label the parts? Of course not. But a little organization early in the process will make it easier for you to find what you need later.

■ **Tip** Want to find a part's sheet faster? Affix a sticky note with the sheet's part letter along the right edge of each sheet and stagger the sticky notes like a Rolodex. Then you can easily thumb to the proper sheet when you begin working on a specific part.

Head to the Discussion Forums

We have done our best to check and double-check things like dimensions, part counts, drill depths, and more. But mistakes are possible. We want to make certain that readers who choose to build the 3D printer have the most current information on the project, but a printed book poses difficulty if an error is found.

As mentioned, in order to provide readers with the most current information on the 3D printer, we're providing an Errata page as well as a forum section dedicated to the book (`www.buildyourtools.com`). Post your questions, share photos of your 3D printer build, and visit with other readers and builders.

Summary

We want the building your own 3D printer to be fun, safe, and as uncomplicated as possible. In the upcoming chapters, we'll show you the steps you need to follow to build your own machine. We won't skimp on the figures (photos, screen captures, etc.) or the details of the tasks you'll need to perform.

We've offered some advice in this chapter and we'll continue to offer more in the book's remaining chapters. But if we can offer a final bit of advice, it is this: don't let this project overwhelm you. The machine you're going to build has been built by others; you can do it, too. Take your time. Walk away if you get frustrated. Use the book's discussion forum to ask questions if you get stumped or need some advice.

You can do this. Enjoy the project, but don't hesitate to step back and ask for help when you need it. Now let's get started!

CHAPTER 4

■ ■ ■

Cutting the Parts I

Okay, we know you're anxious to get started. But there's a lot more information we need to give to you as the project moves forward—how to configure the electronics, how to use the required software, etc.— so we'll break up the book by giving you some hands-on time with building your 3D printer and squeeze in some theory chapters as we go along.

In Chapter 3, we recommended that you read through the entire book before actually beginning any cutting or drilling, but if you're dead-set on getting your hands dirty, this chapter is going to get you started cutting out the first eight parts (of 17) and provide some insight into what these parts are and where they'll be located on the final machine.

So, if you've got yourself a sheet of plywood and your tool of choice for making the initial cuts (table saw, circular saw, or handsaw) and a good ruler and pencil, let's dive in and get some of the 3D printer parts cut out.

Before You Begin

Appendix A contains a complete listing of all the supplies that you'll need to build your own 3D printer. This list consists mainly of the bolts and nuts and electronic parts that you'll need to purchase, but we also suggest purchasing a good quality piece of 4' x 8' plywood with a ¾" thickness.

■ **Note** Yes, we've told you that the parts can be cut out of a 2' x 4' sheet, but that is assuming you'll make every cut perfectly. It's also assuming that you lay out all the parts on the plywood in an efficient manner that reduces waste. If you purchase a 4' x 8' sheet and cut it in half, you'll have the extra plywood you need should you make any mistakes in the cutting or drilling of the parts.

What do we mean by "good quality" plywood? One of the name brands that we've found at a home improvement store is called Sandiply; it's extremely smooth on both sides of the sheet. But you can use other brand names of plywood. A good rule of thumb is to look for cabinet grade; this is plywood suitable for furniture and will be more than suitable for building a 3D printer. Another key is to buy plywood with the smoothest surface you can find. A rough surface may have a negative effect when it comes time to join two pieces. Moreover, if you choose to paint your machine, a smooth surface will provide better final results.

Can you use a material other than plywood, such as Medium Density Overlay (MDO), High Density Overlay (HDO), or Medium Density Fiber (MDF)? MDO is perfectly acceptable; it does cost a little more, but it lacks a grain so parts can be laid out in any direction, which is a good thing. The surface of a MDO sheet is covered with a thin MDF resin that has been applied with pressure and heat (like hardboard) to provide an extremely smooth surface that doesn't require sanding. MDO is used for very smooth concrete forming and has great structural properties. HDO is much more expensive than MDO and has a thicker top surface. For purposes of the 3D printer, HDO is probably not worth the extra price in material; MDO will suffice.

MDF is slightly more expensive than plywood; it's heavier and the dust produced when it is cut can be harmful to breathe if the board contains Urea Formaldehyde (ask your retailer/home improvement center if their stock of MDF contains this chemical). The best advice we can give if you choose to use MDF is to always use a respirator and vacuum the area well after you cut a piece.

■ **Note** One final warning about MDF: as MDF is subject to humidity or direct penetration of water, the material can thicken an additional 70% on top of its initial thickness. However, the material is incredibly stable if coated with a chemical that blocks water permeation (i.e. polyurethane).

The 3D printer parts you see in this book as examples are cut from Sandiply plywood. However, one of the authors (Patrick) used a CNC machine to cut out parts for the 3D printer using MDO. Both materials will work fine. Choose the one that fits your budget.

Once you've got your wood, a ruler, a pencil, and a tool for cutting, it's time to select the first part to cut.

Lower Structural Sides – Parts A and B

You can consult the building plans and start marking and cutting whichever part you like, but we'd like to offer up an order in which to cut the parts. The reason for this is that certain parts are large and others are small, so cutting the large parts first will leave waste material behind that can be used to cut a smaller part. If you cut the smaller parts first, you may find blocks of waste wood left behind that are just an inch or two shorter than you need for cutting a larger part at a later time.

For this reason, we're going to suggest that the first parts you cut are the two pieces that will be used to make the Lower Structural Sides. Figure 4-1 shows the building plan sheet for the parts that will eventually be cut and drilled from these two first pieces.

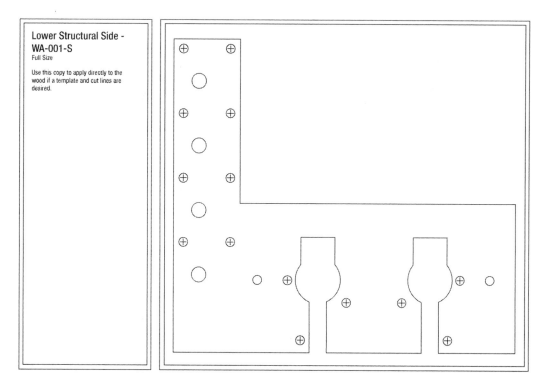

Figure 4-1. *The building plan for the Lower Structural Sides*

Cut these two pieces (and set aside the waste pieces for later) and label them Part A and Part B. Write the letter on both sides in a corner and maybe even on the edges. In a later chapter when you make more detailed cuts and drill holes in these two pieces (indicated by the various holes and curves in Figure 4-1), labeling them will make them easier to distinguish from other similar sized parts (such as the Back – Part O). Whether you choose to label your parts or not, always get in a habit of measuring the parts you pick up; use these measurements to verify the piece you'll be cutting or drilling by checking your building plans.

░ **Note** We suggest that you write a part's letter on its matching building plan sheet. This will help to make sure you don't cut or drill a piece using a different part's dimensions. You might also consider labeling the part in a spot that will be covered up by another part later on.

Figure 4-2 shows Parts A and B cut out and set aside. Chapter 7 will cover how to make the final cuts and drill the holes in the two pieces.

Figure 4-2. Parts A and B are ready for additional cuts and holes.

If you're curious to know what these parts will look like and where they will eventually be located, take a look at the model in Figure 4-3. This model was created using Google SketchUp (http://sketchup.google.com) and we'll be using it throughout the book to demonstrate the location of parts and how they are put together to build the completed machine. Parts A and B are shaded in Figure 4-3 to make it easier for you to see their location in the full 3D printer assembly. They're slightly L-shaped and form the legs of the 3D printer.

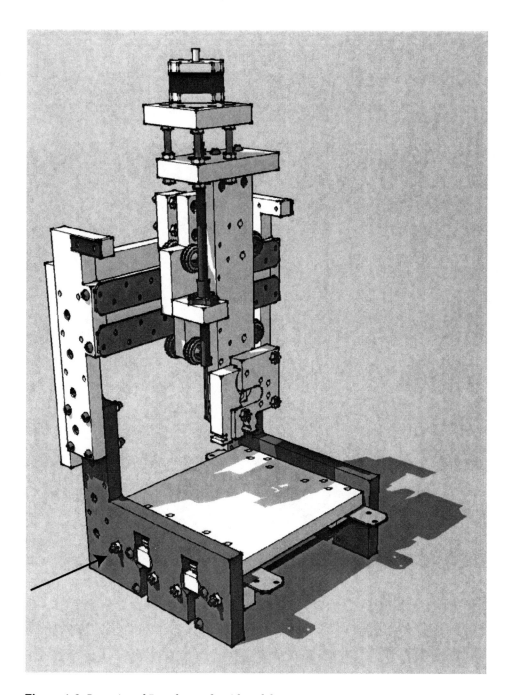

Figure 4-3. Parts A and B make up the sides of the 3D printer.

Table – Part C

The Table is a single piece with dimensions of 8-9/16" x 9-1/16". You might want to write the dimensions on the wood somewhere to indicate which side is of which length. This is important because Part C is almost square and can fool the eye. Later you'll be drilling holes in this piece and it will be important to drill those holes along the 8-9/16" side, not the 9-1/16" edge. Figure 4-4 shows Part C cut out and labeled.

Figure 4-4. Part C is the table (or work surface) of the 3D printer.

Figure 4-5 shows the table (shaded) between Parts A and B. Part C will actually move forwards and backwards via a set of bearings and pulleys.

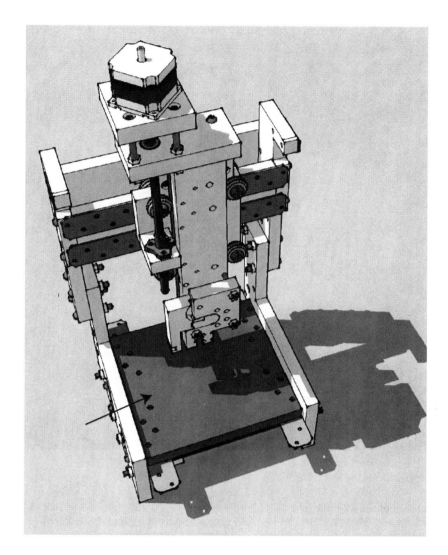

Figure 4-5. Part C moves forward and backward as an object is being printed.

ZY Plate – Part D

The next part you'll be cutting out is the ZY Plate. Its dimensions are 5-3/8" x 7-1/2" and should be labeled Part D. Figure 4-6 shows Part D cut out and labeled. It's a small piece, so you may find that you can cut it out from a waste piece left over from cutting parts A, B, or C.

Figure 4-6. *Part D mounts vertically on the machine.*

Figure 4-7 shows the location of the ZY Plate (shaded). Part D will move left and right along a set of metal rails using a set of bearings and pulleys. (The ZY Plate also serves as part of a slider mechanism, allowing the Z axis to move up and down. This will become more apparent later when you begin assembly.)

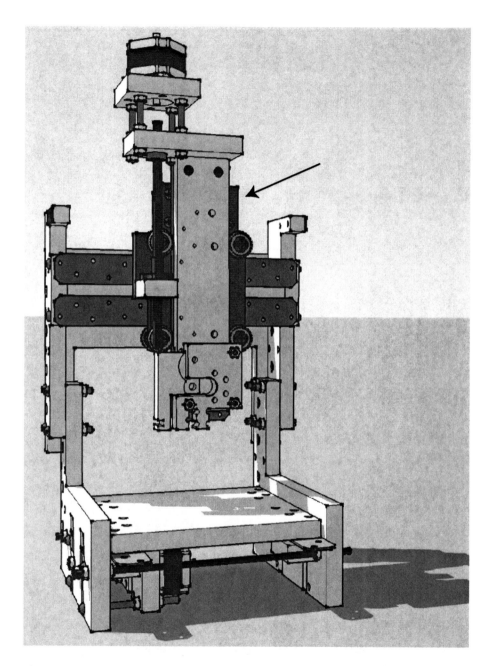

Figure 4-7. Part D moves left and right as an object is being printed.

X-Axis Motor Mount – Part E

The next part to cut is the X-Axis Motor Mount. Its dimensions are 2-5/8" x 5-7/16" and it should be labeled Part E.

■ **Note** We want to offer a quick reminder when cutting out these parts: do your best to cut them as close to the required dimensions as possible. The 3D printer is a small machine, and every part you'll be cutting is touching one or more other pieces. You want to make certain that the pieces do not rub or interfere with other parts. The best way to do this is to check your measurements before cutting and make cuts as accurate as possible.

Figure 4-8 shows Part E cut out. It's another small piece, so check to see if you can cut it from a waste piece left over from cutting parts A, B, or C.

Figure 4-8. *Part E cut out and ready for drilling.*

Figure 4-9 shows the X-Axis Motor Mount (shaded) with a motor attached to it. Part E does not move, but the motor attached to it allows the Table (Part C) to move forward and backward.

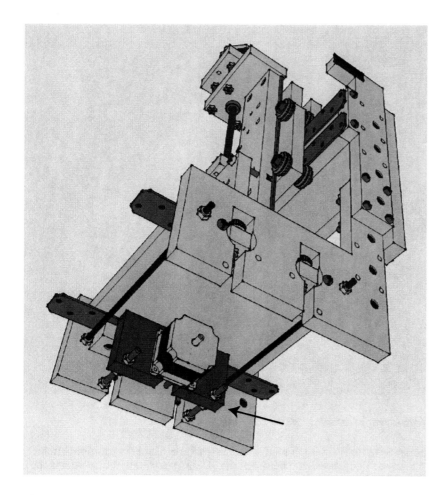

Figure 4-9. *Part E holds a motor that allows the Table to move forward and backward.*

Upper Structural Sides – Parts F and G

The last two parts you'll cut in this chapter are the Upper Structural Sides; the dimensions are 3-1/2" x 10-1/2". Be sure to label one piece Part F and the other Part G. Figure 4-10 shows Parts F and G cut out and labeled.

Figure 4-10. *Part F and G are ready for additional cuts and drilling.*

Figure 4-11 shows the Upper Structural Sides (shaded) attached to Parts A and B. Additional holes in this piece will allow you to increase or decrease the height of the 3D printer, which in turn affects the maximum height of a printable object.

■ **Note** You may be wondering why this raising and lowering feature is available. The high position has the least amount of rigidity but has more clearance for tall 3D print jobs. The low frame position adds a great amount of rigidity for machining operations but has the least amount of clearance, which is appropriate since machining is generally done on low-profile parts. The builder can, for example, consider a high frame setting for foam machining since there will be very little load on the cutter. Ultimately, you'll need to experiment and adjust your 3D printer based on the printing or milling job (using a small router or Dremel device) at hand.

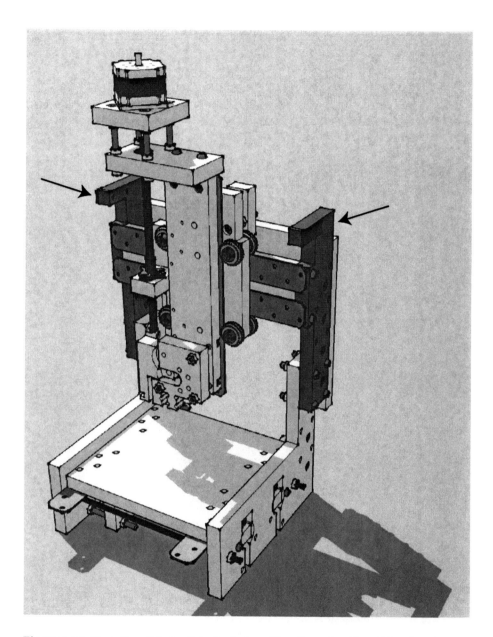

Figure 4-11. Parts F and G attach to Parts A and B to form the sides of the 3D printer.

Summary

We hope you weren't overwhelmed by the number of cuts in this chapter. We chose to start out by cutting just the length and width dimensions of the parts. The additional cuts and drill holes required to shape each piece to match the building plans will be covered in later chapters.

Remember to go slow! You've got nine more pieces to cut out in Chapter 5, but there's no rush. The extra time you take to make your cuts perfect will pay off later when it comes time to assemble your machine. When you finish the cuts specified in this chapter, take a break. You've earned it!

■ ■ ■

Cutting the Parts II

We're going to pick up right where we left off in Chapter 4. At this point, you should have a total of seven pieces of your 3D printer cut out. These pieces are raw in form—just a specific length and width with no special cuts or holes drilled yet.

In this chapter, we're going to finish up the cuts required for the remaining 10 pieces. When you're done, you'll have 17 pieces of plywood, each ready for more detailed cuts and drilled holes. These will make up the frame of your 3D printer. The electronics and other hardware (such as bolts or bearings) will be added to form your machine and give it the ability to move. But that comes later; for now, let's get to the last of the basic cuts you'll need to make.

Y-Axis Rail Support – Part H

The next part to cut out is the Y-Axis Rail Support. Its dimensions are 3-1/32" x 10-13/16" and it should be labeled Part H.

■ **Note** Try to cut Part H as close to the exact dimensions as possible since the Upper Structural Sides (Parts F and G) will be fastened to the ends of Part H and a bearing will ride very close to the top and bottom of Part H.

Figure 5-1 shows Part H cut out and labeled. It's a longer piece, so you may not be able to cut this from any scrap from earlier cuts.

Figure 5-1. *Part H cut and labeled*

Figure 5-2 shows the location of the Y-Axis Rail Support. Part H serves as the guide that will carry the ZY Plate and enable the extruder to move left and right.

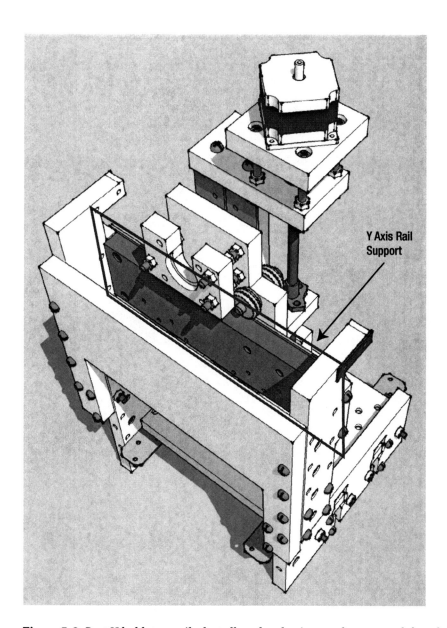

Y Axis Rail
Support

Figure 5-2. Part H holds two rails that allow the plastic extruder to move left and right.

Table Bearing Supports – Parts I and J

Next, you'll cut out the two Table Bearing Supports. The dimensions are 2-1/16" x 6-3/8" and they should be labeled Part I and Part J, as shown in Figure 5-3.

Figure 5-3. *Part I and J cut and labeled*

Figure 5-4 shows the location of the Table Bearing Supports. Parts I and J allow the Table (Part C) to move back and forth. The Table contains a set of rails that will move back and forth between Parts I and J (one on each side of the table). This will be possible since the Parts I and J will contain v-groove bearings that keep the table rails moving along a single path.

■ **Note** You'll noticed two long threaded rods in Figure 5-4 (a threaded rod is a continuous rod that is threaded like a screw). The threaded rods keep the bearings tight against the table rails when the rod is snugly tensioned (more on using tension rods in Chapter 13).

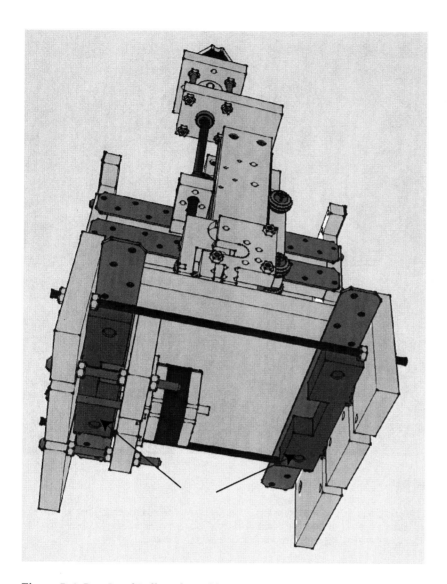

Figure 5-4. *Part I and J allow the Table (Part C) to move forward and backward.*

Z-Axis Rail Support – Part K

Your next cut will be the single piece called the Z-Axis Rail Support. Its dimensions are 2-1/2" x 11-1/2" and it should be labeled Part K, as shown in Figure 5-5.

Figure 5-5. Part K cut and labeled

Figure 5-6 shows the location of the Z-Axis Rail Support. Part K allows the plastic extruder to move up and down on a set of metal rails via a set of bearings and pulleys. The extruder will be fastened to the lower part of this piece and the motor/bearing support will be fastened to the top.

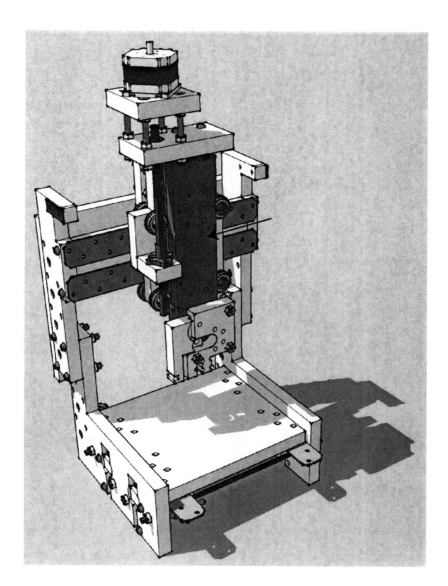

Figure 5-6. Part K allows the plastic extruder to move up and down on a set of metal rails.

Z-Axis Bearing Support – Part L

Up next for cutting is the Z-Axis Bearing Support. Its dimensions are 2-9/16"x5" and it should be labeled Part L, as shown in Figure 5-7.

Figure 5-7. *Part L cut and labeled*

Figure 5-8 shows the location of the Z-Axis Bearing Support. Part L will have a threaded rod inserted through it that connects to the Z-Axis motor and allows the plastic extruder to move up and down.

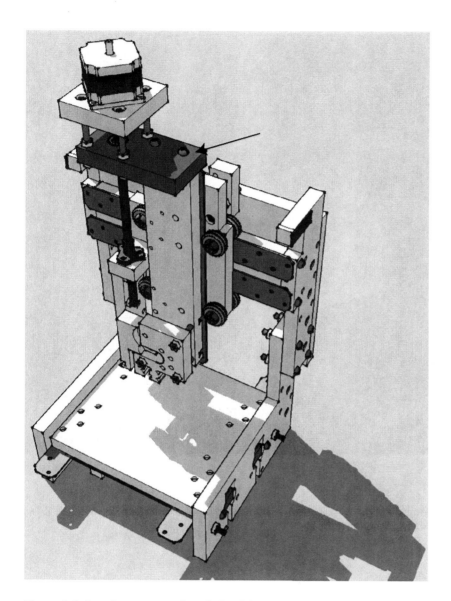

Figure 5-8. *Part L supports a threaded rod that provides the up and down motion.*

Z-Axis Motor Mount – Part M

Next you'll cut out a single piece for the Z-Axis Motor Mount. Its dimensions are 3-1/4" x 3-1/4" (square) and it should be labeled Part M. You can probably use scrap wood for this cut. Figure 5-9 shows Part M cut out and labeled.

Figure 5-9. *Part M cut and labeled*

Figure 5-10 shows the location of the Z-Axis Motor Mount. Part M is the interface between the Z-Axis motor and the Z-Axis Bearing Support (Part L).

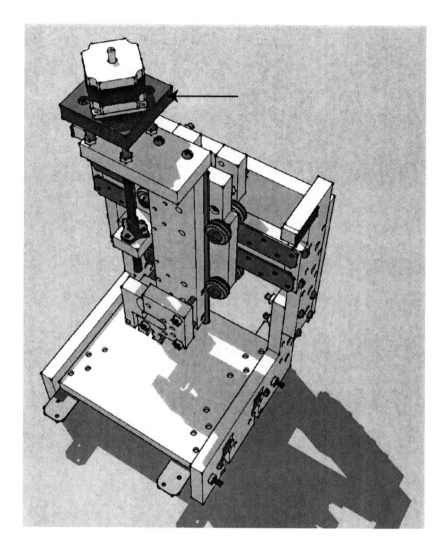

Figure 5-10. Part M connects the Z-Axis motor to the 3D printer.

Z-Axis Nut Mount – Part N

Your next cut is the Z-Axis Nut Mount. Its dimensions are 1-1/2" x 2-1/16" and it should be labeled Part N. This is a small part and you may be able to cut it out of a scrap piece of plywood left over from previous cuts. Figure 5-11 shows Part N cut out and labeled.

Figure 5-11. *Part N cut and labeled*

Figure 5-12 shows the location of the Z-Axis Nut Mount. Part N will hold the anti-backlash nut for the Z-Axis threaded rod. This part will need to be cut as precisely as possible since you will not want this part to rub against the Z-axis rails or rail support and restrict motion.

___

▪ **Note** We'll talk about anti-backlash later in the book. For now, all you need to know is the nut will prevent inaccuracies in the printing caused by changes in direction of the threaded rod.

___

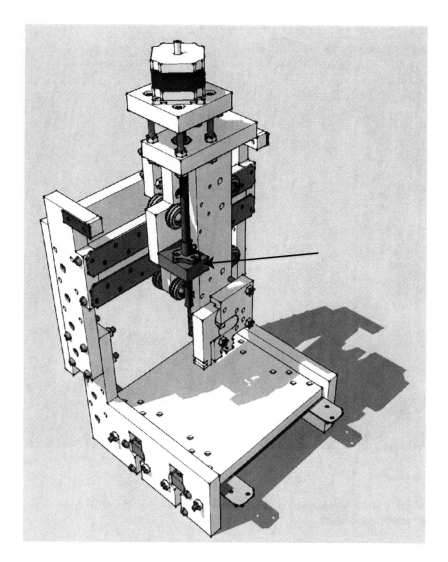

Figure 5-12. Part N will hold the anti-backlash nut and help prevent printing inaccuracies.

Machine Back – Part O

Your next cut should be for the Machine Back. Its dimensions are 9-3/4" x 12-3/16" and it should be labeled Part O, as shown in Figure 5-13. (More cuts will be made later to Part O to remove excess wood so that the Table can move forward and backward without hitting this piece.)

Figure 5-13. Part O cut and labeled

Figure 5-14 shows the location of the Machine Back. Part O does not move but it does help to increase the rigidity of the 3D printer assembly.

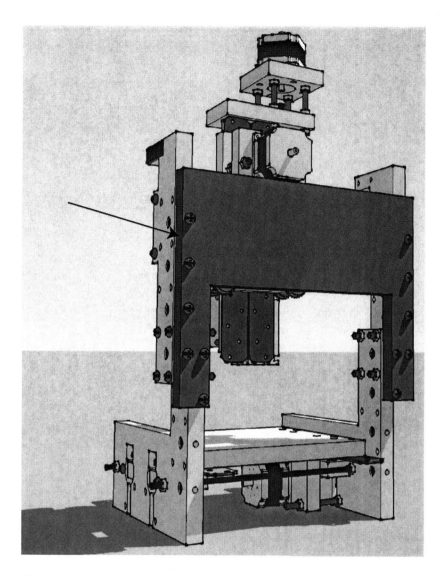

Figure 5-14. *Part O helps strengthen the entire 3D printer structure.*

Extruder Bearing Hinge I – Part P

The next piece to cut is actually a sub-part of a two-piece assembly and is called the Extruder Bearing Hinge I. Its dimensions are 1-13/16" x 3-17/32" and it should be labeled Part P, as shown in Figure 5-15. Part P is a small piece and you may be able to cut it from a piece of waste.

Figure 5-15. *Part P cut and labeled*

Figure 5-16 shows the location of the Extruder Bearing Hinge I. Part P is a moving piece and will work in conjunction with Part Q (Extruder Bearing Hinge II) during the printing process by creating a lever that enables a pinching motion on the PLA or ABS filament (the plastic) so that the motor can push the filament down into the extruder nozzle. A bearing is fastened to this part to create an idler (a part that keeps tension on a belt and reduces slack) on one side of the filament; the other side will have a drive pulley connected to a motor that is installed to Part Q.

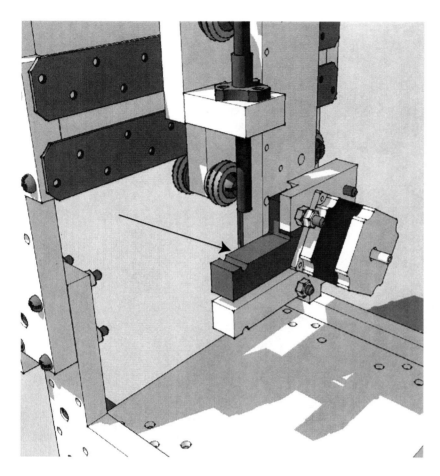

Figure 5-16. Part P connects to Part Q (Extruder Bearing Hinge II).

Extruder Bearing Hinge II – Part Q

The next piece to cut is a sub-part of a two-piece assembly and is called the Extruder Bearing Hinge II. Its dimensions are 3-5/8" x 5-1/2" and it should be labeled Part Q, as shown in Figure 5-17. Part Q is a small piece and you may be able to cut it from a piece of waste.

Figure 5-17. *Part Q cut and labeled*

Figure 5-18 shows the location of the Extruder Bearing Hinge II. Part Q works in conjunction with Part P (Extruder Bearing Hinge I) during the printing process and it holds the motor. Part Q also holds the extruder nozzle where the heating of the plastic filament takes place and is pushed through.

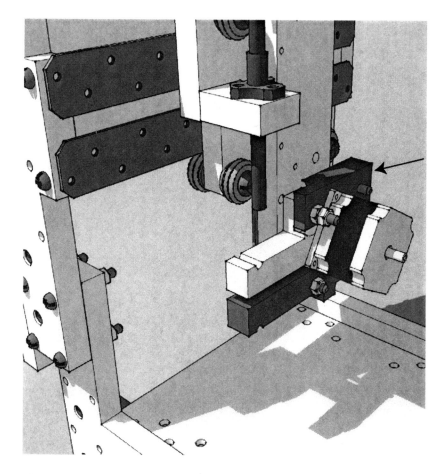

Figure 5-18. Part Q connects to Part P (Extruder Bearing Hinge I).

Summary

You made a few more cuts in this chapter than in the previous one. We hope the process went smoothly and that you're beginning to see how some (or maybe all) of the parts will fit together.

So now that you have all 17 parts cut out and labeled, it's time to move on to the more advanced cuts that some parts require and to the drilling of holes. Warning: there are a lot of holes to drill. Again, the key is to take your time. (During the drilling operation of one key piece, we rushed it and ended up ruining the part, so we had to cut another one.)

In Chapter 6, we're going to walk you through the detail work needed to finish each wood piece. Again, we recommend that you read the chapters ahead (or, even better, the entire book) so that you'll have an idea of what to expect. Note that you're free to perform the remaining cuts and drilling tasks in any order you see fit; we chose the order of the next few chapters based on the perceived complexity of the work required.

■ ■ ■

CHAPTER 6

Advanced Cuts and Drilling I

We hope you're feeling pretty good about your progress thus far. At this point, you should have 17 pieces of plywood (or other material) cut out that match the length and width of the pieces seen in the building plans.

Before you begin to assemble your 3D printer, however, you need to make some more cuts and you need to drill a bunch of holes. This chapter is titled "Advanced Cuts and Drilling" but don't let that description scare you; all we're talking about is making more cuts to give a part a more definite shape than just the rectangular pieces you see before you now.

Over the next four chapters, we're going to show you how each and every part must be cut and drilled. We'll offer up our best advice on making these cuts plus tips on how to ensure that your cutting and drilling are as accurate as possible. As with every task we describe in this book, we'll tell you again to take it slow. Cut a few parts, drill a few holes, and then take a break. Rushing the process will only result in mistakes or damage to your 3D printer pieces.

This chapter will cover the cutting and drilling of just two pieces. This will give you the chance to understand what you're seeing in our figures and why there may be some deviations in how our parts look compared to your own. This introduction should make the other Advanced Cuts and Drilling chapters much easier to understand.

Z-Axis Nut Mount – Part N

Part N, or the Z-Axis Nut Mount, is the smallest of the pieces you have cut. Verify that the piece you've cut has dimensions of 1-1/2" x 2-1/16" before moving forward. If you find the piece does not match these dimensions, verify the dimensions you do have against the building plans (because there could very well be a typo in this book).

After you've got Part N cut to the correct length and width, it's time to drill a series of holes in the piece. Figure 6-1 shows a portion of the building plans.

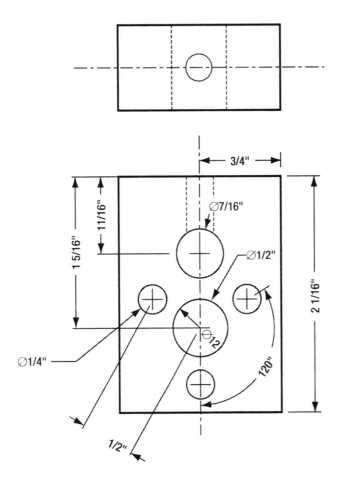

Figure 6-1. *Part N needs six holes drilled: five on its face and one on its edge.*

One of the first things to notice is that the three smaller holes on the face of Part N are spaced using a measurement of degrees and a distance from the larger hole centered between the three small holes. (These holes are used to fasten the flange of a nut to this piece. If you have the nut handy, this is an alternative to marking the holes if you don't have a full-scale version of the plans.) We'll leave it up to you to decide how you wish to mark these on your Part N piece for drilling, but we can tell you that it was easier for us to drill these holes by simply taking accurate measurements from the building plans that were printed at actual size.

When the building plans are printed at actual size, you can take a ruler (with 32^{nds} of an inch increments) and actually measure out the center points of the holes to be drilled. Figure 6-2 shows a close-up of both the plans (printed at actual size) and Part N prior to drilling the holes. Notice that we've used a pencil to draw accurate lines on Part N. We've also written (in pencil) some of our measurements of the holes on the plans themselves.

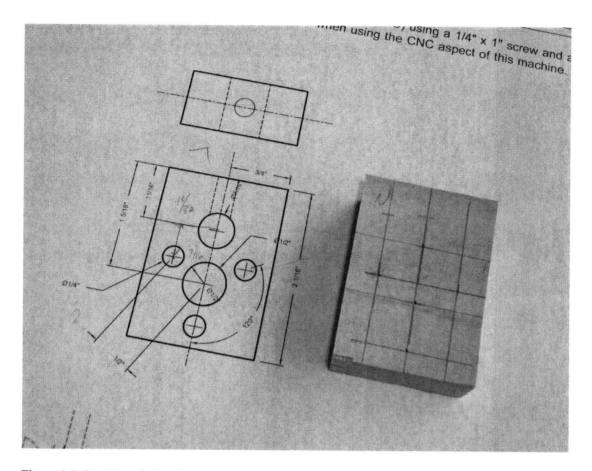

Figure 6-2. Part N marked with penciled lines to indicate drill points

Notice in Figure 6-2 how the actual Part N is identical in size to the drawing. This is a benefit to printing out the building plans at actual size.

The three small holes you'll drill on the face of Part N have a diameter of 1/4" to match the flange holes of the three nuts to be inserted. The hole centered between the three small holes has a diameter of 1/2" that serves as the pass-through hole for the lead screw. Finally, the mid-size hole drilled above the 1/2" hole has a diameter of 7/16" and is the hole that will intersect the 1/4" hole drilled into the edge of Part N. This hole will carry the cross dowel (barrel nut) and the edge hole will receive the 1/4" screw to screw into the cross dowel for mounting to the ZY Plate.

Don't forget this edge hole! In Figure 6-2 you can see that the 1/4" edge hole is drilled in such a way that it intersects the 7/16" hole on the face of Part N. The dashed lines in the drawing represent the depth of the 1/4" hole drilled on the edge.

After you've drilled the face holes, your piece should look like the one in Figure 6-3.

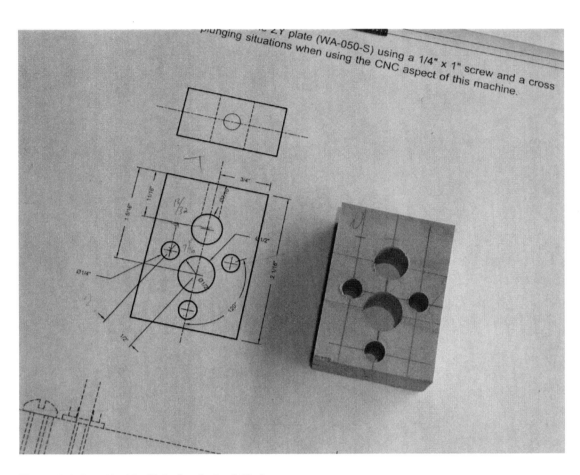

Figure 6-3. *Part N with all the face holes drilled*

Figure 6-4 shows the final 1/4" hole drilled into the edge. If you look carefully, you can see how the hole intersects the 7/16" hole on the face of Part N.

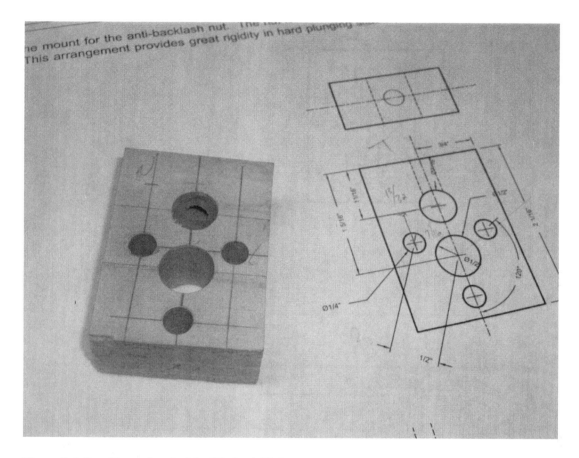

Figure 6-4. Part N completed with all holes drilled

Before we move on to the next part to be drilled, take a look at Figure 6-5. It shows another portion of the building plans for Part N. Its shape doesn't match the one you're holding, does it?

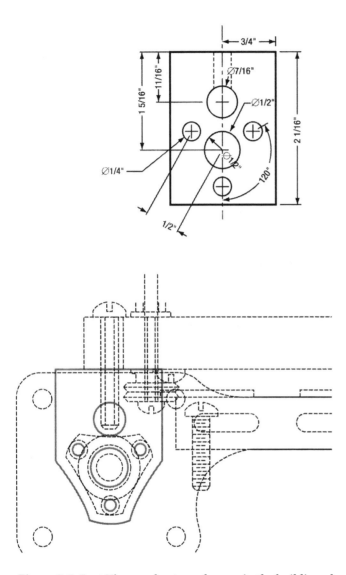

Figure 6-5. *Part N's curved cuts can be seen in the building plans.*

There are quite a few parts in the building plans that have curved cuts applied to them. There's a very good reason for this: Patrick, one of this book's authors, used a CNC machine (instead of a table saw) to cut out parts for his 3D printer. The CNC machine uses a milling bit that is round, which makes it difficult to make 90 degree cuts in corners. But he also applies a bit of artistic flair to some of the pieces by shaving away material that won't be missed when the machine is assembled.

Those nice curved edges along the bottom left and bottom right of Part N in Figure 6-5 look great, but they're not required. You can easily leave your Part N in its rectangular shape with no further cuts. But if you'd like to use a bandsaw (or other tool) to cut away some material so your Part N looks like the one in Figure 6-5, go right ahead! Just be careful not to trim away too much.

▓ **Note** You're free to make drastic changes to the parts if you so desire. Use the diagrams in the plans/book and the pictures in each chapter to determine the flexibility of each part. We will also provide occasional suggestions regarding certain parts. Just make sure when creating these changes that the part will not conflict with other parts or assemblies.

Conversely, you can choose to make no additional cuts to a part unless you find that the part, when added to the 3D printer assembly, interferes with the movement or function of another part. We'll let you know in later chapters when a part requires a cut and when any additional cuts are just for aesthetics.

Figure 6-6 shows a marked-up plywood Part N and a completed Part N cut from MDO with a CNC machine. Yes, the machined part looks pretty, but the rectangular piece will serve its purpose as-is with no further cuts required. Ultimately, it's up to you if you'd like to modify your Part N to match the curved piece in Figure 6-6.

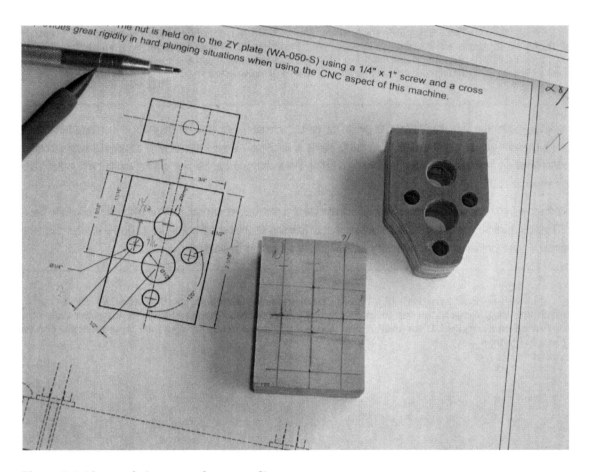

Figure 6-6. *It's your choice: rectangle or curved?*

Z-Axis Motor Mount – Part M

Part M, or the Z-Axis Motor Mount, will have a total of nine holes drilled plus a channel cut into it. Verify that your Part M has dimensions of 3-1/4" x 3-1/4" (square) before continuing. If so, it's time to mark and drill the nine holes in the piece. Figure 6-7 shows a portion of the building plans displaying the nine holes to be drilled. (Consult the actual building plans for the drill hole diameters—the numbers may be a bit difficult to read in this figure.)

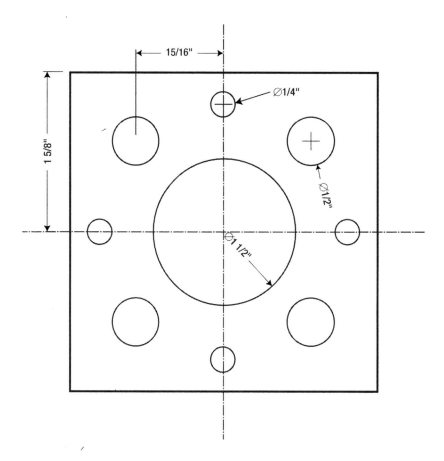

Figure 6-7. *The building plans displaying the nine holes to be drilled into Part M*

Figure 6-8 shows our Part M with all the drill holes marked. We took the measurements directly from the actual size building plans and transferred those measurements to our piece with a pencil prior to drilling.

Figure 6-8. Part M with the drill hole locations marked using the actual size plans

Take a look at Figure 6-9. It contains another portion of the building plans, but this one shows two new items: a channel to be cut into the piece (for inserting an Allen wrench later to adjust the coupling that will be fastened to the motor shaft) and four counterbore holes drilled into the face of Part M. The large hole in the center will provide room for this coupling.

So what is a coupling and why is it needed? The motor shaft will need to turn a lead screw (a long screw without stub ends). There are two challenges for the motor to turn the lead screw. First, the shaft and the screw are two separate components and something needs to connect the two while allowing some flexibility for slight misalignment. Second, the shaft and the screw are two different sizes in this machine. A coupling is simply a small assembly that solves both of these problems with a hole on each end and a rubber component at the midpoint for flexibility. This coupling has a set screw to tighten against the shaft of the motor and the lead screw. The set screw for the shaft of the motor will be adjustable through this slot created in this part. (We'll cover the coupling during the assembly portion of the project later in Chapter 13.)

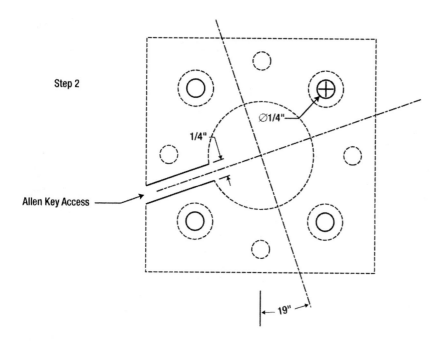

Step 2

Ø1/4"

1/4"

Allen Key Access

19"

Figure 6-9. Counterbore holes must also be drilled into Part M.

What's a counterbore hole? A counterbore hole is a hole that is drilled partially, but not completely, into the wood. It allows a bolt's head, when inserted into the hole, to sit just below the flat surface of the piece. This helps prevent two moving pieces from scraping (or stopping altogether) against one another. Figure 6-10 shows an example of a bolt inserted into a counterbore hole. Notice how the bolt head sits below the surface and will not be felt if you drag a flat piece of wood across the part's face. For Part M, these counterbore holes will allow the motor to sit flat against the part and still contain enough material for the screws to fasten to the part below.

Figure 6-10. *A bolt inserted into a counterbore hole with its head just below the surface*

The 1/2" counterbored holes will be drilled first, as shown in Figure 6-11. Feel free to use some scrap wood to drill a test counterbore to get the feel of it.

Figure 6-11. Insert the head of a bolt into a counterbore hole to test it for depth.

After drilling the four counterbore holes, use their centerpoints and drill a single 1/4" hole into the counterbore holes and through the other side of the wood. (The drilling operation will typically leave a small dimple or mark that you can use to find the center of the hole again.) Remember to place a piece of scrap wood underneath Part M to prevent your drill bits from breaking through the plywood and damaging the smooth back surface.

Drill the remaining holes as described in the building plans. The large center hole has a diameter of 1-1/2" and can be drilled easily with a Forstner bit all the way through Part M. The four small remaining holes are each 1/4" diameter and are drilled completely through Part M as well. These four 1/4" holes will be used to fasten the motor flange to this piece. The motor flange specification is NEMA 23. Figure 6-12 shows Part M completed with all the holes drilled, including the four counterbore holes.

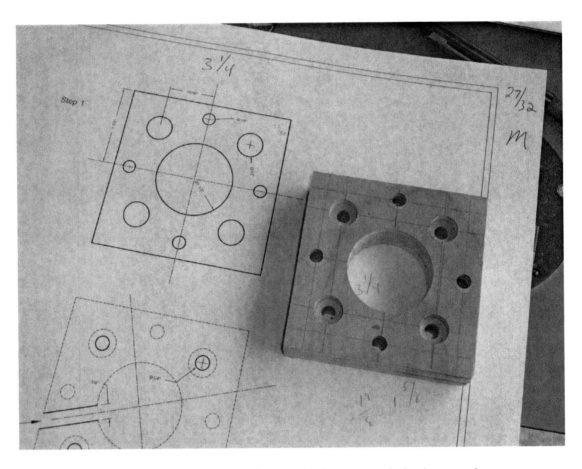

Figure 6-12. *Part M will hold the anti-backlash nut and help prevent printing inaccuracies.*

Next, you'll finish up Part M by cutting out a small channel, as seen in Figure 6-9. Mark your Part M using the actual size building plans or take measurements for where the cuts are to be made. Figure 6-13 shows us cutting the channel out of Part M using a bandsaw.

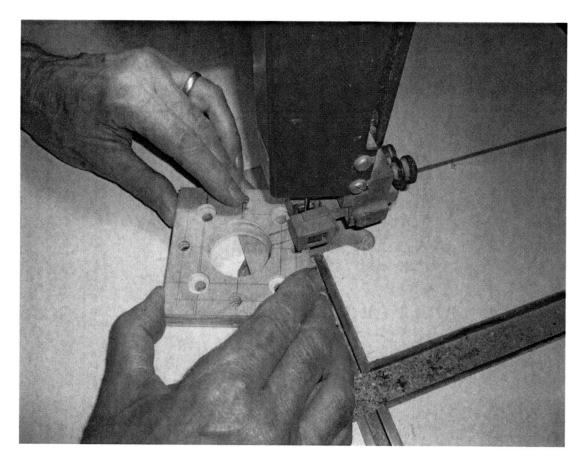

Figure 6-13. *Cutting the channel in Part M with a bandsaw*

And Figure 6-14 shows the final piece with all holes drilled and the channel cut out.

Figure 6-14. Part M with all cuts and drilled holes completed

Finally, Figure 6-15 shows how Part M looks when cut out with Patrick's CNC machine. It's no longer square-shaped as many of its edges have been shaved down. Feel free to modify your Part M if you like, but the square version of Part M will work just fine in the final 3D printer assembly.

■ **Note** Go wild! If you choose to modify Part M, the top edge of the part (as shown in Figure 6-15) is the only side of the part that should maintain close tolerance to its dimension as this side will come close to the top of the ZY plate.

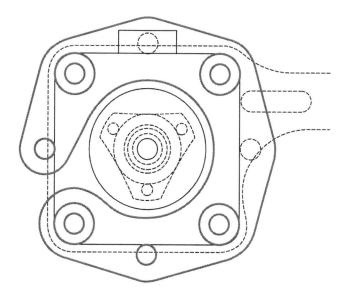

Figure 6-15. *Part M can have its edges trimmed away but it's not required.*

Figure 6-16 shows the Part M cut from MDO using Patrick's CNC machine alongside a square version cut from plywood with a bandsaw.

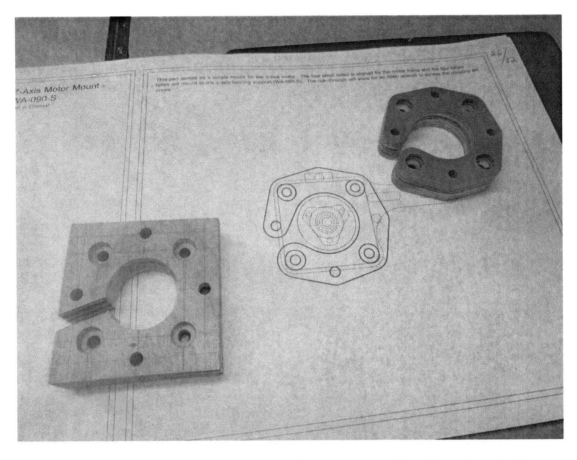

Figure 6-16. *A Part M cut from MDO using a CNC machine next to a Part M cut from plywood with a bandsaw.*

Summary

We wanted to keep this chapter short on the cutting and drilling so as not to overwhelm you with a lot of work. We also wanted to introduce the concept of counterboring and show you how the building plans can offer up an occasional modification to a piece's final look.

In upcoming chapters, we'll cover the cutting and drilling of the remaining 15 pieces. By the time you're done with Chapter 9, you'll have 17 pieces all ready to be bolted together to form the frame of your 3D printer. So take a break. When you're ready to continue, Chapter 7 will show you the cuts and drill holes for the next five pieces.

CHAPTER 7

■ ■ ■

Advanced Cuts and Drilling II

So you've got two pieces of your 3D printer cut and drilled completely. Let's continue with the cutting and drilling of the remaining fifteen pieces. This chapter and the next two will provide you with photos and notes about the various pieces that you'll be cutting. We'll discuss the pieces that might be a bit tricky, and we'll show you some alternative methods for cutting and drilling.

In Chapter 6, we used dimensions taken directly from the building plans to mark where cuts were to be made and where holes were to be drilled. But remember that the building instructions contain actual-size templates for all the parts. We'll show you how to use the actual-size templates to mark cuts and drilling locations versus using measurements from the building plans.

Let's get started. This chapter will walk you through the cutting and drilling of five new pieces. As always, take your time, double and triple-check all your measurements, and be careful! Put on your safety goggles, watch your fingers, and don't rush it.

Z-Axis Bearing Support – Part L

Part L, or the Z-Axis Bearing Support, is not a difficult piece to complete. It does have one counterbore hole that must be drilled (in addition to some regular holes) but, as you can see from Figure 7-1, the part retains its rectangular shape and no extra cuts are required—just drilling.

Your Part L dimensions should be 2-9/16" x 5" but be certain to verify your cut piece's measurements with those provided in the building plans. You'll use the plans to mark the holes to be drilled. Here's an important tip: drill the counterbore hole first! If you use a Forstner or Brad point bit, the counterbore drilling step will leave a dimple in the wood that will allow you to later drill the 1/2" hole directly in the center of the 7/8" counterbore hole.

Figure 7-1 shows our completed Part L with six 1/4" holes and a 1/2" hole drilled all the way through the piece. The 7/8" counterbore hole was drilled to approximately half the thickness of the piece (3/8"). You can still see the pencil lines we used to mark the locations of the holes to be drilled.

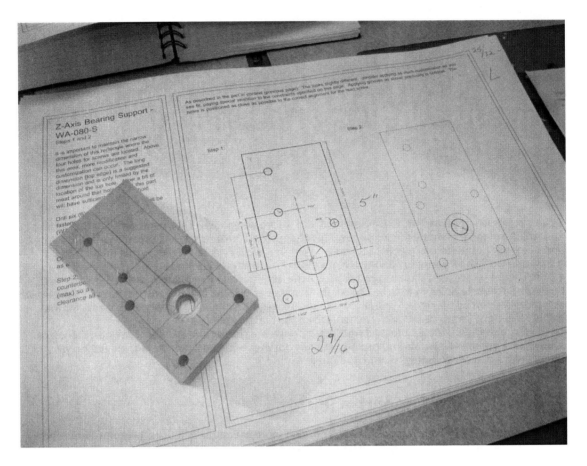

Figure 7-1. Part L with lines for drilling the 1/4" and 1/2" holes and counterbore hole

If you look at your building plans, you'll notice that this part can be modified slightly with some additional cuts. Figure 7-2 shows a Part L with the basic cuts and drilled holes alongside a Part L cut from a CNC machine.

Figure 7-2. The Part L on right was cut from MDO using a CNC machine.

Take a closer look the Part L cut by the CNC machine; you may notice that two of the 1/4" holes have been elongated to form two 1/4" wide channels. These two channels are to allow for adjustment when bolting Part L to another part. To recreate this, you'll need to drill multiple 1/4" holes along a straight line and use a file or bit of sand paper to smooth down the inner edges. The Part L on the left side of Figure 7-2 still has the pencil line running vertically down the piece that connects the two 1/4" holes.

You'll see these channels in many more parts. When you begin to assemble your 3D printer, you may find that two parts do not line up perfectly where a bolt needs to be inserted through them. Channels like the ones in Figure 7-2 allow you to move a part slightly to obtain a proper fit. Just keep in mind that you don't have to cut these channels unless you find two parts that don't fit well together.

Y-Axis Rail Support – Part H

The Y-Axis Rail Support, or Part H, will require the use of two Simpson Strong-Tie metal straps (or brackets), as seen in Figure 7-3. (Actually, you'll need to purchase a total of six of them. These are a standard piece of hardware with standard thicknesses and holes drilled into the metal. Strong-Tie is the brand, and you'll want to purchase the HRS12 version, which is 12" long and 1/8" thick.)

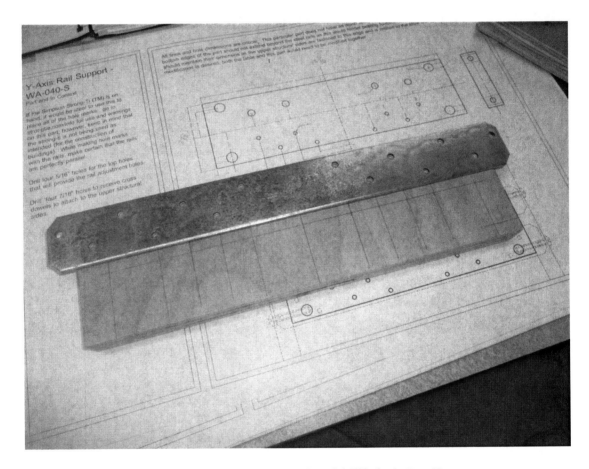

Figure 7-3. The Strong-Tie brackets will be used to mark and drill holes in Part H.

After marking Part H, go ahead and drill the four corner holes that will be used to hold a barrel nut. The plans call for these holes to be drilled using a 7/16" bit, but we found that using a 13/32" bit provided a more snug fit for the barrel nut. Either bit will work, but a 13/32" bit might not be in your bit collection. Figure 7-4 shows Part H with the holes drilled for the barrel nuts.

Figure 7-4. Part H with the four corner holes drilled

Next, you're going to drill one half of the 5/32" holes shown in the building plans. The reason for this is that you'll attach a Strong-Tie to Part H after drilling one set of holes. You'll use the attached Strong-Tie to help place the second Strong-Tie and mark the holes that will be used to hold the second Strong-Tie. The two Strong-Tie brackets must be perfectly parallel to one another, so we'll walk you through how we did this. Figure 7-5 shows half of the holes used to bolt a single Strong-Tie to Part H drilled.

■ **Note** We chose to use a 15/64" bit to make the 5/32" holes slightly larger. This allowed us to make very fine adjustments to the Strong-Tie. You can still use a 5/32" bit to drill these holes because the plans will have you later drill 5/16" holes for the second Strong-Tie—these larger diameter holes will allow the second Strong-Tie to be adjusted with respect to the first Strong-Tie.

Figure 7-5. *Part H with holes drilled to hold a single Strong-Tie*

Bolt on a Strong-Tie with a few #8 or #10 x 1-1/4" machine screws. You should be able to match up the holes in the Strong-Tie so that the bracket sits on Part H with its ends extending evenly beyond the edges of Part H, as shown in Figure 7-6.

Figure 7-6. Part H with a Strong-Tie bolted on

Next, you'll need to obtain a 1/2" spacer. This spacer will be used to ensure that the two brackets are perfectly parallel when bolted to Part H. We used a metal spacer that is precision cut for this kind of task, but as long as you can find an object that has a consistent thickness of ½", you should be fine. Insert the spacer between the first and second Strong-Tie brackets, as shown in Figure 7-7.

Figure 7-7. *Use a spacer to make certain the brackets are perfectly parallel.*

Use a transfer punch or sharp bit to mark the eight holes to be drilled to hold the second Strong-Tie to Part H. You can choose to drill these holes at 5/32" if you are confident in the accuracy of your marks or, if you're like us, you can drill the holes for the second bracket slightly larger. These larger holes can be either 5/16" (as shown in the plans) or at 15/64" (as we chose to do). Figure 7-8 shows these holes drilled into Part H.

■ **Note** Figure 7-8 shows more holes than the plans call for. The extra holes are due to a mistake I made in drilling the part. The extra holes won't hurt anything, so I used the part as I drilled it.

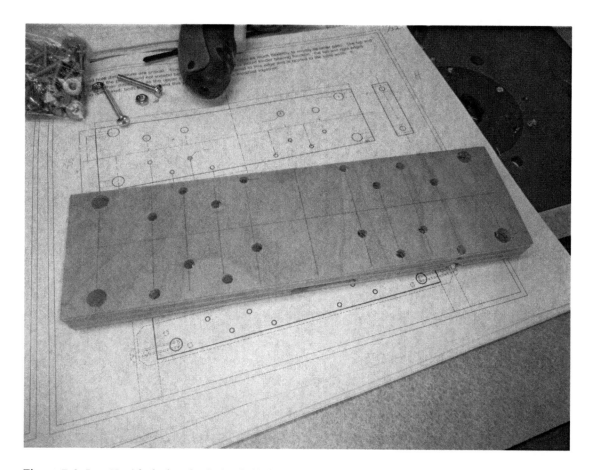

Figure 7-8. Part H with the bracket holes drilled

All that's left is to drill the 1/4" holes on the edges of the piece for the bolts that will be screwed into the barrel nuts. Mark a center line down both the left and right edges (the shorter 3-1/32" edges). We recommend using a drill press to drill these holes because you want them as perfectly perpendicular to the barrel nut holes as possible. Using a hand drill is possible, but just make certain you're drilling the holes as close to perpendicular as you can. (The two holes we drilled into Part H in Figure 7-9 were done by hand and are slightly off center, so we switched to a drill press shortly after this!) Figure 7-9 shows two of the edge holes drilled.

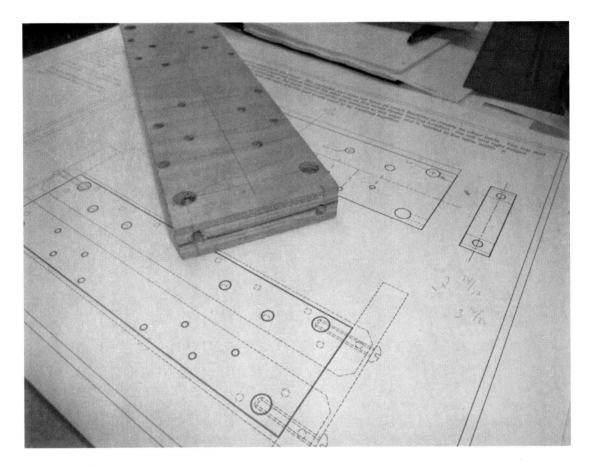

Figure 7-9. *Edge holes drilled into Part H*

Figure 7-10 shows our cut and drilled part compared to Part H from the CNC machine. Note that the machined part has channels that will allow one of the brackets to be adjusted so that it's parallel to the other.

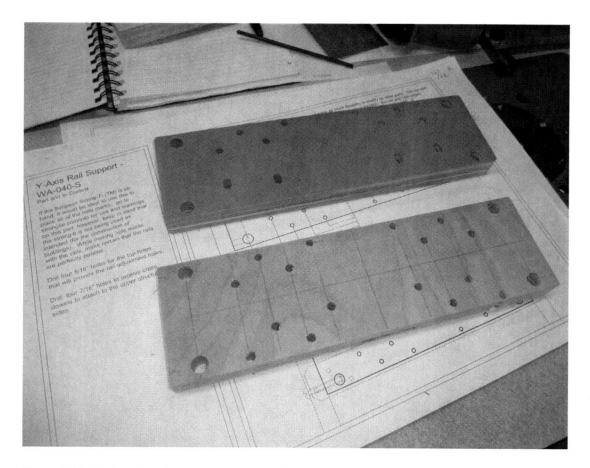

Figure 7-10. The Part H at the top was cut and drilled from MDO using a CNC machine.

■ **Note** Sharp-eyed readers may notice in Figure 7-10 that instead of the four larger diameter holes called for in the plans, there are eight small diameter holes. This was a mistake, plain and simple. But it still worked, so we didn't have to cut a new piece. Cut the four holes and you'll have wiggle room for attaching the Strong-Tie brackets and positioning them correctly.

Machine Back – Part O

The Machine Back, or Part O, is a fairly simple part to drill, but it does require a few additional cuts. Use the building plans to mark a set of lines and points for the 1/4" holes that will be drilled along the left and right sides. Figure 7-11 shows Part O with the first set of holes drilled down the left side.

Figure 7-11. The first set of holes drilled down the left side of Part O

Drill the remaining holes and then mark the wood for the section to be cut out. Find the center of the piece (vertically) and draw a line down the center. Use this centerline as the starting point for measuring and marking the lines where you'll cut away wood from Part O. Figure 7-12 shows the remaining holes drilled as well as the area that will be cut away (marked with large Xs).

Figure 7-12. Part O with holes drilled and sections marked for removal

Finally, use a bandsaw (or jigsaw or coping saw) to cut away the bottom interior section of Part O. Figure 7-13 shows our Part O compared to the same part cut with the CNC machine.

Figure 7-13. *A Part O cut by us and and one by Patrick's CNC machine.*

Lower Structural Side – Part A and B

There are two Lower Structural Sides that we've labeled Parts A and B. You can use the building plans to measure and mark the locations of all the holes to be drilled as well as the extra material that must be cut away, but we'd like to walk you through another method that we used for these two parts.

First, these two parts are mirror images, and neither part has any counterbore holes that must be drilled. This means that we can put Part A on top of Part B and drill and cut through both parts at the same time. This will ensure that all holes and cuts match up—and it will save us time. Here's how we did it.

First, we cut out the actual-size template from the building plans. Note that this will only work if you print out the building plans on 11x17 paper with no reduction! You can use a ruler to measure the actual-size template against the building plan sheet that has the measurements on it. If the actual-size template matches, you're in good shape. Figure 7-14 show the actual-size template being cut out.

Figure 7-14. Parts A and B will but cut and drilled using the actual-size template.

Attach the cut-out template to the top of Part A (with tape) and use a sharp point to mark the centerpoints of all the holes to be drilled. In addition, we used our sharp edge to mark the corners of the lines that will be used for cutting away additional material. Figure 7-15 shows us marking the points.

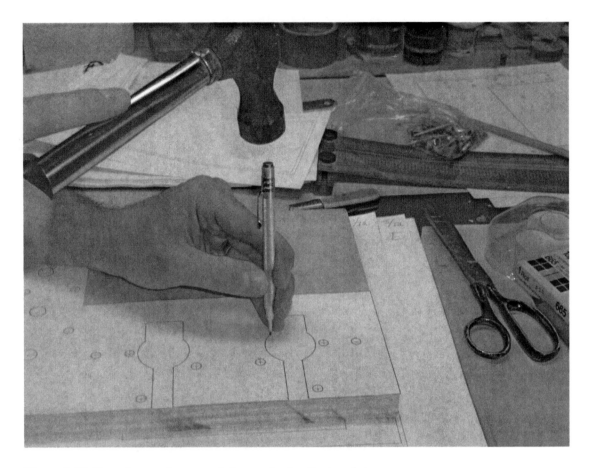

Figure 7-15. Use a sharp point to mark the wood using the template.

In Figure 7-16, the template has been removed and the marks in the wood are easy to find (for us—however, they may be difficult to see in the photo).

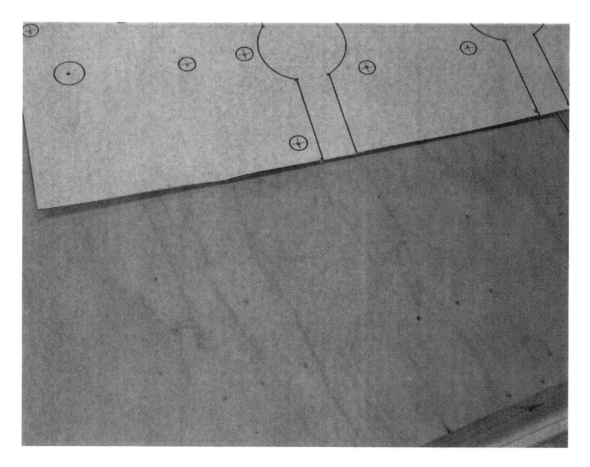

Figure 7-16. Part H has dimples in the wood indicating where we will drill or cut.

Figure 7-17 shows us applying the double-sided tape to Part B and Figure 7-18 shows both parts stuck together (with blue painter's tape that won't leave any residue when you remove it). You can see that the 1/4" holes have been drilled through both parts.

Figure 7-17. Parts A and B need to be taped together.

Figure 7-18. *Parts A and B with all 1/4" holes drilled*

Next, you need to drill the two large holes (and cut the grooves) that you can see back in Figure 7-15. We used a Forstner bit to drill the two holes (with a diameter of 1-3/8"), as shown in Figure 7-19.

Figure 7-19. Parts A and B each have two large holes drilled.

Now it's time to drill the four 7/16" holes for the barrel nuts. Figure 7-20 shows these four holes drilled through Parts A and B. We used a 13/32" bit, but a 7/16" bit will work fine.

Figure 7-20. *Holes drilled through Parts A and B for the barrel nuts*

Next, drill the 1/4" holes along the left edges of Parts A and B, as seen in Figure 7-21. These holes are where the 1/4" bolts will be inserted and screwed into the barrel nuts.

■ **Note** We recommend drilling pilot holes of 1/8" or less to start these 1/4" holes. The pilot holes will help ensure that the 1/4" bit will drill the holes perpendicular to the 7/16" barrel nut holes.

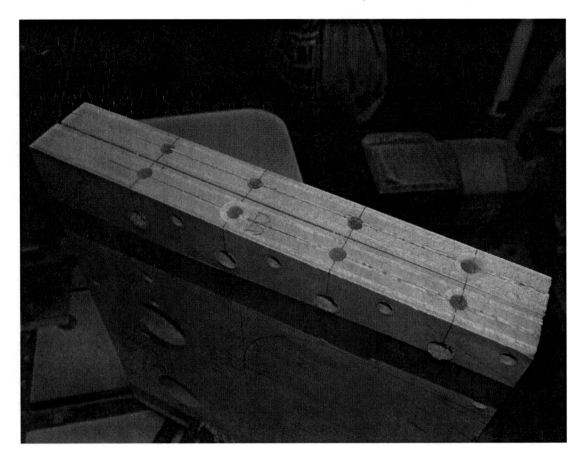

Figure 7-21. Holes drilled through the edges of Parts A and B for the barrel nuts

And finally, use a bandsaw, jigsaw, or coping saw to cut away the excess material and give Parts A and B their final shape. Figure 7-22 shows our Parts A and B along with the same two parts cut and drilled with a CNC machine.

Figure 7-22. Plywood Parts A and B along with the MDO parts from the CNC machine

X-Axis Motor Mount – Part E

The final part that we'll cut and drill in this chapter is the X-Axis Motor Mount, or Part E. For Part E, the order in which you drill the holes is very important. We're going to first drill pilot holes in specific locations where counterbore holes will also be drilled. The pilot holes (drilled all the way through Part E) will help us retain the center point on those holes where a counterbore hole will be placed. A counterbore hole will often leave a dimple or small mark where the centerpoint of the drill bit eats into the wood—but not always—so pilot holes will be critical for Part E.

First, take a look at Figure 7-23. This figure shows our Part E with all the holes marked carefully in pencil.

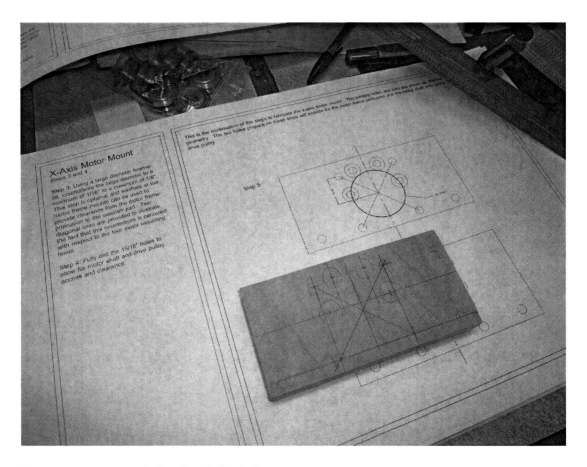

Figure 7-23. Part E marked and ready for drilling

Now, just follow along as we progress through the proper order to drill Part E. First, we'll drill two pilot holes for the two counterbore holes that will be located at the 3 o'clock and 9 o'clock positions (around the larger hole seen in the plans in Figure 7-23.) Drill the pilot holes using a 1/8" bit and then drill the two counterbore holes seen in Figure 24 to a depth of 13/32" (or as close as you can get it). Look closely at the figure and you can see the pilot holes inside the counterbore holes.

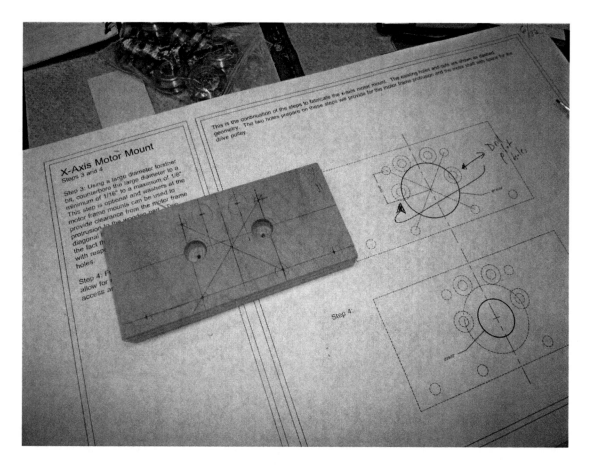

Figure 7-24. *Part E with first two counterbore holes drilled*

Next, drill two more 1/8" pilot holes followed by two counterbore holes (drilled to a depth of 1/4") at the 11 o'clock and 1 o'clock positions, as seen in Figure 7-25.

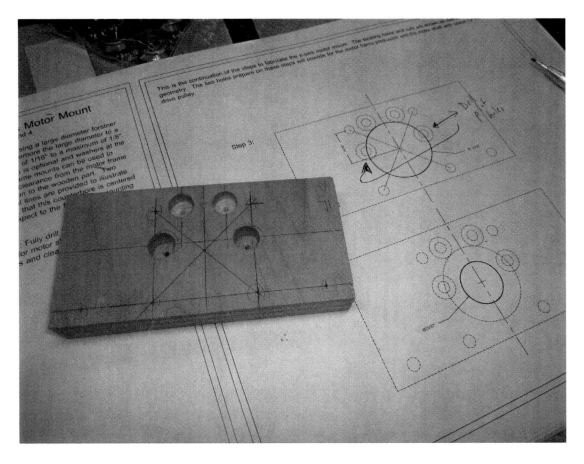

Figure 7-25. *Part E with the next two counterbore holes drilled*

Next, you'll drill another counterbore at a much larger diameter. The plans call for using a 1-21/32" bit but we used a 1-5/8" bit with no problems. Drill this counterbore hole to a depth of 13/64" (or as close as you can get it). Figure 7-26 shows this larger hole drilled. (Notice the dimple in the center—this will be used to drill the next hole completely through Part E.)

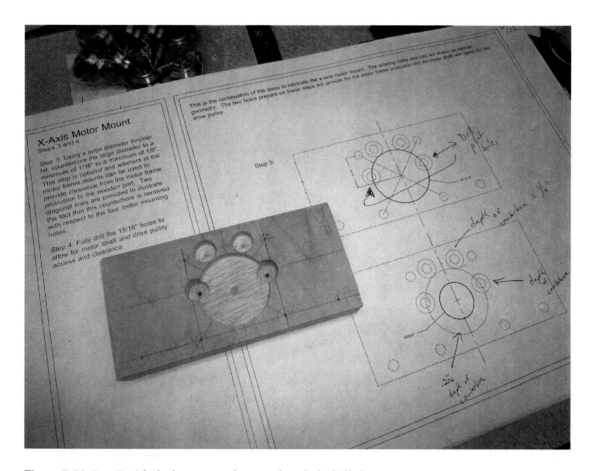

Figure 7-26. Part E with the large central counterbore hole drilled

Now drill the inner hole using a 7/8" bit. (The plans call for using a 29/32" bit but we didn't have this odd size. A 7/8" bit will work fine.) Figure 7-27 shows this hole drilled.

Figure 7-27. *The central hole drilled through Part E*

Now drill the 1/4" holes indicated in the building plans. Figure 7-28 shows Part E with all but two final holes drilled.

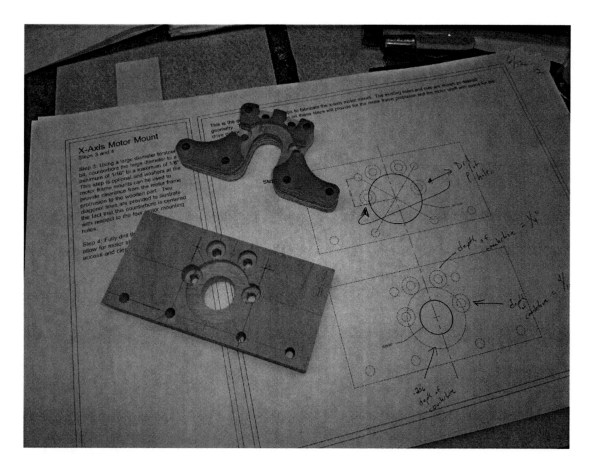

Figure 7-28. *Part E with the 1/4" holes drilled*

Flip Part E over and mark the two lines shown in Figure 7-29. Cut away this part to leave the large opening in Part E.

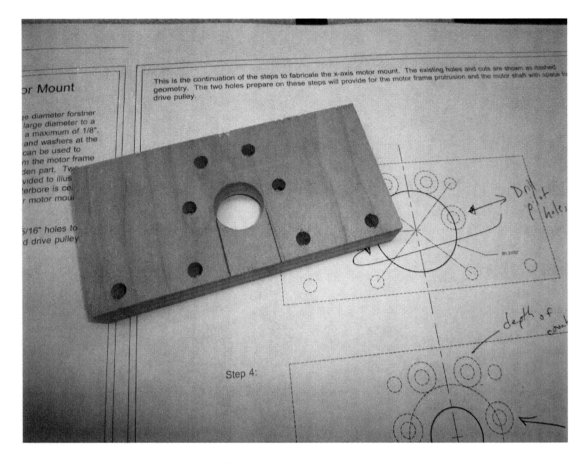

Figure 7-29. *Two cuts and two more 1/4" holes are needed on Part E.*

Figure 7-30 shows Part E complete and sitting beside the same part from the CNC machine.

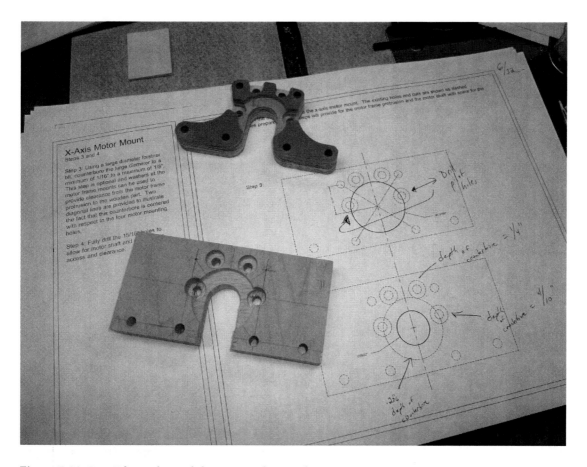

Figure 7-30. *Part E from plywood (bottom) and Part E from MDO (top)*

Summary

There's not much to say at this point other than to keep moving forward. Feel free to take a break at this point—you've accomplished a lot. But there are 11 more pieces to be cut and drilled! Chapter 8 covers the cutting and drilling of the next five pieces.

CHAPTER 8

■ ■ ■

Advanced Cuts and Drilling III

Eight parts down and ten to go! By now, you should be familiar enough with the process of either taking measurements from the building plans or using the actual-size templates to mark your cuts and locations for drilling, so let's jump right back in.

This chapter will walk you through the cutting and drilling of the next six pieces. Remember to go slow and check your measurements before performing any cutting or drilling. You'll be passing the halfway point when it comes to finishing up the plywood pieces for your 3D printer, so take your time and avoid mistakes.

Upper Structural Sides – Parts F and G

Parts F and G are identical with no counterbores required; this means you can easily drill the holes in both pieces if you properly clamp or tape them together before drilling. Mark one of the parts (Part F in Figure 8-1 below) using a center point punch or other sharp object where you need to drill.

Figure 8-1 shows Parts F and G taped together (with double-sided carpet tape) with the actual-size template cut out from the building plans and taped to the surface of Part F.

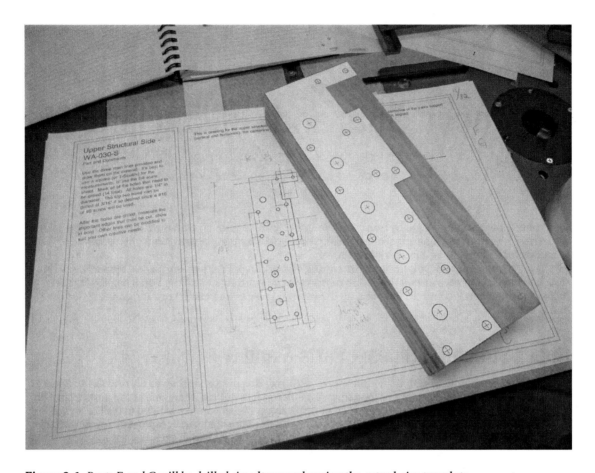

Figure 8-1. *Parts F and G will be drilled simultaneously using the actual-size template.*

Figure 8-2 shows the 1/4" holes drilled all the way through Parts F and G. All that's left is to drill the 7/16" holes for the barrel nuts and the 1/4" holes along the edges. Note that we've used a pencil to mark where additional cuts will be made.

Figure 8-2. *Parts F and G with the 1/4" holes drilled.*

Next, use a 7/8" drill bit (we used a 13/32" for a tighter fit for the barrel nuts, but either bit size will work fine) and drill the remaining holes on the face of parts F and G, as shown in Figure 8-3.

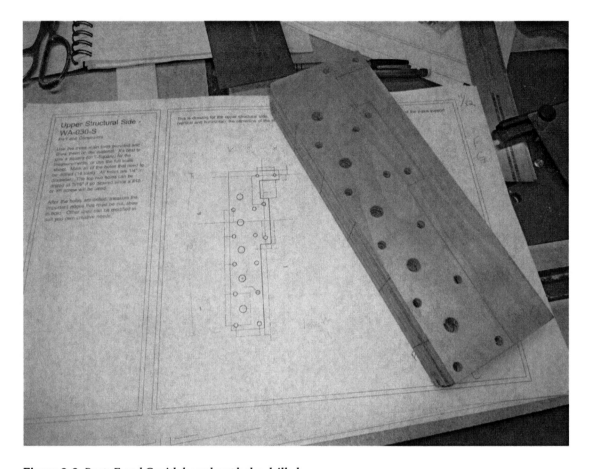

Figure 8-3. *Parts F and G with barrel nut holes drilled.*

And finally, drill the 1/4" holes into the edges of Parts F and G for the bolts that will be screwed into the barrel nuts. Figure 8-4 shows these holes drilled; we used a drill press for better accuracy than can be obtained with a hand drill. Note that we're using a small vise to stabilize the pieces while drilling.

Figure 8-4. Drill the 1/4" holes along the edge of Parts F and G.

To finish up Parts F and G, use a saw (a bandsaw works best) to cut along the lines specified in the building plans. This will give Parts F and G their distinctive shape. Figure 8-5 shows Parts F and G in plywood and MDO.

Figure 8-5. *Parts F and G in plywood (left) and MDO (right)*

As with many of the parts for the 3D printer, you may have to enlarge some holes or cut channels to get a better fit during the assembly portion. In Figure 8-5, you can see that some of the 1/4" holes in the MDO pieces on the right have been extended into channels.

ZY Plate – Part D

The ZY Plate, or Part D, is not a difficult piece to cut and drill, but it does require three counterbore holes. Figure 8-6 shows the initial part with lines for cutting drawn on the face of the piece and a few of the holes drilled, including the counterbore holes. The counterbore holes are drilled to a depth of 1/4". Note that we've written Xs on the waste material that will be cut away.

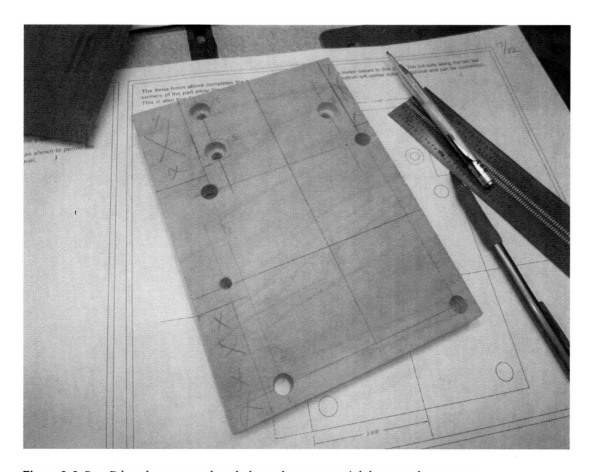

Figure 8-6. Part D has three counterbore holes and some material that must be cut away.

Figure 8-7 shows the final part (with all the holes drilled) sitting beside the same piece created with the CNC machine. The CNC machine has applied some nice curves to the piece but these curves are not required.

Figure 8-7. *Part D in plywood (on left) and MDO (on right)*

Y-Axis Motor Mount – Part R

Part R, or the Y-Axis Motor Mount, is a fairly simple part to drill. Rather than use the actual-size template, we chose to mark out the locations for the 1/4" holes. As you can see in Figure 8-8, we've connected four points on Part R to find the center for the large hole that will be drilled in the piece.

Figure 8-8. *Part R marked for drilling and a centerpoint penciled in for the large hole*

Drill the 1/4" holes as shown in Figure 8-9. Note that instead of the 1-19/32" diameter hole specified in the building plans, we used a 1-5/8" bit; this larger hole is visible in Figure 8-9. We've also penciled in the two lines where we'll cut away material to open up the large hole.

Figure 8-9. *All holes drilled in Part R*

Figure 8-10 shows the final piece next to the MDO piece. The part done with the CNC machine features some optional angled cuts.

Figure 8-10. Part R in plywood (on bottom) and MDO (on top)

Table Bearing Supports – Parts I and J

Parts I and J, the Table Bearing Supports, are two of the oddest looking pieces that you'll be cutting and drilling. We actually used rulers to take accurate measurements from the full-sized building instructions just to be certain about the placement of the cuts and holes. Fortunately, these pieces are small and easy to make, even thought they might look difficult. In fact, you can clamp or tape them together to drill and cut them simultaneously. Figure 8-11 shows the two pieces taped together and ready for drilling.

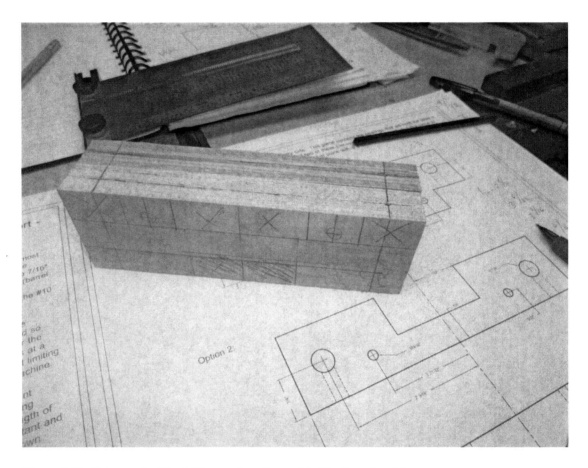

Figure 8-11. Holes marked for drilling and cut lines added for Parts I and J

Note If you examine the building instructions, you'll find that there are two options for the final shape of these two pieces. Option 1 requires the largest number of cuts but it will also allow you to print larger objects with your 3D printer. Option 2 requires fewer cuts but picking this option will reduce the size of the objects you will be able to print.

We chose to first drill the 1/4" holes on the edges using a drill press. Figure 8-12 shows this part of the process.

Figure 8-12. Parts I and J with 1/4" edge holes drilled by a drill press.

Next, you'll drill the 7/16" holes on the face of Parts I and J. Figure 8-13 shows Parts I and J with these holes completed. (Again, we substituted a 13/32" bit for the 7/16" bit for a snug fit for the barrel nuts.)

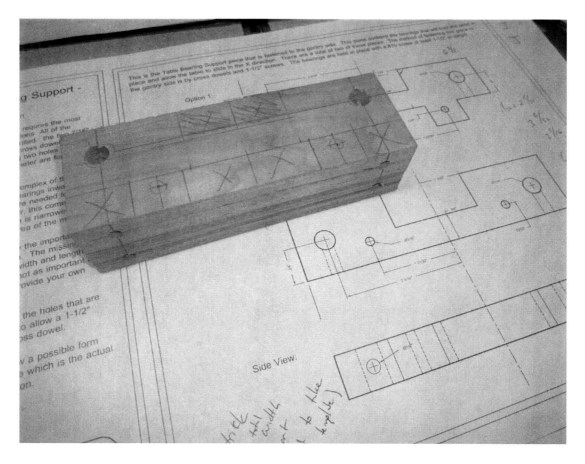

Figure 8-13. Parts I and J with 7/16" holes drilled for barrel nuts.

The 3/16" holes are drilled next, followed by cuts made with a bandsaw specified by Option 1 in the building plans. Figure 8-14 shows Parts I and J being cut with the bandsaw. If you look closely, you can see that the 3/16" holes have already been drilled.

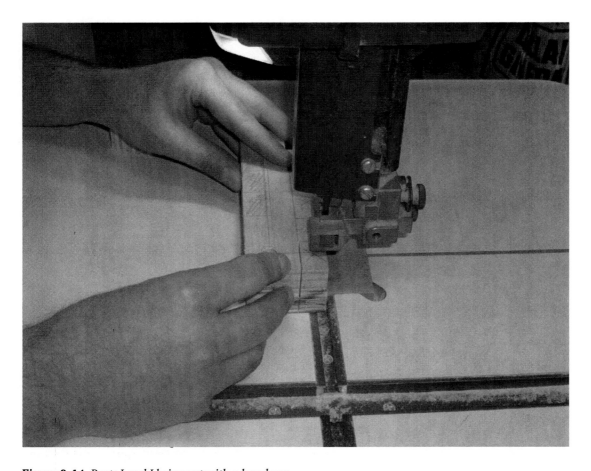

Figure 8-14. Parts I and J being cut with a bandsaw.

Figure 8-15 shows Parts I and J in plywood compared to the same parts finished by the CNC machine. Those curved cuts you see in the MDO pieces in Figure 8-15 are optional.

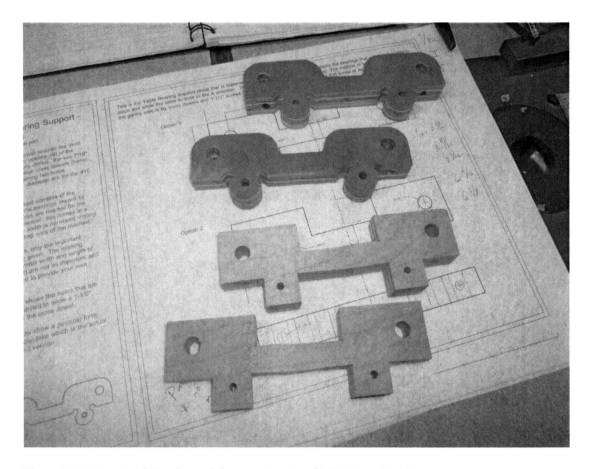

Figure 8-15. *Parts I and J in plywood (bottom pieces) and MDO (top pieces).*

Summary

So now you have completed fourteen parts! Only four more pieces to cut and drill and then you'll be ready to start assembling your 3D printer. Chapter 9 will finish up the instructions for the remaining pieces, so take a break and then let's wrap up the cutting and drilling portion of the project!

■ ■ ■

Advanced Cuts and Drilling IV

Four more pieces to cut and drill—that's all that is left before you can begin the assembly of your 3D printer and start adding in the electronics and other hardware. This chapter will walk you through that last bit of work. Let's get started!

Extruder Bearing Hinge 1 – Part P

The Extruder Bearing Hinge consists of two pieces. Part P is the Extruder Bearing Hinge 1, and its starting dimensions should be 1-13/16" x 3-17/32" (verify these dimensions with the full-sized plans). Figure 9-1 shows Part P marked for drilling. Drill the first counterbore hole to a diameter of 1-1/2" and a depth of 3/8" (half the thickness of the plywood).

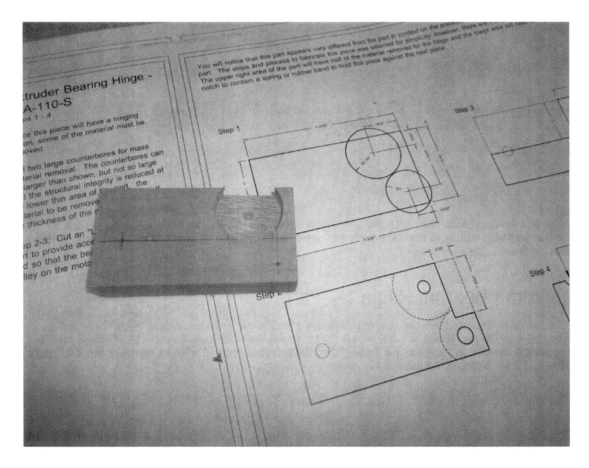

Figure 9-1. Part P with the first counterbore hole drilled.

Next, drill the second largest counterbore hole specified in the building plans. It's a 1" diameter hole also drilled to a 3/8" depth. Figure 9-2 shows Part P with the second counterbore hole drilled.

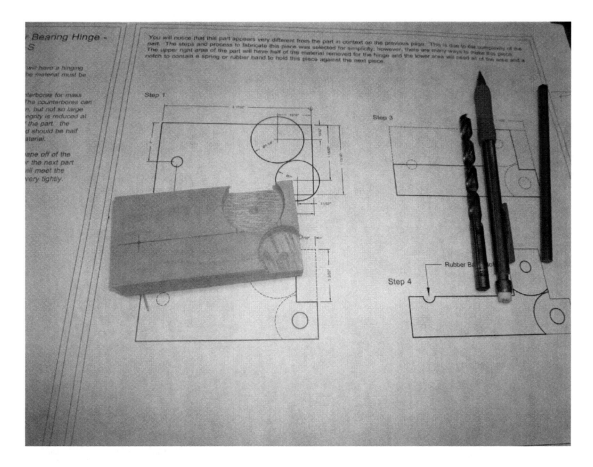

Figure 9-2. Part P with the addition of the second largest counterbore hole.

Next, use a 1/4" drill bit to drill the three holes all the way through Part P, as shown in Figure 9-3. Note that two of these holes are drilled into the counterbore holes. We used Forstner bits for the counterbore holes, which left a small dimple in the center of the hole that helped us find the center of the 1/4" holes.

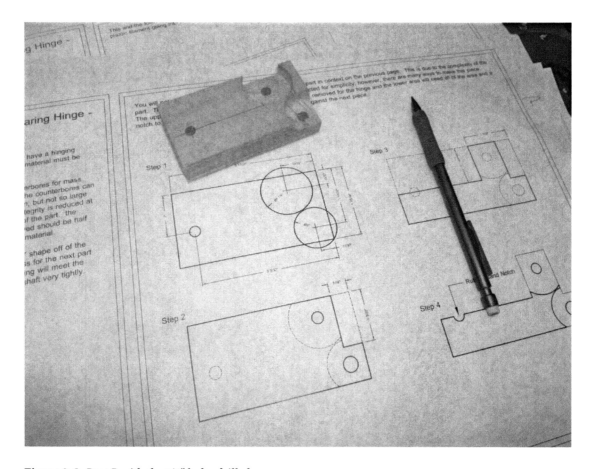

Figure 9-3. *Part P with the 1/4" holes drilled.*

Mark up Part P to indicate the waste material to be cut away. (It's easier to mark these lines before any drilling is done, but you can also mark the cuts on the back of the piece—just make sure to draw your lines reversed from the lines shown on the plans.)

Figure 9-4 shows the complete plywood Part P with all holes drilled and the cuts finished. The MDO piece (cut using Patrick's CNC machine) is provided for comparison.

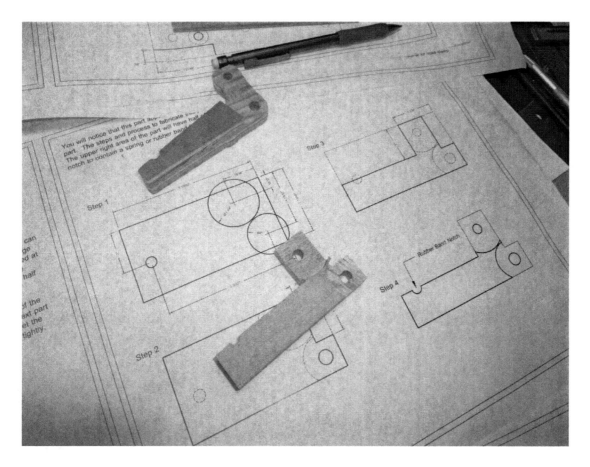

Figure 9-4. Part P in plywood (bottom) and MDO (on top).

Extruder Bearing Hinge 2 – Part Q

Part Q is the second part of Extruder Bearing Hinge 2. Its starting dimensions should be 3-5/8" x 5-1/2". Figure 9-5 shows Part Q marked for drilling, including lines for later cutting away the waste material.

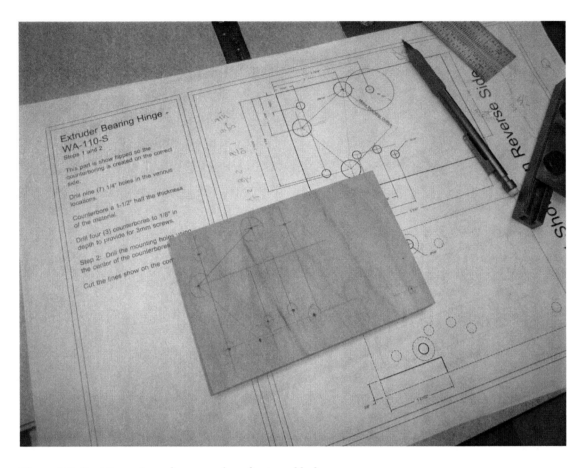

Figure 9-5. Part Q requires a large number of cuts and holes.

First, drill the counterbore hole into Part Q. Figure 9-6 shows the first (and the largest) counterbore hole drilled. It's a 1-1/2" diameter hole that is drilled to a depth of 3/8" or half the thickness of the plywood.

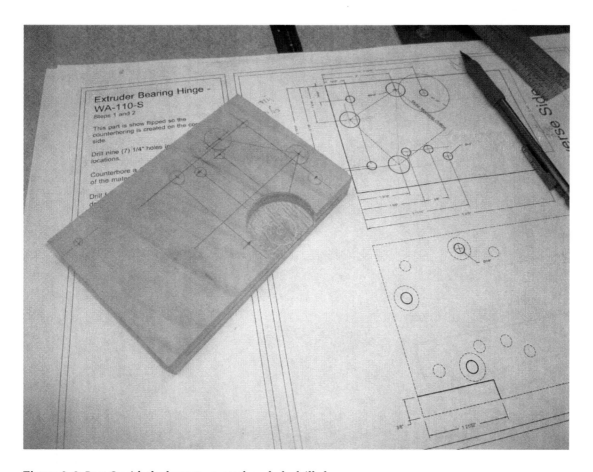

Figure 9-6. Part Q with the largest counterbore hole drilled.

Next, drill the three smaller counterbore holes using a bit diameter of 9/16". Drill these three counterbore holes to a depth of 1/8" and then drill 1/4" holes centered in the four counterbore holes, plus the remaining 1/4" holes indicated in the building plans. Figure 9-7 shows Part Q with the three new 9/16" counterbore holes drilled along with all the 1/4" holes.

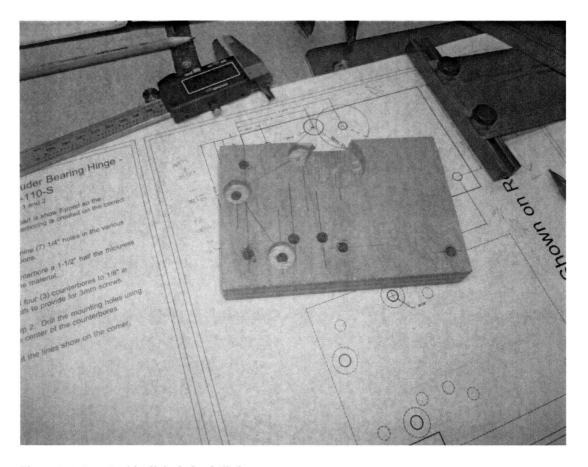

Figure 9-7. *Part Q with all the holes drilled.*

Finally, you'll finish Part Q by cutting away the waste material specified in the building plans. Flip the piece over and draw the cut lines, as shown in Figure 9-8. (Note that waste material is X'd out in the figure.)

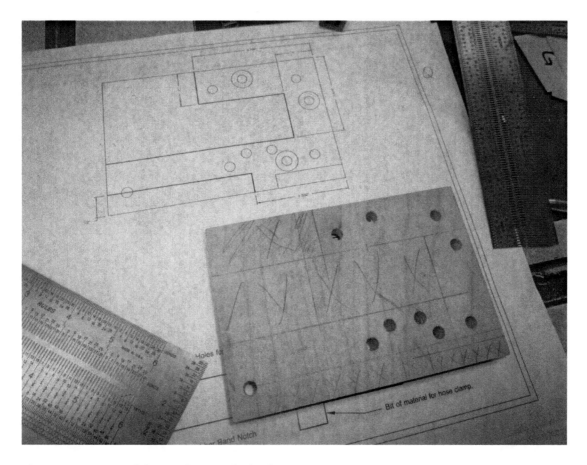

Figure 9-8. Part Q with lines indicating the final cuts.

Figure 9-9 shows a finished plywood Part Q as well as the MDO piece finished with a CNC machine.

Figure 9-9. Part Q completed in plywood (bottom) and MDO (top).

Table – Part C

Part C, or the Table, will require two Strong-Tie brackets. The starting dimensions of this piece are 8-9/16" x 9-1/16". This piece requires no additional cuts, but you must make certain to drill the holes along the 8-9/16" side (the shorter side) and not the 9-1/16" side.

You can cut out the full-size template and tape it to the top of Part C to mark the drill holes if you like, but we wanted to make absolutely certain that the Strong-Tie brackets were mounted parallel to one another and bolted down accurately, so we chose instead to draw centerlines both horizontally and vertically on Part C, as seen in Figure 9-10. Note that we also took a 1-5/16" measurement from the building plans for the lines that indicate where the edge of the Strong-Tie rails will be located. If you refer to the building plans, you'll see the dotted lines we drew on Part C indicate the Edge of Rail lines (2) and the middle lines that crisscross the part.

Figure 9-10. Part C with all lines marked for proper placement of brackets.

Using a sharp edge of a bit, scratch a line in the exact middle of two Strong-Tie brackets, as shown in Figure 9-11.

Figure 9-11. Mark a centerline in a bracket and match it up on Part C.

Place the bracket so that the centerline you scratched on the metal lines up with the line that bisects the 8-9/16" side. Also make certain the edge of the bracket is lined up perfectly with the line you drew for the Edge of Rail. When you've got the bracket properly placed, use a center point punch or drill bit to mark the eight holes that will be drilled to hold the bracket to Part C. Figure 9-12 shows this being done on one side. Perform the same action on the opposite side.

Figure 9-12. Part C with holes and bracket on one side.

The instructions recommend drilling all sixteen counterbore holes with a 5/16" drill bit but we chose to drill them slightly larger with a 11/32" bit. Drill the counterbores to an approximate depth of 3/16" and then finish up by drilling 1/4" holes completely through the centers of the counterbore holes. Figure 9-13 shows Part C completed with all holes drilled.

Figure 9-13. *Part Part C with all holes drilled.*

Z-Axis Rail Support – Part K

Part Z, or the Z-Axis Rail Support, begins with dimensions of 2-1/2" x 11-1/2"; it won't require any additional cuts, but it will require two Strong-Tie brackets. Start by marking the piece with centerlines down the long and short face, as shown in Figure 9-14.

Figure 9-14. *Mark Part K with centerlines down the horizontal and vertical face.*

Place a Strong-Tie bracket against Part K so that the bracket is flush with one end of Part K. Make certain the long edge of a bracket runs parallel to the line drawn vertically down the piece, as shown in Figure 9-15.

Figure 9-15. The Strong-Tie must run parallel to the vertical centerline.

Use a transfer punch or drill bit to mark the location of the eight holes that you will use to bolt the Strong-Tie bracket to Part K. Perform the same action on the other side—temporarily bolt on the first Strong-Tie and place the edge of the second bracket against the edge of the bolted-on bracket to mark the eight additional drill holes. Figure 9-16 shows the holes being marked for the first Strong-Tie.

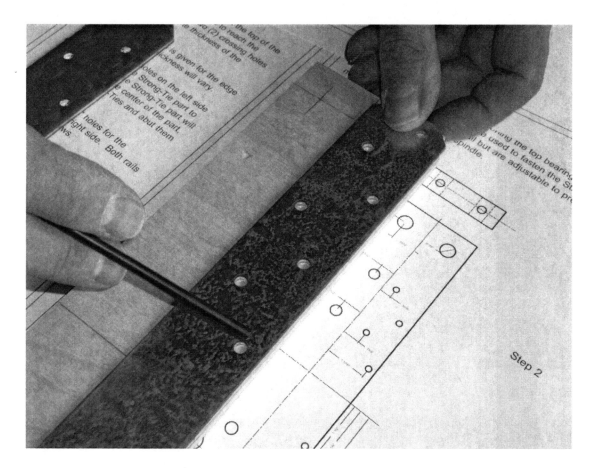

Figure 9-16. Use the Strong-Tie to mark holes to be drilled.

The two Strong-Tie brackets will touch, as shown in Figure 9-17.

Figure 9-17. Proper placement of the two Strong-Tie brackets on Part K.

Remove the Strong-Tie brackets and drill the holes as specified in the building plans. The barrel nut holes will be drilled using a 7/16" bit at the top of Part K. Also, don't forget to drill the two 1/4" holes on the top edge of Part K for the bolts that will be screwed into the barrel nuts.

Drill the four 1/2" counterbore holes to a depth of 3/8" and then drill the remaining face holes using a 5/32" bit to provide the holes that will be used to bolt the Strong-Tie brackets to Part K. Figure 9-18 shows Part K with all the drilling completed. (Note that we used a much larger bit than was specified in the plans for the four highlighted holes in Figure 9-18—this will allow us to adjust the left Strong-Tie bracket if necessary.)

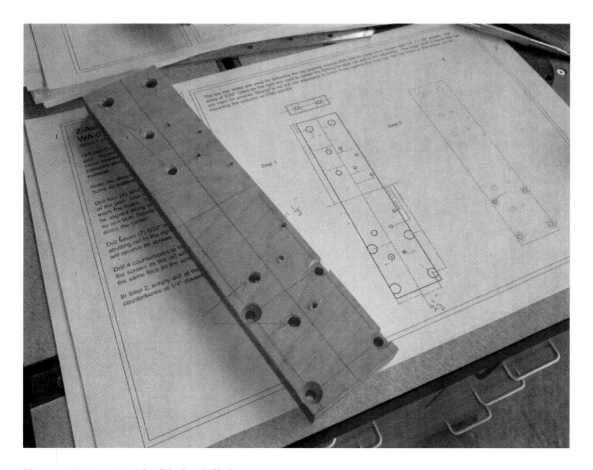

Figure 9-18. Part K with all holes drilled.

Summary

Congratulations! You've finished drilling and cutting all of the plywood parts for your 3D printer. Keep in mind that you're working with plywood here, so you may need to re-drill some holes later if you find that two pieces don't match up perfectly, but you shouldn't encounter this problem too often.

Now, set aside your parts and read over Part II of the book if you haven't already. Part II covers the assembly portion of the project, including adding the electronics.

CHAPTER 10

■ ■ ■

Beginning Assembly

Now it's time to see the efforts of your labor take shape, literally. In this and the next three chapters, we'll walk you through the process of assembling the basic framework of the 3D printer. The electronics (including the motors) will come later, but for now you'll need to grab some basic tools such as Philips and slot screwdrivers (electric/portable versions are even better) and start putting these pieces you've cut and drilled together.

At the beginning of each of these chapters, we'll provide you with a summary of the hardware you'll need, including sizes, quantity, length, etc. (If after reading the chapter you have any doubt about what hardware you need to use, you can always jump on the book's forum discussion and post your question there.)

Required Hardware and Parts Summary

For Chapter 10, you will be using the following plywood pieces and hardware:

- Part K – Z-Axis Rail Support
- Part D – ZY Plate
- Part L – Z-Axis Bearing Support
- Part N – Z-Axis Nut Mount
- Qty-3 of 2-1/2" length bolts, 1/4" diameter
- Qty-9 of 1/4" nuts
- Qty-2 Strong-Tie metal brackets
- Qty-4 #6 machine screws, 1" length
- Qty-7 #6 nuts
- Qty-4 #6 nylon spacers, 1/2" length
- Qty-7 #8 bolts, 1" length
- Qty-7 #8 nuts
- Qty-3 of 3" length bolts, 1/4" diameter

- Qty-4 of 2-1/4" bolts, 3/8" diameter

- Qty-4 3/8" nuts

- Qty-8 small red washers for 3/8" diameter bolts

- Qty-8 3/8" washers, 1" diameter

- Qty-8 3/8" V-groove bearings, 1-1/4" diameter

- Qty-3 of 1-1/2" bolts, 1/4" diameter

- Qty-3 barrel nuts

Extruder Placeholder and Z-Axis Rails

You haven't yet built the actual plastic extruder (sometime called the Plastruder), but you're going to need to add some bolts to the Z-Axis Rail Support (Part K) that will have their heads hidden underneath the two Strong-Tie rails. It's easier to place these bolts now rather than have to remove the Strong-Tie brackets later.

Figure 10-1 shows Part K with the three 2-1/2" bolts inserted into the counterbored holes. One hole was drilled but not used; you'll see why later in the assembly.

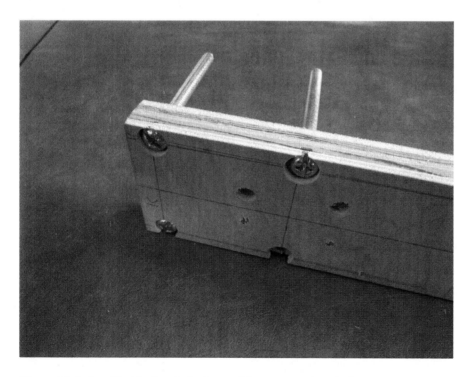

Figure 10-1. Part K with three bolts inserted into counterbore holes

Next, place two 1/4" nuts on each of the bolts. Tighten the first nut down before adding the second nut on top of the first. Figure 10-2 shows all three bolts with the double-nuts tightened.

Figure 10-2. Add two nuts to each of the bolts inserted into Part K.

Grab a single Strong-Tie bracket along with four each of the 1" #6-32 Phillips round head machine screws (9/64" diameter), the #6-32 nuts, #6 nylon spacers, and the washers. Figure 10-3 shows this hardware assembled and ready to use.

■ **Note** When it comes to washers, you should learn to treat them as an "as needed" piece of hardware. Most of the time you won't need them. But every now and then you may have a hole that is slightly larger (due to shaking of the drill, for example) and thus requires a washer. We recommend purchasing a small number of #6, #8, and 1/4" washers for the various machine screws you'll use throughout this project.

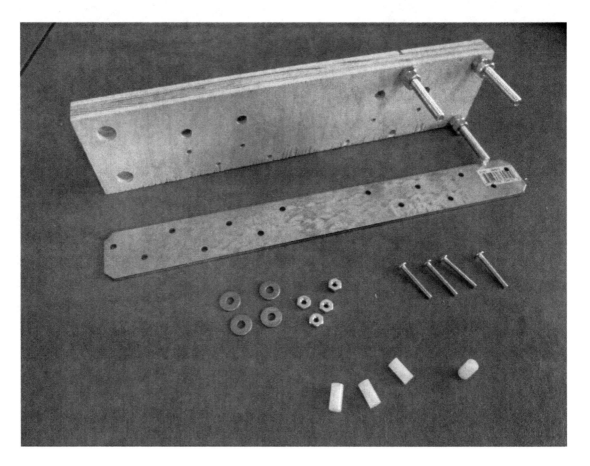

Figure 10-3. Hardware to be used to attach Strong-Ties to Part K

■ **Note** The washers are optional; you may or may not find them necessary. If the #6 nuts are getting pulled down into the holes you drilled, use the washers to prevent this.

Place the Strong-Tie bracket into position over the four holes you drilled, as shown in Figure 10-4.

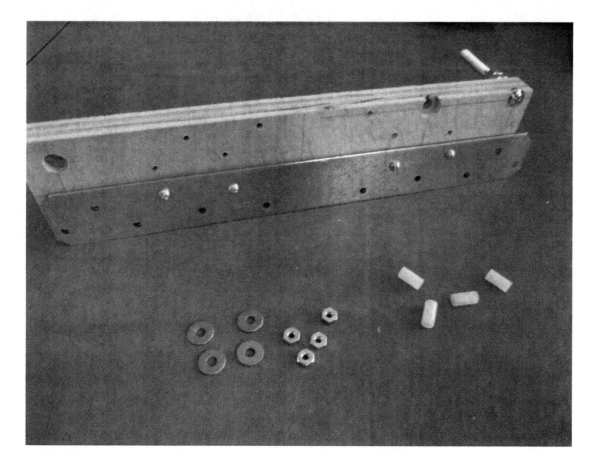

Figure 10-4. Insert the four #6 screws into the Strong-Tie bracket and through Part K.

On the other side of Part K, insert the spacers into the holes over the bolts. Follow this up with the washers (if required) and the #6 nuts and then finger tighten them for now. Figure 10-5 shows all four #6 bolts secured. Take note that the Strong-Tie bracket will extend 1/2" past the top of Part K (to the right in Figure 10-4) and will be flush at the bottom (to the left in Figure 10-4).

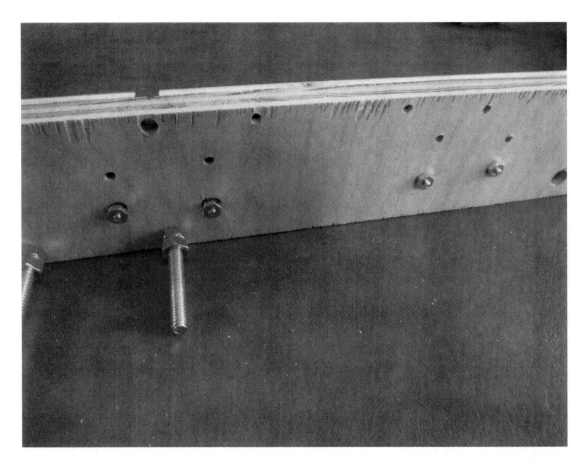

Figure 10-5. *Part K now has one Strong-Tie bracket attached.*

Next, grab another Strong-Tie bracket and seven each of the #8-32 bolts and #8-32 nuts, as shown in Figure 10-6.

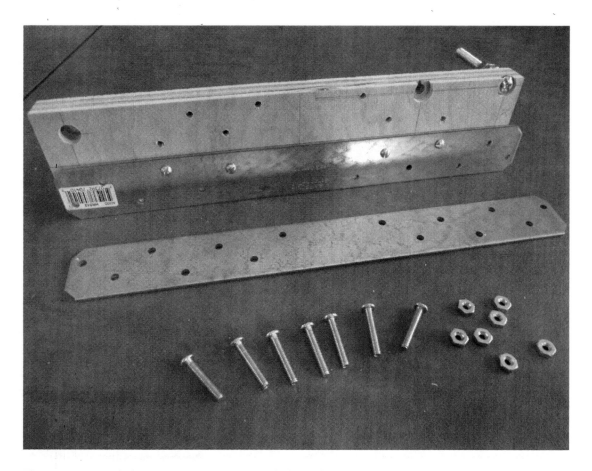

Figure 10-6. Attach the next Strong-Tie using #8 bolts and nuts.

Match up the Strong-Tie so it is runs parallel to the bracket already attached to Part K. Make certain the ends of the brackets are flush and match up and then use the bolts and nuts to secure the second one. Figure 10-7 shows the second Strong-Tie attached.

Figure 10-7. Part K with both Strong-Tie brackets bolted on

Attach the Z-Axis Bearing Support

Now find the Z-Axis Bearing Support (Part L) and grab two bolts of length 1-1/2" (diameter 1/4") and two barrel nuts, as shown in Figure 10-8.

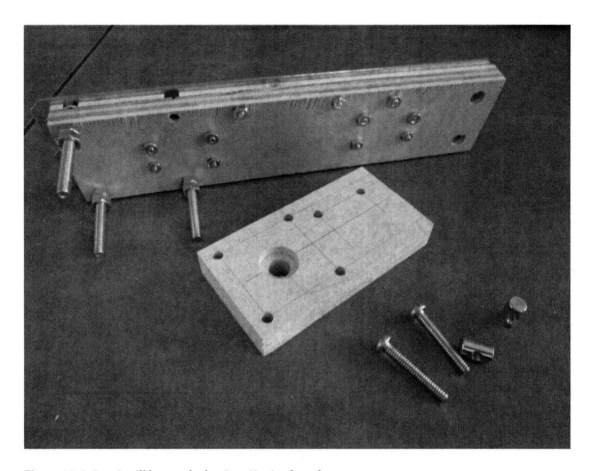

Figure 10-8. *Part L will be attached to Part K using barrel nuts.*

Place Part L perpendicular to Part K, as shown in Figure 10-9, and insert the two bolts, securing them with the two barrel nuts. Use the fact that one side of Part L has a counterbore hole and the other doesn't to help orient Part L with respect to Part K. You'll need to use a slot screwdriver to properly align the barrel nuts so that the bolts can be properly screwed into place to secure Part L. In Figure 10-9, you can just barely see the barrel nuts and their two slots at the extreme right.

Figure 10-9. *Part L attached to Part K*

Set this partial assembly aside for now and locate the ZY Plate (Part D) for the next step.

Attach V-Groove Bearings to ZY Plate

Find three of the 3" length bolts (1/4" diameter) and insert them into the ZY Plate, as shown in Figure 10-10. Secure each with a 1/4" nut (also shown in Figure 10-10).

Figure 10-10. *Part L with three bolts inserted*

Next, you'll want to gather up the parts for four different V-groove bearing assemblies. Each bearing assembly will consist of two V-groove bearings, one 2-1/4" bolt (3/8" diameter), one 3/8" nut, two small red washers, and two 3/8" washers (1" diameter), as shown in Figure 10-11. (Remember that you're making four of these assemblies, so you'll need four of everything you see in Figure 10-11.)

Figure 10-11. *These eight pieces will make one V-groove bearing assembly.*

Start by placing a single V-groove bearing onto the bolt followed by a small red washer, as shown in Figure 10-12.

Figure 10-12. Place a V-groove bearing followed by a small red washer on to the bolt.

Next, place the 3/8" washer (shown in Figure 10-12) over the small red washer and then insert this assembly into Part L, as shown in Figure 10-13. (Insert the bolt opposite of the three 3" bolts previously inserted into Part D.)

Figure 10-13. *Part D with partial V-groove assembly inserted*

Next, place a 3/8" washer followed by a small red washer onto the bolt, as shown in Figure 10-14.

Figure 10-14. A 3/8" washer and small red washer are added next.

Place a final V-groove bearing followed by a 3/8" nut and tighten. Figure 10-15 shows the final assembly of one V-groove bearing.

Figure 10-15. *A completed V-groove assembly*

■ **Note** In Figure 10-15 you may notice that the machine screw does not go all the way through the nut. You can easily increase the length of the machine screw if you prefer.

Assemble three additional V-groove bearing assemblies as previously described and place them in the locations shown in Figure 10-16.

Figure 10-16. All four V-groove bearing assemblies mounted to Part D

Attach Z-Axis Nut Mount

The last bit of assembly you'll perform in this chapter is to attach the Z-Axis Nut Mount (Part N) to Part D. You will do this using a single 1-1/2" bolt (1/4" diameter) and a single barrel nut. Figure 10-17 shows Part N, the barrel nut, and the bolt already inserted into the remaining drilled hole on Part D.

Figure 10-17. Part N will be bolted to Part D with a single bolt and barrel nut.

Insert the barrel nut into Part N and use a slot screwdriver to hold it in place as you screw the bolt into the barrel nut. Figure 10-18 shows Part N properly attached.

Figure 10-18. Part N attached to Part D

Summary

It may not look like much, but you've already assembled about a quarter of the entire machine. If you don't yet understand how all these sub-assemblies will come together and function, don't worry! Just keep moving forward; we'll include some discussion in the remaining chapters about what you're seeing and the function of these sub-assemblies.

CHAPTER 11

■ ■ ■

Sub-Assembly Work

In this chapter, you'll continue to put together various sub-assemblies; the machine isn't quite in its final form yet, but it's getting close. We'll continue to provide you with a hardware summary of the various bolts, nuts, and other pieces you'll need (including some optional hardware that will be explained). Remember to visit the book's forum discussion if you have any questions related to the assembly process in this chapter or any other chapter.

Required Hardware and Parts Summary

For Chapter 11, you will be using the following plywood pieces and hardware:

- Part H – Y-Axis Rail Support
- Parts F and G – Upper Structural Sides
- Part C – Tabletop
- Qty-4 Strong-Tie metal brackets
- Qty-16 #8-32 machine screws, 1" length
- Qty-32 #8-32 nuts
- Qty-4 of 1/4" machine screws, 1-1/2" length
- Qty-4 of 1/4" barrel nuts, 7/16" length
- Qty-16 #8-32 screws, 3/4" length
- (Optional) #8-32 machine screws, 1" length
- (Optional) #8 washers

Preparing the Y-Axis Rail Support

You're going to prepare the Y-Axis Rail Support (Part H) in a similar manner to that of the Z-Axis Rail Support (Part K). You will be attaching two Strong-Tie rails to Part H using #8 screws of 1" length.

Figure 11-1 shows Part H with the two of the #8 bolts inserted through the Strong-Tie and into the plywood piece.

Figure 11-1. Part H with two #8 bolts holding a Strong-Tie in place

Finger-tighten two #8 nuts onto the #8 bolts through the Strong-Tie and into the plywood. Attach the second Strong-Tie to Part H using two additional #8 bolts (1" length). Figure 11-2 shows the two Strong-Tie rails attached.

▨ **Note** Why are you finger-tightening only two bolts on each rail? You'll be inserting Part H (with the two Strong-Tie rails attached) into the sub-assembly you put together in Chapter 10. The rails will be inserted through the v-groove bearings and must roll smoothly. You may have to adjust the Strong-Tie rails by pushing them outward or inward in order to obtain a proper fit between the v-groove bearings. Finger-tightening now will allow you to more easily adjust the rails before adding the additional 12 #8 bolts and tightening all of them down securely.

Figure 11-2. Two Strong-Tie rails attached to the Y-Axis Rail Support

Your first task will be to insert the Z-Axis Rail Support (from Chapter 10) into the ZY Plate, as shown in Figure 11-3. Note the orientation of Part L (at top); it is pointed to the left and its counterbored hole will be directly over the larger center hole of Part N.

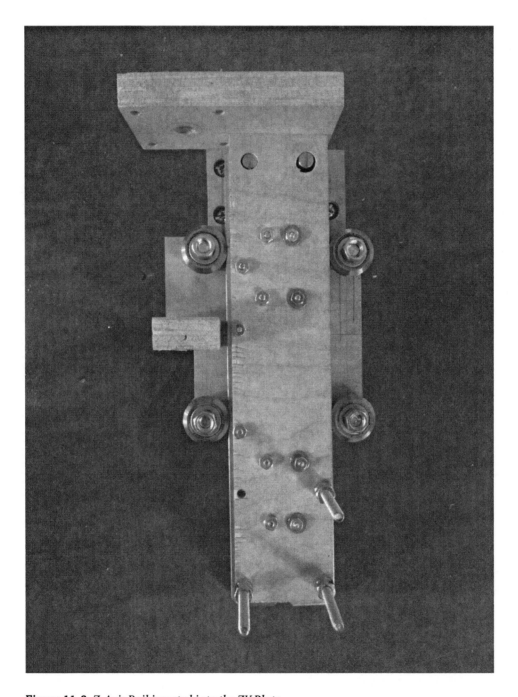

Figure 11-3. Z-Axis Rail inserted into the ZY Plate

Next, flip the ZY Plate over so that the v-groove bearings not currently being used (on the backside of the ZY Plate) are facing up. Insert Part H as shown in Figure 11-4.

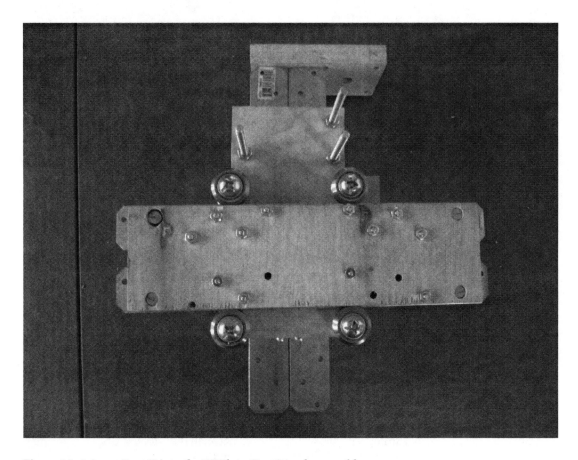

Figure 11-4. Insert Part H into the ZY Plate (Part D) sub-assembly.

When inserting a rail, push one of the Strong-Tie rails firmly against the v-groove bearings (the rail's edge should fit in the center of the v-groove bearings) and then tighten down the two #8 bolts before adding the additional six #8 bolts (and nuts). By locking down one rail, you can now move the remaining rail in or out so that it fits snugly into the v-groove bearings on the right. If you tighten down the Strong-Tie rails properly, Part H should roll back and forth in a smooth manner on the v-groove bearings. If your rails are still not rolling smoothly, you may need to drill out one or two of the v-groove bearing holes to allow you to adjust the bearings for a tighter fit.

Figure 11-5 shows two of the holes used for the v-groove bearings. These holes have been enlarged to allow the bolts more freedom of movement. We chose to enlarge one hole to allow the bolt to move only up and down (along the z-axis); the other hole was enlarged to allow its bolt to move left and right (along the y-axis). (This is one of those times where you will have to examine the movement of your rails and determine what adjustments need to be made to allow for smoother movement.)

Figure 11-5. *Enlarge one or two of the v-groove bearing holes so you can adjust them.*

If you still can't get the two Strong-Tie rails securely seated between the v-groove bearings, you may have to enlarge the holes under only one of the Strong-Tie rails. By enlarging these holes, you will give the two bolts (used to hold the rail in place) more room to move, allowing the Strong-Tie rail to be pushed into the v-groove bearings and securing it with additional bolts. Just make certain the rails are perfectly parallel to one another or they will not move between the v-groove bearings smoothly.

Attaching the Upper Structural Sides

Once you have both the Z-Axis and Y-Axis rails moving smoothly on their v-groove bearings, it's time to attach the Upper Structural Sides (Parts F and G). You will attach one side to each of the shorter edges of Part H using two 1-1/2" bolts (1/4" diameter) and two barrel nuts.

Figure 11-6 shows one of the sides held against Part H in the location where it will be bolted. Notice that the "arm" of the Upper Structural Side is pointing down towards the Z-Axis motor mount.

Figure 11-6. *An Upper Structural Side will be bolted to Part H.*

Insert a single 1-1/4" bolt and secure it with a barrel nut, as shown in Figure 11-7. You'll need a slot screwdriver to hold the barrel nut so that the slot is parallel to the inserted bolt.

Figure 11-7. Using a bolt and barrel nut to secure the Upper Structural Side

In Figure 11-7, you'll notice one problem we encountered. Sometimes, when drilling the holes for the bolt to be inserted into a barrel nut, the hole is drilled in such a way that the bolt does not line up perfectly and will not easily be screwed into the barrel nut. The only solution is to enlarge the hole. In Figure 11-7, you can see that the bottom bolt is visible in the barrel nut hole and is slightly closer to the top of the hole than it is centered. We used a large bore drill bit and just drilled out more of the wood near the top of the hole (we removed the bolt first).

Attach the other Upper Structural Side to Part H with two 1-1/2" bolts and barrel nuts. Figure 11-8 shows Parts F and G attached to Part H. Notice the barrel nut on the top-left side of Figure 11-8 is sitting higher; it doesn't look pretty but it holds the side securely. This is the hole we had to enlarge for the bolt to properly screw into the barrel nut.

Figure 11-8. *Parts F and G bolted to the sides of Part H*

Preparing the Tabletop

Your final sub-assembly for this chapter is the Tabletop (Part C). You'll be using Part C and two more
Strong-Tie rails, as shown in Figure 11-9.

Figure 11-9. Part C will have two Strong-Tie rails bolted to it.

Insert eight #8 bolts of 3/4" length through a Strong-Tie rail and into the counterbore holes of Part C, as shown in Figure 11-10.

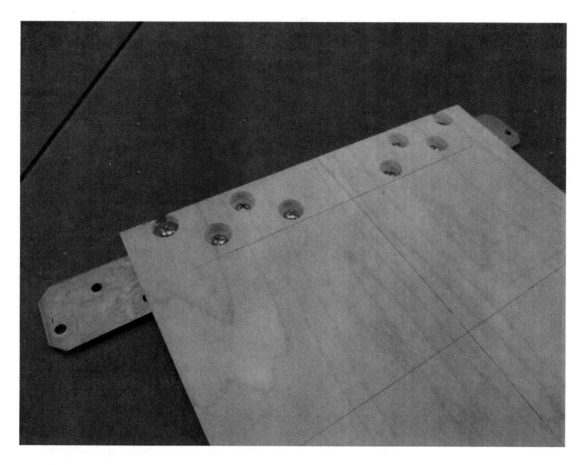

Figure 11-10. *Bolts inserted into the counterbore holes on Part C*

Flip Part C over and finger-tighten eight #8 nuts onto the bolts. (You'll be finger-tightening these nuts for now so that you'll be able to adjust the rails more easily into v-groove bearings in Chapter 12.) Figure 11-11 shows the bolts tightened and holding the rail in place.

Figure 11-11. Part C with one Strong-Tie rail attached

■ **Note** If you find that there is not enough length on the 3/4" bolts, you can use 1" length bolts instead, but nothing longer. You may also find that the #8 bolt heads, when tightened down, sink into the drilled holes; if this happens, you can use #8 washers underneath the bolt heads to prevent this. Note that if you choose to use washers, you will need to use the 1" length bolts as there will not be enough of the ¾" bolt shaft to secure properly with a nut.

Attach the second Strong-Tie rail to Part C in a similar manner, finger tightening the nuts for now. Figure 11-12 shows both rails attached to Part C.

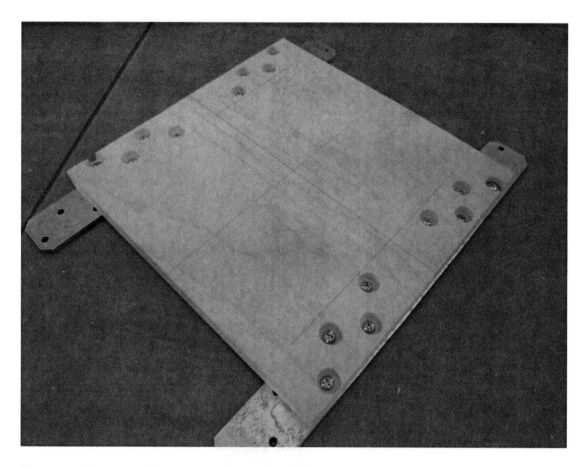

Figure 11-12. *Part C with two Strong-Tie rails attached*

Summary

Keep moving forward! Your 3D printer should be taking shape before your eyes. In the next chapter, you'll attach some parts that will bring the device closer to its final form.

■ ■ ■

CHAPTER 12

Adding Structure

By the time you finish the work in this chapter, you'll have a substantial portion of your 3D printer completed. This will provide a good look at what the final structure will look like (minus motors and a few last remaining plywood pieces).

We hope that you're starting to gain a better understanding of how to modify the existing plywood pieces by drilling out existing holes to allow for a better assembly. The machine itself is very forgiving when it comes to lining up parts and squaring up rails, but you don't want to see any major errors when it comes to bolting the pieces together. This is a build-it-yourself machine, and as such we're relying on you to examine your machine and make the necessary fixes (if any are required) to get the machine assembled properly.

Required Hardware and Parts Summary

For Chapter 12, you will be using the following plywood pieces and hardware:

- Sub-Assembly from Chapter 11 (Z-Axis Rail, Y-Axis Rail, ZY Plate)

- Parts I and J

- Parts A and B

- Qty-1 4140 Alloy Steel Precision Acme Threaded Rod, 11" length

- Qty-1 3/8"-10 ,1/5" Travel/turn, 2 Start

- Qty-1 Anti-Backlash Nut ,3/8-10, 2 Start

- Qty-3 #6 machine screws, 1-1/4" length

- Qty-3 #6 washers

- Qty-3 #6 nuts

- Qty-2 bearings, 3/8" (inner diameter) x 7/8" (outer diameter)

- Qty-1 3/8" collar
- Qty-1 motor couple (3/8" to lead screw and 1/4" to motor)
- Qty-4 3/16" v-groove bearings
- Qty-4 #10 machine screws, 1-1/2" length
- Qty-8 #10 washers
- Qty-8 #10 nuts
- Qty-4 1-1/2" machine screws, 1/4" length
- Qty-4 barrel nuts
- Qty-8 2" machine screws, 1/4" length
- Qty-8 1/4" nuts

Adding the Z-Axis Lead Screw

The Z-axis is the only axis that will move (up and down) using a lead screw. (The X and Y axes are each belt-driven.) Before you go any further with the assembly, it's time to attach the lead screw.

You'll start by inserting the lead screw into the anti-backlash nut (ABN). This can be tricky; you want the lead screw to screw into the ABN centered perfectly. The lead screw threads will be difficult to turn initially; the threads are actually going to "cut" into the plastic of the ABN and create a threaded path (similar to a nut) for the lead screw to move through.

Screw the ABN onto the lead screw as shown in Figure 12-1. You want to have the ABN about two inches from one end of the lead screw.

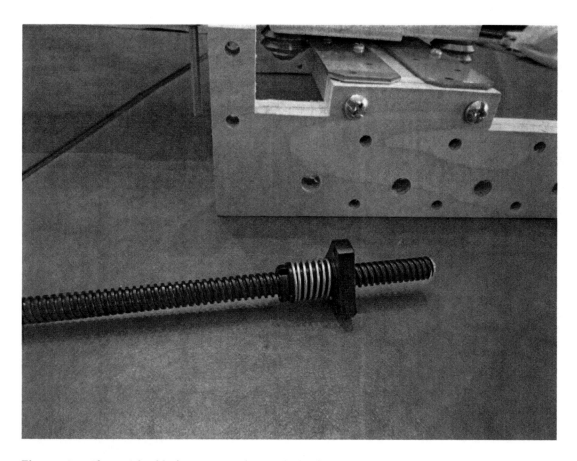

Figure 12-1. The anti-backlash nut screwed on to the lead screw

Next, insert the collar and then a single bearing, as shown in Figure 12-2. Don't tighten the collar yet, and push the collar and bearing to the mid-point of the lead screw. If you find that the bearings don't slide easily onto the lead screw, use 600 grit Emery paper and carefully sand about 4" on one end of the lead screw. This removes the thickness of the paint on the lead screw and the bearing should slip on with ease.

Figure 12-2. *A collar and a bearing inserted onto the lead screw*

Insert the lead screw end closest to the bearing (hold the collar and bearing so they don't slide off) through the counterbored hole on the Z-Axis Bearing Support (Part L). The other end of the lead screw (with the ABN) will be inserted through the large center hole of Part N (Z-Axis Nut Mount). Next, use three #6 machine screws (1-1/4" length) inserted through the three holes surrounding the lead screw in the ABN and insert these into the holes of Part N, as shown in Figure 12-3.

Figure 12-3. *Insert the lead screw through Parts L and N.*

Use three #6 nuts and three washers to secure the three #6 machine screws and tighten them to keep the ABN attached securely to Part N, as shown in Figure 12-4. (You'll notice in Figure 12-4 that we need to add a final nut over the washer to secure the ABN.)

Figure 12-4. *Secure the anti-backlash nut to Part N with three machine screws.*

Next, insert a bearing on the other end of the lead screw (again, you may need to sand a bit of the paint finish off of the lead screw if the bearing doesn't slide on easily) and push it into the counterbored hole, as shown in Figure 12-5. (If the bearing doesn't fit flush with the surface of Part N, this is okay, but it shouldn't protrude more than 1/16" or so.)

Figure 12-5. *Bearing inserted in counterbore hole to hold the lead screw*

Now add one half of the motor couple to the lead screw (only one of the two pieces will fit properly), as shown in Figure 12-6. The end of the lead screw should sit flush with flat surface of the couple.

Figure 12-6. *Tighten the motor collar on to the lead screw.*

Move the Z-Axis rail away from Part L until the motor couple is up against the inserted bearing, and then use an Allen wrench to tighten the set screw. Tighten the set screw(s) good and tight so the couple will not come off of the lead screw.

On the other side of Part N, push the bearing and collar up against Part N and use an Allen wrench to tighten the collar against the lead screw; again, tighten it securely so it doesn't loosen on the lead screw. Figure 12-7 shows the bearing and collar tightened against Part N.

Figure 12-7. Tighten the bearing and collar against Part N.

Assemble Table Bearing Supports

Next, you're going to assemble the two Table Bearing Supports (Parts I and J). This work will require four of the smaller 3/16" v-groove bearings plus the additional hardware shown in Figure 12-8.

Figure 12-8. *Parts I and J will each hold a set of v-groove bearings.*

Start by placing a single v-groove bearing onto a #10 machine screw (1-1/4" length), followed by a washer and then a nut tightened up against the v-groove bearing, as shown in Figure 12-9.

Figure 12-9. *A v-groove bearing assembly for Part I*

Insert the machine screw into one of the small holes on Part I and push it completely through. Secure the machine screw with a single washer and nut, as shown in Figure 12-10.

Figure 12-10. *Secure the v-groove bearing with a washer and nut.*

Perform the previous actions for the remaining hole on Part I and the two smaller holes of Part J. Figure 12-11 shows Parts I and J with the v-groove bearing assemblies added.

Figure 12-11. Parts I and J with the v-groove assemblies added

Add Bearing Supports to Lower Structural Sides

You're going to now attach Parts I and J to the two Lower Structural Sides (Parts A and B). For each Table Bearing Support, you will need one Lower Structural side, two 1-1/2" long machine screws, and two barrel nuts (see Figure 12-12).

Figure 12-12. A Lower Structural Side with hardware to attach a Table Bearing Support.

Insert a Table Bearing Support (Part I or J; it doesn't matter) with the v-groove bearing towards the top of the Lower Structural Side and insert two machine screws through the holes seen in Figure 12-13.

Figure 12-13. *Insert a Table Bearing Support into a Lower Structural Side.*

On the other side of the Lower Structural Side, you will use two barrel nuts. Screw the machine screws into the barrel nuts and tighten them to secure the Table Bearing Support. Figure 12-14 shows the underside of one of the Table Bearing Supports; notice how the slot on the barrel nut runs parallel to the machine screw that is screwed into it.

Figure 12-14. *Use barrel nuts to secure the Table Bearing Supports.*

Figure 12-15 shows parts A and B, each with a Table Bearing Support attached.

Figure 12-15. Parts A and B have their Table Bearing Supports secured.

Attach Lower Structural Sides

Now it's time to attach Parts A and B to the larger sub-assembly that you put together in Chapter 11. Figure 12-16 shows Part A (or B; you want the Table Bearing Support facing inwards) placed against the Upper Structural Side and four machine screws ready to be inserted. (Note the orientation of the Z-Axis rail; it's on top and the "arms" of the Lower Structural Sides are pointing down towards the tabletop.)

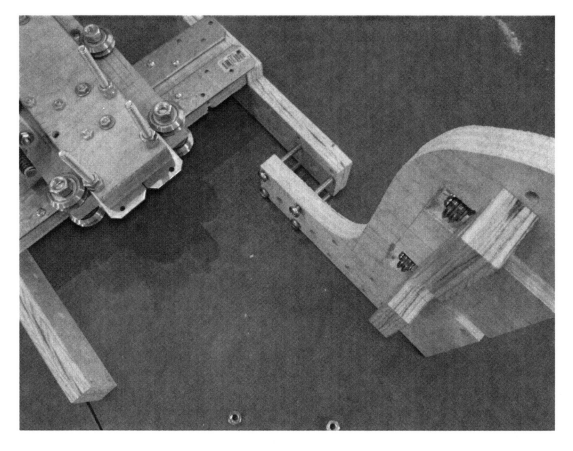

Figure 12-16. A Lower Structural Side ready to attach to the Upper Structural Side

Do the same with the other Lower Structural Side. Push four machine screws through each of the Lower and Upper Structural Sides and secure them with 1/4" nuts, as shown in Figure 12-17.

Figure 12-17. Upper and Lower Structural Sides bolted down and tightened

Stand up the assembly at this point and take a look! Your 3D printer is really coming together and should look like the one in Figure 12-18.

Figure 12-18. *Your 3D Printer should look like this one.*

Summary

Although the 3D printer is looking nice, it's not done yet! You've still got a few plywood pieces to attach and the electronics to add. Speaking of electronics, let's take a break from the assembly and prepare the motors before you attach them to your machine.

■■■

CHAPTER 13

Motors and Movement

Your 3D printer is now ready for the motors that will control movement and allow the Plastic Extruder to "print" on the tabletop. There are three axes of movement: X, Y, and Z. The X-axis consists of the Table that will move forwards and backwards (front to back), the Y-axis will move the Extruder left and right, and the Z-axis will allow the Extruder to move up and down. Each of these axes has a dedicated stepper motor that will be added to the machine. (A fourth motor will be added later that is not involved in movement.)

There are two methods of movement that will be used; the Z-axis movement will use a lead screw and the X and Y axes will be belt driven. Read over the chapter completely before beginning your work and make certain you understand how all the moving parts are connected and assembled. When done, you'll have your 3D printer (minus Extruder) ready for testing.

Required Hardware and Parts Summary

For Chapter 13, you will be using the following plywood pieces and hardware:

- 3D Printer Assembly from Chapter 12
- Part E (X-Axis Motor Mount)
- Part M (Z-Axis Motor Mount)
- Part R (Y-Axis Motor Mount)
- Qty-3 NEMA 23 stepper motors (with wires already attached)
- Qty-4 4" machine screws, 1/4" length
- Qty-4 3-1/2" machine screws, 1/4" length
- Qty-42 1/4" nuts
- Qty-6 bearings (1/4" inner diameter)
- Qty-2 1-1/2" machine screws, 1/4" length

- Qty-12 #6-32 x 1-1/4" (or 1-1/2") machine screws
- Qty-12 #6 nuts
- Qty-12 #6 washers
- Qty-2 belt pulleys
- Qty-2 belts
- Qty-1 Motor collar
- Qty-1 Motor mating piece
- Qty-2 Threaded Rod, 13" length x 1/4" diameter
- Qty-4 #8-32 x 1-1/4" machine screws
- Qty-6 #8 nuts
- Qty-2 metal brackets (a.k.a. mending plates)Home Depot part#339-482 for attaching belt for Y-axis
- Optional: Qty-4 of the metal brackets in lieu of screws/washers/nuts for attaching belt to X-axis Strong-Ties
- Qty-2 #8-32 machine screws, 1" length
- Qty-8 #8 washers
- Qty-4 fender washers (optional)

Adding the X-Axis Motor and Motor Mount

The X-axis motor will control the forward and backward movement of the Table (Part C). The motor will sit underneath the Table and use a nylon belt and notched timing pulley to control the movement.

Figure 13-1 shows the three stepper motors that will be used to control the X, Y, and Z axes. Each axes has its own motor mount; a motor will first be attached to the motor mount and then the motor mount will be added to the 3D printer body you've assembled so far.

▪ **Note** You can purchase these types of motors with or without wires already attached, but we recommend that you buy them with the wires already attached instead of soldering wires yourself. If you buy motors without wires, you will need to solder wires to the motors or use another method for attaching the wires.

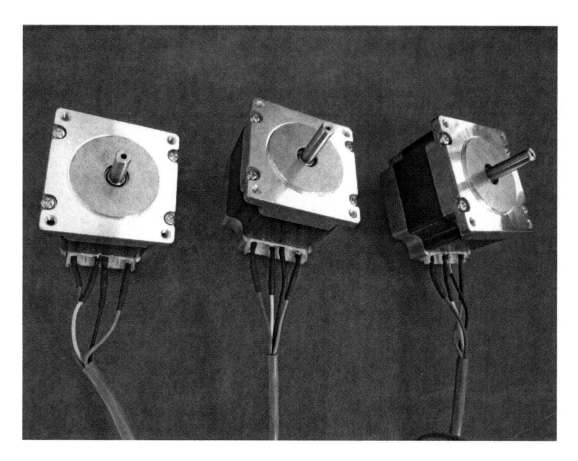

Figure 13-1. *Three stepper motors for the X, Y, and Z axes*

Start with the X-axis motor and prepare the X-Axis Motor Mount (Part E). Start by inserting two 4" x 1/4" machine screws (3" can also be used). The two machine screw heads will be on the same side as the large counterbore hole. On the other side of Part E, thread two 1/4" nuts on each of the machine screws, as shown in Figure 13-2.

Figure 13-2. *Preparing the X-Axis Motor Mount*

Next, insert two 1-1/2" x 1/4" machine screws (through the holes just above the longer 4" machines screws). Flip Part E over and, on each 1-1/2" machine screw, add a nut, two bearings (1/4" inside diameter), and a final nut; then screw the nuts down tight, as shown in Figure 13-3.

Figure 13-3. Add bearings to the X-Axis Motor Mount.

Now it's time to attach one of the stepper motors. Use four #6-32 x 1-1/2" (1-1/4" length will also work) machine screws along with four washers and insert them into Part E, as shown in Figure 13-4.

Figure 13-4. Use machine screws and washers to hold the motor to the motor mount.

Hold the #6 nuts against the motor before screwing in the #6 machine screws; the small corners on each motor will make it difficult to rotate the nuts so it's easier to place the nuts first and then screw in the #6 machine screws. Figure 13-5 shows the X-axis motor attached to the motor mount. You want the motor's wire leads to point in the direction of the rear of the machine; simply position this assembly as it would be bolted to the side of the frame and you'll be able to determine if the motor's wires are pointing to the rear of the machine. If not, take the motor off and reposition it.

Figure 13-5. *The stepper motor attached to the X-Axis Motor Mount*

Add the belt pulley to the end of the X-axis motor and use an Allen wrench to tighten it. Make certain the notches (teeth) on the pulley are over the bearings below, as shown in Figure 13-6.

Figure 13-6. *Tighten the belt pulley over the bearings with an Allen wrench.*

Lay your 3D printer frame down with the Lower Structural Sides pointing towards you. Insert the X-Axis Motor Mount as demonstrated in Figure 13-7. Push it as far as possible so that the 1-1/2" machine screws holding the bearings are touching (or almost touching) the notch cut into the Table Bearing Support.

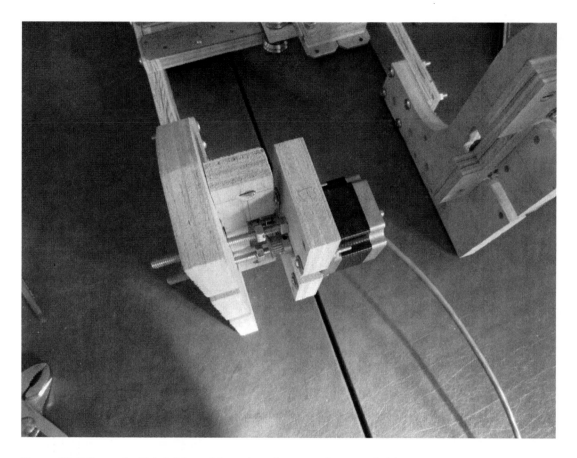

Figure 13-7. Insert the X-Axis Motor Mount into the Lower Structural Side.

Use two 1/4" nuts on the outside of the Lower Structural Side (on the two 4" machine screws) and also secure the two nuts between the motor mount and the inside wall of the Lower Structural Side, as shown in Figure 13-8.

Figure 13-8. Tighten the nuts to hold the motor mount securely.

Insert two 4" machine screws, as shown in Figure 13-9, and secure them in the same manner as the other two 4" machine screws. Use two nuts on the inside that will be tightened against the motor mount and the inside wall of the Lower Structural side and a single nut to tighten against the outer wall of the Lower Structural Side.

Figure 13-9. Two additional machine screws are added to strengthen the motor mount.

Adding the Z-Axis Motor and Motor Mount

Now it's time to prepare the Z-Axis Motor Mount (Part M). Insert four 3-1/2" machine screws and then add two nuts to each of the machine screws, as shown in Figure 13-10.

Figure 13-10. Prepare the Z-Axis Motor Mount with four machine screws.

■ **Note** You may find later when adding the Z-Axis Motor Mount to the 3D printer body that one of the 3-1/2" machine screws needs to be removed if it rubs against one of the Strong-Tie brackets attached to the Y-Axis Rail Support. This is not a problem, but prepare four 3-1/2" machine screws just in case.

Next, attach a stepper motor to the Z-Axis Motor Mount using four #6-32 x 1-1/2" machine screws (1-1/4" length will also work) and #6 nuts and washers. Unlike the X-axis motor, however, this time insert the #6 machine screws through the motor first and secure with the nuts and washers on the underside of the Z-Axis Motor Mount, as shown in Figure 13-11.

Figure 13-11. Attach the motor with #6 machine screws, nuts, and washers.

Next, add the other piece of the motor collar to the Z-axis motor shaft and tighten with an Allen wrench. The end of the motor shaft should be flush with the motor collar, as shown in Figure 13-12.

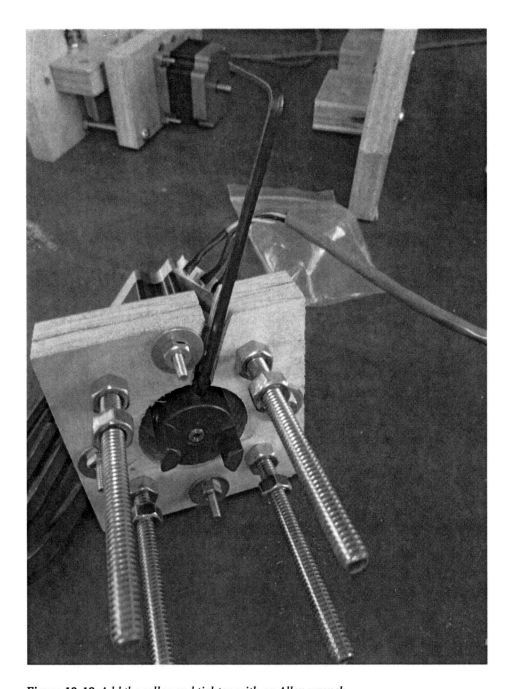

Figure 13-12. Add the collar and tighten with an Allen wrench.

On the 3D printer body, add the small collar mating piece to the collar already attached to the lead screw, as shown in Figure 13-13.

Figure 13-13. Add the collar mating piece to the collar attached to the lead screw.

Carefully insert the Z-Axis Motor Mount by pushing the four (or three) 3-1/2" machine screws into the holes on the Z-Axis Bearing Support (Part L). Push down until the collar on the Z-Axis Motor Mount is secured properly in the collar mating piece. This may require some patience; don't rush it or push too hard. When the collars are mated, secure the four (or three, if you had to remove one) 3-1/2" machine screws with four nuts, as shown in Figure 13-14. Use the other two nuts on each 3-1/2" machine screw to tighten (push) against the and the Z-Axis Bearing Support. Note in Figure 13-14 that the motor's wires are pointed towards the rear of the machine (this will be helpful later during the wiring portion of the project).

Figure 13-14. *Secure the motor mount with the nuts.*

Adding the Y-Axis Motor and Motor Mount

Now attach a stepper motor to the Y-Axis Motor Mount (Part R) using four #6-32 x 1-1/2" machine screws, nuts, and washers as demonstrated in Figure 13-15.

Figure 13-15. *Add a motor to the Y-Axis Motor Mount.*

On the back of the ZY Plate (Part D), add one nut to each of the two machine screws on the right side, as shown in Figure 13-16. You'll also add two bearings followed by a single nut on the machine screw on the left side.

Figure 13-16. *Prepare the ZY Plate to hold the Y-Axis Motor Mount.*

Place the belt pulley onto the Y-axis motor shaft and then add the motor mount, as shown in Figure 13-17. Tighten the belt pulley with an Allen wrench so that the pulley is directly in line with the bearings (also seen in Figure 13-17) and tighten the nuts on the other two machine screws so that they are snug against the ZY Plate and the motor mount.

Figure 13-17. *Attach the Y-Axis Motor Mount with belt pulley to the ZY Plate.*

Secure the motor mount with three nuts, as shown in Figure 13-18.

Figure 13-18. Add nuts to secure the motor mount to the ZY Plate.

Adding Tension Rods and the Table

To allow the Table to move forward and backward smoothly on the v-groove bearings, you're going to need to add two tension rods that can be adjusted to allow the table to be held snug but still allow for smooth movement.

You will need two 12" lengths of 1/4" threaded rod. Threaded rod can be found at most hardware stores in 2' lengths, so you will need to cut two 12" pieces. If you have to cut the two pieces, remember to add nuts to the threaded rod before cutting. The threads on the rod can become damaged during the cutting and putting nuts on the rod will allow you to unscrew them and "repair" any thread damage.

▪ **Note** You might also consider buying a 3' length of threaded rod and cutting two 13" lengths instead. This will give you a longer bit of rod sticking out from each side of the machine but you can later use this extra length to secure the machine to a plywood base, for example, where you can mount the power supply (see Chapter 18) and make the machine more stable.

Insert a single threaded rod, as shown in Figure 13-19. Note that each rod will have two nuts between the Lower Structural Sides as well as one on the outside of each Lower Structural Side.

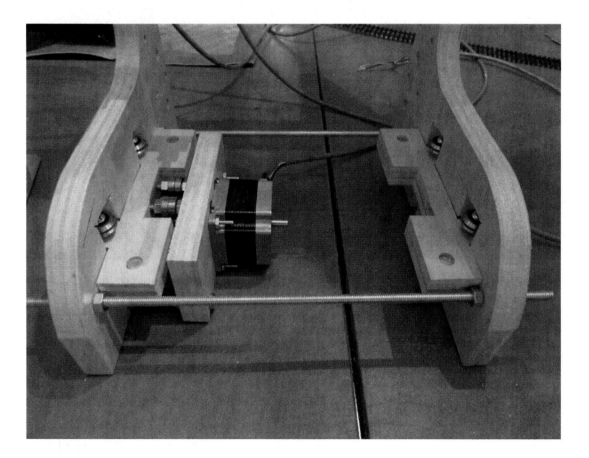

Figure 13-19. Add two threaded rods to control the tension on the Table.

Do not tighten the inner nuts yet; you'll perform this step once the Table has been added. Add the second threaded rod to the rear of the machine (see Figure 13-19) and secure it with nuts. Figure 13-20 shows the two tension rods added and secured with nuts.

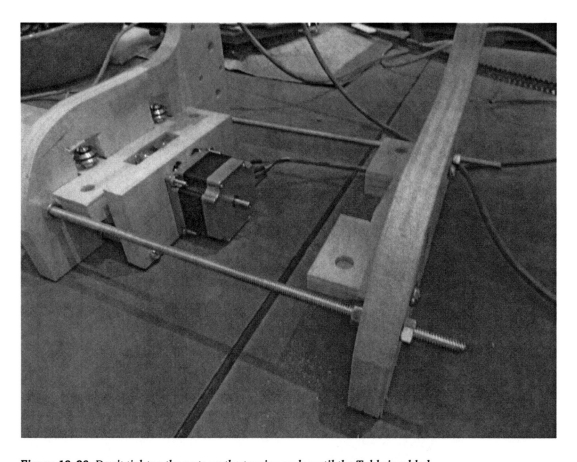

Figure 13-20. Don't tighten the nuts on the tension rods until the Table is added.

Insert the Table (assembled in Chapter 11) so that the edges of the Strong-Tie brackets ride between the v-groove bearings. An extra set of hands will come in handy here as you'll need to adjust the outside nuts so that they squeeze the Lower Structural Sides together and allow the v-groove bearings to hold the Table securely but not too tightly.

Figure 13-21 shows the Table inserted properly. Once you have your Table rolling smoothly, tighten the nuts on the tension rods against the Lower Structural Sides.

Figure 13-21. Add the Table and adjust nuts until the Table rolls smoothly.

Adding Belts to X and Y Axes

The final task for this chapter will be to add the belts to the X and Y motors. You'll start by cutting the two belts (that are sold as a looped belt) and setting them aside until needed.

Next, use two #8-32 machine screws (you can also use 1-1/4" machine screws) through the holes at the top of the Upper Structural Side to hold the small metal bracket in place, as shown in Figure 13-22.

Figure 13-22. A single bracket added to the Upper Structural Side

Next, take one of the cut belts and feed it through the pulley and bearings as demonstrated in Figure 13-23. One end of the belt will be secured by two metal brackets (see Figure 13-22), and the other end, after looping through the pulley and bearings, will be secured in an identical manner on the other Upper Structural Side.

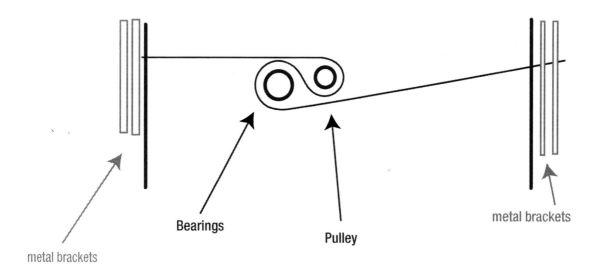

metal brackets

Bearings

Pulley

metal brackets

metal brackets

Figure 13-23. *Feed the belt through the pulley and bearings of the Y-axis motor.*

Pull tightly on one end of the belt (and make certain it stays lined up properly with pulley and bearings) and secure it by placing a second metal bracket over the first; tighten it down with two #8 nuts, as shown in Figure 13-24.

Figure 13-24. Secure the belt with a second metal bracket.

Keeping tension on the other side of the belt (and verifying that it is still feeding through the pulley and bearings, as shown in Figure 13-23), secure the other end of the belt on the opposite side using two metal brackets, #8 machine screws, and #8 nuts.

Next, you'll add the last belt to the X-axis motor; this one can be a bit tricky as you need to keep tension on the belt so it doesn't come off the pulley and bearings, so try to find a partner to assist if you can. (You can also use binder clips to hold the belt to the tension rods.)

Remove the Table and carefully tip your 3D printer back so that the X-Axis Motor Mount is exposed; see in Figure 13-25.

Figure 13-25. Remove the Table to add the belt to the X-axis motor.

Figure 13-26 shows how the belt will loop through the bearings and around the pulley. Take your time; this can be a time-consuming activity (especially if you don't have an assistant). Once you have the belt looped properly, you can either secure it to the tension rods with clips (see Figure 13-25) or have your assistant hold the ends of the belt so that it doesn't slip.

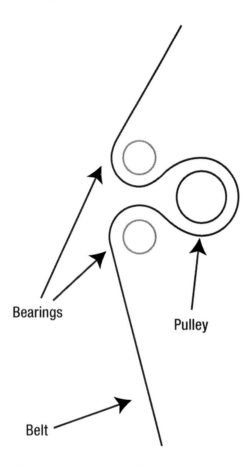

Figure 13-26. *Route the belt through the pulley and bearings.*

Figure 13-27 shows a close-up view of the belt wrapped over the bearings and around the pulley. Keeping tension on the ends of the belt will help prevent the belt from slipping off the pulley and bearings.

Figure 13-27. *The belt wrapping over the bearings and around the pulley*

Carefully insert the Table between the v-groove bearings. You're going to secure one end of the belt to one end of the Strong-Tie bracket using a single #8 x 3/4" machine screw (1/2" length will also work), four fender washers, and a nut. Two washers will be on one side and two washers and the nut on the other. You will feed the belt between the washers on one side, around the Strong-Tie bracket, through the other two washers, and then tighten the nut to hold the belt securely. Figure 13-28 shows one end of the belt held in place with the washers.

Figure 13-28. *Secure the ends of the belt with washers pinching the belt above and below.*

Make certain that the belt is still in place on the pulley and bearings and secure the other end to the Strong-Tie bracket on the opposite end of the Table.

Summary

You now have three (of four) motors attached. All that's left of the assembly portion is to build and attach the Extruder and mount the motor drivers and 3DP controllers to the machine. After that, you'll turn your attention to the software and actually getting your 3DP to do something.

You're almost there, so take a well-deserved break and admire the machine that you've built.

■ ■ ■

CHAPTER 14

The Extruder

Of all the parts on your 3D Printer, the one that makes your machine an actual 3D printer versus just some interesting looking device sitting on your desk is the Extruder. The Extruder is the business end of the machine; without it, you won't be doing any plastic printing.

That's not to say that it's the most important part of your machine, but it is a fairly important element. Although it has no moving parts, it's a component that you should take your time assembling and handle carefully. It consists of a small collection of parts that come together to give your machine the ability to heat up the filament and extrude it from a nozzle using controlled movements.

We're dedicating an entire chapter to just assembling the Extruder, so read over it carefully and gather the required components. You'll purchase a complete kit from Makerbot.com that contains all the parts you need to build the Extruder (plus some extra parts that aren't necessary for your DIY 3D printer).

Required Hardware and Parts Summary

For Chapter 14, you will be using the following components and supplies:

- Mark-5 Extruder Kit from MakerBot

- Minimum 9" of ceramic tape

- Roll of Kapton tape

- Thermocouple

- Qty-2 20-gauge stranded wire, 12" (preferably in two colors)

- Shrink tubing

- Soldering iron (any type used for smaller, more delicate electronics will suffice)

- Solder

Some Soldering Required

Before you begin, you need to be aware that building the Extruder is going to require soldering. This means that a soldering iron and solder will be used at one point in the assembly for making solid connections between wires and certain components in the Extruder.

If you don't know how to solder or are uncomfortable soldering, we highly encourage you to outsource this part of the project. It's highly likely that you know someone (a friend or co-worker, maybe) that has the proper equipment and knowledge. The required soldering will take less than 15 minutes total so it's not going to require a huge time investment.

Another option to consider is placing a "help needed" request on a site such as craigslist.com; you should expect to pay anywhere from $25 to $50 for the soldering work if you choose to hire someone.

If you've never soldered and would like to learn how, you're in luck; for less than $30 you can purchase a decent soldering iron from Radio Shack that will be more than adequate; tubes of solder can typically be found for less than $10. You could spend more, but unless you expect to be doing a lot of soldering in the future, try to keep your costs down by buying the minimum tools that you need. In all honesty, you're not going to need a $100 soldering setup for the work required here, so don't go crazy.

Some great soldering tutorials can be found on the Web; one such tutorial that can help you decide if you'd like to tackle the job yourself is on the Instructables web site at www.instructables.com/id/How-to-solder/. Check it out; we think you'll find that soldering isn't as scary and complicated as you might think.

▓ **Note** Soldering produces fumes that can be dangerous to inhale. Read all instructions on your soldering equipment as well as the actual solder purchased and follow the guidelines to stay safe.

Prepare the Extruder

Your first step in assembling the Extruder is to screw in the nozzle and feed the cylinder into the heater core. Before you do this, however, you need to coat the threads on both the nozzle and feed cylinder with the anti-seize grease that will help prevent corrosion and rust inside the component over time (it's included with the Extruder kit). Collect all four components as shown in Figure 14-1.

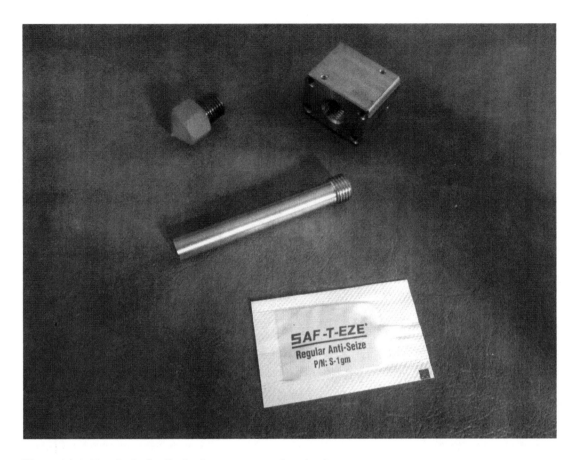

Figure 14-1. *Nozzle, feed cylinder, heater core, and anti-seize grease*

Cut the end off the small package and squeeze half of the anti-seize grease onto the end of a finger. Roll the threaded end of the feed cylinder through the grease, making certain to get it into the grooves and covering the entire threaded surface, as shown in Figure 14-2. Squeeze the remaining grease onto your finger and roll the threaded end of the nozzle through the grease as well.

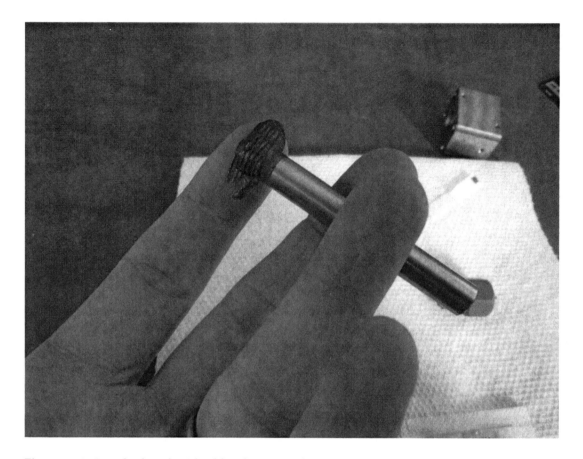

Figure 14-2. Coat the threads with a liberal amount of anti-seize grease.

Screw in the nozzle to the heater element; it goes into the hole on the side *without* the four smaller threaded holes in the corners; see Figure 14-3.

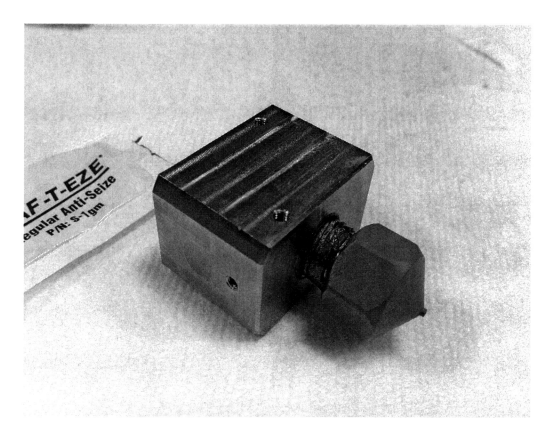

Figure 14-3. *Add bearings to the X-Axis Motor Mount*

Use two wrenches to tighten the nozzle. (The nozzle head requires a 13mm wrench; hold the heater core with the other wrench.)

Next, insert the feed cylinder into the other side of the heater nozzle (the side with four small screw holes in the corners) and finger tighten as much as possible. Figure 14-4 shows both the nozzle and feed cylinder inserted.

Figure 14-4. Heater core with feed cylinder and nozzle inserted

The next step is to insert the PTFE tube (PTFE is a heat resistant material) shown in Figure 14-5 into the feed cylinder.

Figure 14-5. *Insert the PTFE tube into the feed cylinder.*

Push the PTFE tube into the feed cylinder (pointed end first) as far as possible. You can use a sharp blade or pen to make a small mark on the tube at the end of the feed cylinder. Pull out the tube and place it over the feed cylinder and heater core so that the mark you made matches up to the end of the feed cylinder. If the tapered end of the tube doesn't extend to the tip of the nozzle, you didn't push it in far enough; try again and make another mark until you get it all the way into the nozzle.

Once the tube is inserted properly, use a sharp blade to cut the tube so that it is flush with the end of the feed cylinder, as shown in Figure 14-6.

Figure 14-6. Cut the PTFE tube so it is flush with the end of the feed cylinder.

Next, you'll attach the two power resistors to the heater core, one per side. Use the small 1/16" Allen screws seen in Figure 14-7 with an Allen wrench.

Figure 14-7. *Attach one power resistor to each side of the heater core.*

Figure 14-8 shows one of the power resistors attached. Attach the second power resistor to the opposite side (see Figure 14-9).

Figure 14-8. One power resistor attached with two Allen screws

Figure 14-9. Both power resistors now attached to heater core

Soldering the PTFE Wire

Now it's time for some soldering. You'll be using the PTFE wire for this part of the project; the PTFE coating can endure the high temperatures that will be generated by the power resistors that heat the heater core.

The first thing you'll want to do is cut four 2" lengths of PTFE wire and strip off 1/4" from each end with a sharp blade. *Don't use wire strippers for this as the PTFE may not cut properly;* instead, a sharp blade can be used to whittle away the outer coating and leave the wire intact. Be very careful not to cut some of the wires inside; they are very thin and easily cut. Figure 14-10 shows all four wires prepared and ready for soldering.

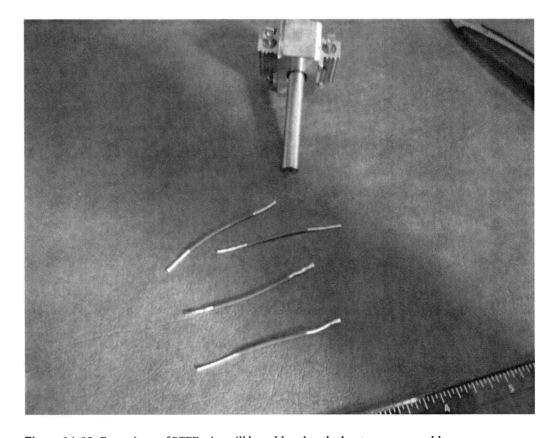

Figure 14-10. Four pieces of PTFE wire will be soldered to the heater core assembly.

What you'll be doing in the next step is soldering one wire between the two leads of one power resistor. Insert one of the stripped wire ends through the hole in one lead and loop the wire around to secure it for soldering; you can trim any wire ends to create a cleaner joint for soldering. Solder this wire to a lead, as shown in Figure 14-11. Don't be stingy with the solder; put a nice blob on both sides if you can. We'll call this wire a lead wire because it will be soldered between the leads.

Figure 14-11. Solder one end of a piece of PTFE wire to one power resistor lead.

Next, before soldering the other end of the lead wire to the other lead, grab another 2" piece of PTFE wire (we'll call this the extension wire). Insert the stripped ends of both the lead wire and the extension wire through the other lead's hole and wrap the ends around so they are secured to the lead before soldering. You can see this in Figure 14-12.

Figure 14-12. *The lead wire and the extension wire wrapped around the other lead*

Place a good bead of solder on both sides of the lead to secure the lead wire and the extension wire, as shown in Figure 14-13.

Figure 14-13. *Solder the lead wire and the extension wire away from the body of the heater core.*

Flip the heater core over and do the exact same thing with the remaining two pieces of PTFE wire, making sure that the second extension wire is pointing in the same direction as the first extension wire, as shown in Figure 14-14.

Figure 14-14. Both lead wires and extension wires soldered to the heater core

---

■ **Note** The extension wires are important; the heater core is going to generate a lot of heat and the PTFE extension wires have a coating that will resist that heat. Standard shielded wire (speaker wire) won't handle the heat, so the extension pieces provide a place to connect to regular wire without worrying about the high temperatures.

The last bit of soldering will be done to add two 12" lengths of 20 gauge stranded wire to each of the extension wires. Cut the two 12" lengths (we used one black wire and one red wire, but the colors really don't matter here) and strip 1/4" or so from one end of each wire. Solder one wire to each of the extension wires, as shown in Figure 14-15.

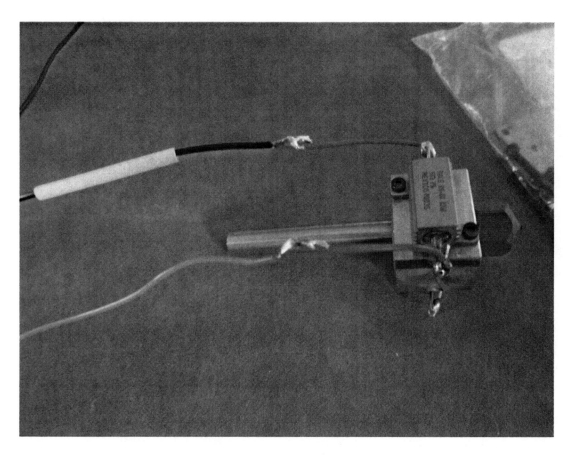

Figure 14-15. Solder one piece of 12" wire to each of the extension wires.

Cover each of the solder joints with a bit of shrink tubing, as shown in Figure 14-16, and put away the soldering iron.

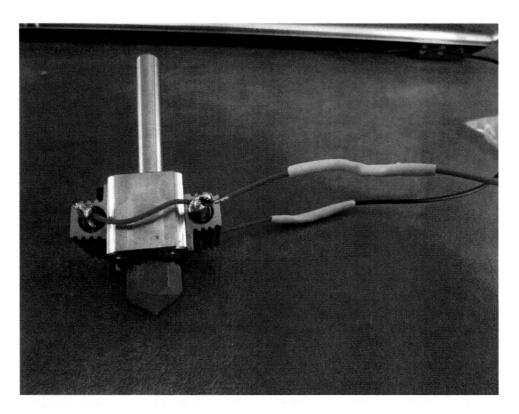

Figure 14-16. Shrink tubing will protect the solder joints.

Add the Thermocouple

Next, you're going to attach the thermocouple, a device that will allow the temperature of the heater core to be monitored by another piece of electronics (more on that in Chapter 17). For now, however, all you need to gather are the thermocouple wire, the small Allen screw, the M2 washer, and a #6 washer (see Figure 14-17). You'll also need about 1" or so of Kapton tape to wrap around the end of the thermocouple.

■ **Note** Technical editor Darrell Kelly had this to say about attaching the thermocouple using the small washers: "I took this washer and with a pair of pliers bent it on one side not quite through the middle. This formed a small clamping area for the thermocouple to fit into. I was able to mount the thermocouple on the first try without any trouble. The washer is easy to bend when held with pliers and pushed against a piece of wood or countertop.

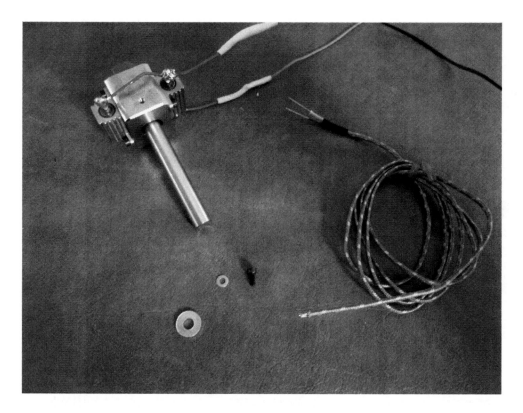

Figure 14-17. *The thermocouple wire will be attached to the heater core.*

Don't wrap the thermocouple with too much Kapton tape. One or two layers should work fine; any more and you may have a hard time keeping it in place under the washer in the next step.

Angle the thermocouple wire so that it is coming off of the heater core at approximately a 45 degree angle away from the nozzle, as shown in Figure 14-18, and then tighten it down.

Figure 14-18. Angle the thermocouple wire away from the nozzle.

Add Ceramic Tape and Wrap

Cut two 4" lengths of ceramic tape, as shown in Figure 14-19.

Figure 14-19. *Two pieces of ceramic tape cut to 4" length*

Mark the center of each piece of tape as shown in Figure 14-20. By "center," we mean both vertically and horizontally (think of balancing the tape on the head of a pin). Make the mark as close to center as possible (this means 2" from the left or right edge and 1/2" from the longer top or bottom edges).

Figure 14-20. Make a small mark in the center of each piece of ceramic tape.

Place the end of the feed cylinder over the mark and twist the cylinder back and forth. It will cut into the soft ceramic tape, making a small hole in each piece, as shown in Figure 14-21.

Figure 14-21. *A hole is cut into each piece of ceramic tape.*

Insert the feed cylinder into the hole of one piece of ceramic tape and then through the other. Orient the two pieces of ceramic tape so they form a cross and fold one piece down and under the lead wires, as shown in Figure 14-22.

Figure 14-22. Place the ceramic tape so it can be wrapped around the heater core.

Fold down the other edges of the ceramic tape towards the nozzle. One piece of ceramic tape will need to be fed under the two lead wires, as shown in Figure 14-23.

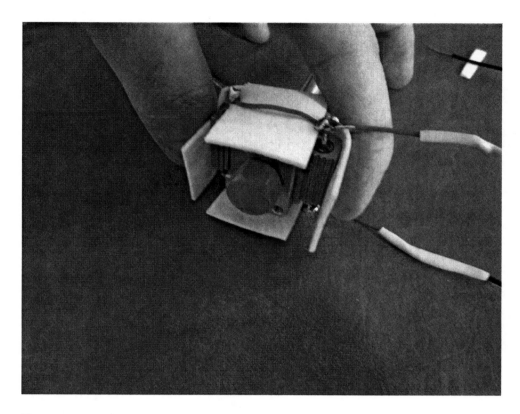

Figure 14-23. *Fold down the ceramic tape to surround the nozzle.*

Trim back the edges of the ceramic tape so they are even with the end of the nozzle and then cut two 6" pieces of Kapton tape (which is resistant to high temperatures). Use these two pieces of Kapton tape to wrap the ceramic tape as demonstrated in Figure 14-24.

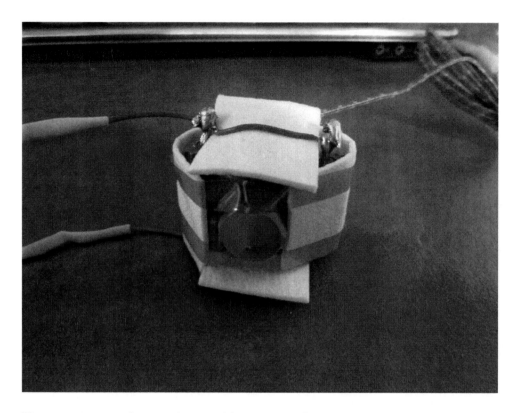

Figure 14-24. Wrap the ceramic tape with two pieces of Kapton tape.

The tape can touch the nozzle slightly as demonstrated in Figure 14-24 but don't allow it to get too close to the end of the nozzle. Use another two pieces to secure the other piece of ceramic tape, as shown in Figure 14-25.

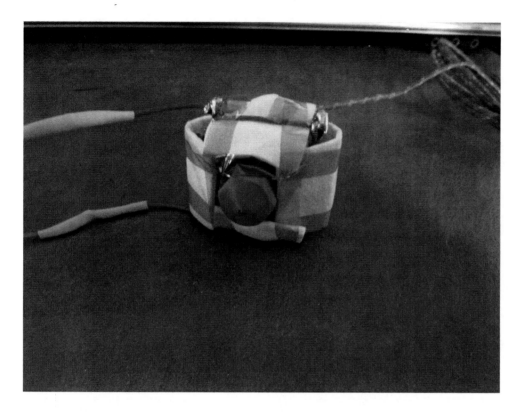

Figure 14-25. *The ceramic tape is held in place by four pieces of Kapton tape.*

Finally, use the roll of Kapton tape to completely wrap the heater core assembly, including the solder beads on the lead wires. The idea is to completely cover all the ceramic tape and solder leads while avoiding the nozzle. Figure 14-26 shows the final result of approximately 25 to 30 circles around the assembly.

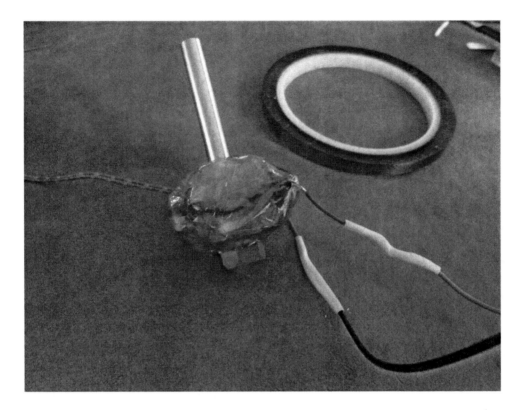

Figure 14-26. *The completed Extruder, including the Kapton tape wrapping*

Summary

Now that the Extruder is done, it's time to attach it to the 3D printer assembly. We'll cover that in Chapter 15, where you'll also add the servo motor that will be used to feed the plastic filament into the Extruder.

▪ **Note** Be sure to read the Addendum chapter at the end of the book. Modifications were made to the Extruder that, although not required, may produce a stronger connection between the Extruder and the 3D printer frame.

■ ■ ■

The Filament Feeding Mechanism

Now that your Extruder is complete, it's time to bolt it onto your 3D printer frame. Your 3D printer works by feeding a plastic filament into the heater core of the Extruder. The plastic melts and is then forced through the Extruder's nozzle and applied to the worktable to print three dimensional objects.

You've still got some electronics to handle (all those little circuit boards that actually allow the machine to work) but you'll deal with those parts in the next chapter. This chapter will be short and sweet; you're going to connect the Extruder and the last stepper motor to the machine.

Required Parts Summary

For this chapter, you'll be using the following components:

- Parts P and Q (Extruder Bearing Hinge I and II)
- Extruder (from Chapter 14)
- Qty-1 5/16" bearing
- Qty-1 5/16" hex head bolt, 1" length
- Qty-1 5/16" nut
- Qty-3 #6-32 machine screws, 1" length
- Qty-3 #6 washers
- Qty-3 #6-32 nuts
- Hose clamp (approx 1-1/2" diameter)
- Zip tie
- Qty-5 1/4" nuts
- Qty-1 1/4" machine screw, 1-1/2" length
- Qty-1 serrated collar

- Qty-1 heat sink for feed cylinder on extruder
- Qty-1 NEMA 23 Stepper Motor

Attach Extruder Bearing Hinges I and II

The Extruder will be bolted to a mechanism that consists of Parts P and Q, the Extruder Bearing Hinges I and II.

Figure 15-1 shows Parts P and Q along with the single 1/4" x 1-1/2" bolt and two nuts that will connect the two parts together.

Figure 15-1. *Parts P and Q will be bolted together.*

Insert the 1-1/2" machine screw through Part P and into Part Q, as shown in Figure 15-2.

Figure 15-2. Insert a machine screw through Part P first and then into Part Q.

Flip the two pieces over and secure the machine screw with two 1/4" nuts. Finger tighten the first nut. The second nut must be tightened against the first nut, but not so tight as to prevent Part P from pivoting around the inserted machine screw. Figure 15-3 shows the two parts bolted together.

Figure 15-3. *Add bearings to the X-Axis Motor Mount*

Next, you need to insert a plastic zip tie through the holes shown in Figure 15-4. Don't close the tie yet; it will be used later to secure the Extruder in place. Note that the tie will be closed on the side with the 1-1/2" bolt head and not the two 1/4" nuts previously added.

Figure 15-4. Insert a zip tie but don't close it.

Add the Stepper Motor

Now it's time to add the stepper motor. You will use three #6-32 x 1" machine screws along with three #6 washers and three #6-32 nuts to secure the motor to Part Q. The motor will press down on a piece of the plastic tie; this is normal.

Figure 15-5 shows the three screws inserted first into the washers and then into the counterbored holes on Part Q. (The plastic tie has been removed temporarily so you can see the proper counterbored holes where the machine screws are inserted.)

Figure 15-5. *The stepper motor is bolted to Part Q with three #6-32 machine screws.*

Place the motor so that the wires on the motor are facing away from Part P (the smallest of the two wood parts) and secure the motor with the three nuts. Figure 15-6 shows the motor added to Part Q and secured with three #6-32 nuts.

▪ **Note** It helps to hold a nut in place over the holes on the stepper motor as you screw in the machine screws. The nuts can't rotate due to the small edges on the motor, so just hold them with your finger as you tighten the screws. Tighten the screws a little at a time; the motor has a tiny protruding circular surface around the motor shaft that will prevent the motor from bolting to Part Q flush. The motor will be slightly raised from Part Q (about the thickness of a washer); this is normal.

Figure 15-6. *Mount the stepper motor to Part Q.*

Attach the Filament Feed Components

After the stepper motor is attached, flip it over to expose the motor shaft, as shown in Figure 15-7. Note that the plastic tie is still not closed. You'll also need the 5/16" bearing and 5/16" hex head bolt.

Figure 15-7. Flip the mechanism over to expose the motor shaft.

Insert the 5/16" bearing on the 5/16" hex head bolt and then screw it into the mechanism as demonstrated in Figure 15-8. You may need a wrench for this; the 1/4" hole you drilled will hold the bolt tight, and you will secure it once it's been screwed in with a 5/16" nut on the opposite side.

Figure 15-8. Attach the filament tensioning bearing on Part P.

Next you'll add the serrated collar to the end of the motor shaft, as shown in Figure 15-9. You can use the bearing to apply pressure to hold the collar in place until you tighten it with an Allen wrench. Note that the serrated curved edge of the collar matches up with the bearing edge.

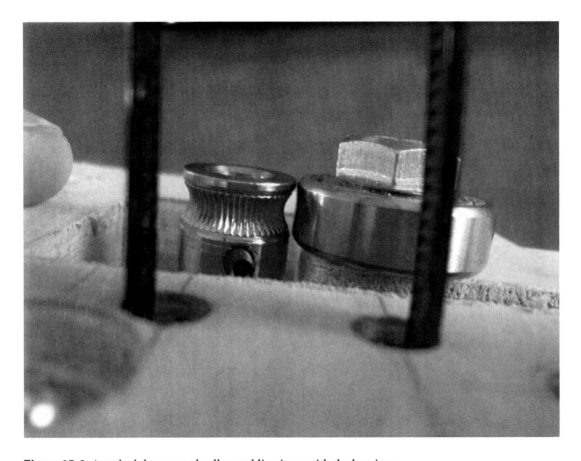

Figure 15-9. *Attached the serrated collar and line it up with the bearing.*

The plastic filament that will be melted and applied to the 3D printer's worktable will be fed into the Extruder through the tight space between serrated collar and bearing. The serrated edges will help "grab" the filament and feed it into the heater core.

Figure 15-10 shows the mechanism so far; next, you'll attach the actual Extruder.

Figure 15-10. The feeding mechanism ready for the Extruder to be attached

Attaching the Extruder

And now it's time to attach the Extruder. Figure 15-11 shows the filament feeding mechanism and the Extruder along with the heat sink.

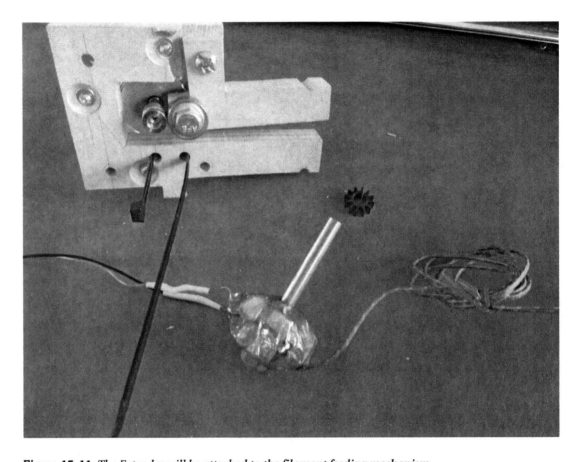

Figure 15-11. The Extruder will be attached to the filament feeding mechanism.

Use a pair of pliers to bend the hose clamp so it fits over the notch in Part Q, as shown in Figure 15-12. You'll have to experiment a bit and maybe loosen the clamp with a slot screw driver, but the idea is to allow yourself enough space at the top to allow the feed cylinder to slide under the clamp before the clamp is tightened down.

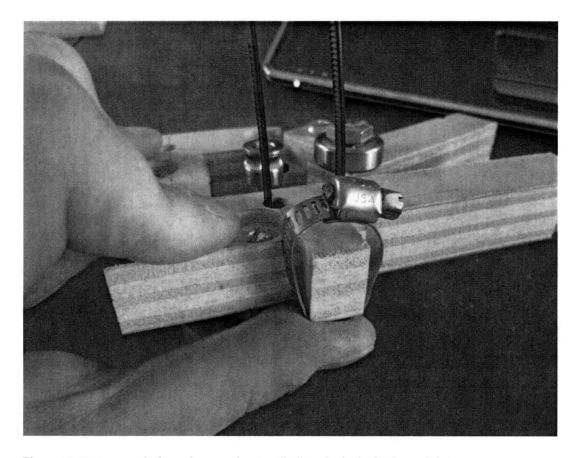

Figure 15-12. Prepare the hose clamp so that it will allow the feed cylinder to slide in.

Next, slide the heat sink over the feed cylinder and then insert the Extruder so that the feed cylinder goes under the hose clamp, as shown in Figure 15-13. You'll also want to cut a small piece of ceramic tape to wrap around the feed cylinder. The zip tie, when closed, will hold the ceramic tape in place over the feed cylinder.

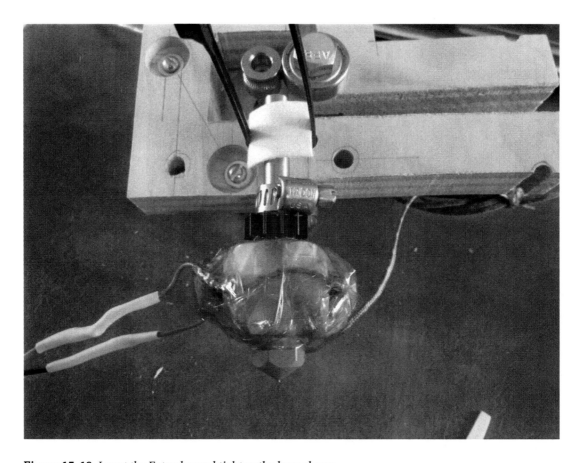

Figure 15-13. Insert the Extruder and tighten the hose clamp.

Tighten the zip tie over the ceramic tape and continue to tighten the hose clamp if possible. You want to have the nozzle pointing perpendicular to the bottom edge of Part Q (see Figure 15-13) and tightened down as much as possible using the zip tie and the hose clamp.

Figure 15-14 shows the zip tie tightened as much as possible along with the hose clamp. Cut the zip tie close to the feed cylinder.

Figure 15-14. The Extruder attached to the filament feed mechanism

Attach the Filament Feed Mechanism and the Extruder to the 3D Printer

The last step is to attach the filament feed mechanism and Extruder to your 3D printer. There are three holes in Part Q that will match up to the three machine screws on the front of your 3D printer (found on the Z-Axis Rail Support). You will want two 1/4" nuts on each of the three screws behind the mechanism. An additional three 1/4" nuts will be used to secure the mechanism in place.

Figure 15-15 shows the mechanism being pushed onto the three machine screws.

Figure 15-15. Add the mechanism to the front of the Z-Axis Rail Support.

Push the mechanism back as far as possible. Ideally, you want about 1" or so of space between the Z-Axis Rail Support (Part K) and Part Q. On each of the three machine screws, tighten one 1/4" nut against the Z-Axis Rail Support and another 1/4" nut against the back of Part Q.

Secure everything by tightening one 1/4" nut onto each of the three machine screws, as shown in Figure 15-16.

Figure 15-16. Add three 1/4" nuts to secure the mechanism in place.

Summary

Next you'll attach the final plywood piece (the Machine Back – Part O) along with a nice collection of circuit boards that will be used to control the Extruder and motors. You'll also add on the motherboard that controls everything else.

CHAPTER 16

■ ■ ■

Mounting Electronics

Your 3D printer needs a handful of electronics to control the Extruder and motors, and that's what you'll be working on in this chapter. While you could easily mount all of the electronics on a separate piece of plywood, that would also involve having many long wires running from motors and Extruder to the various controller components.

Because most of the electronics for the 3D printer are small, you can mount them right on the 3D printer frame. This will keep the machine portable but also help to reduce the clutter that comes with lots of long lengths of wiring.

Required Parts Summary

For Chapter 16, you will be using the following components:

- 3D Printer (frame with motors and Extruder mounted)
- Arduino Mega
- MakerBot Motherboard (this book uses v2.4)
- Qty-4 Stepper Motor Drivers (this book uses v3.3)
- Qty-1 Extruder Controller (this book uses v3.5)
- Qty-24 1/4" long x 1/4" outer diameter x .14" inner diameter nylon spacers
- Qty-24 #4 flat head Phillips wood screws, 3/4" length

Attach Arduino Mega and Motherboard

Your first task will be to attach the Arduino Mega (also simply called Mega) and the MakerBot Motherboard to the 3DP. Before you do this, however, plug in the motherboard to the Mega. The pins on the underside of the motherboard can only be inserted one way into the Mega. Figure 16-1 shows the motherboard as it should be inserted into the Mega.

Figure 16-1. *Connecting motherboard and Arduino Mega*

Push the pins on the underside of the motherboard firmly into the Arduino Mega; apply equal pressure on all sides so you don't bend any pins. Before pushing completely in, make certain all pins are being properly inserted into the Mega's headers (those black rectangles with little holes that line the perimeter of the Mega). Figure 16-2 shows a side view of the motherboard inserted into the Mega.

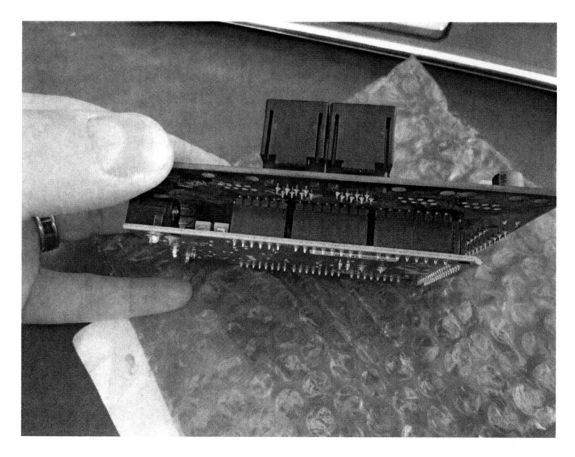

Figure 16-2. Motherboard inserted completely into Arduino Mega

After you've inserted the motherboard into the Mega, place the two boards against the left side of the 3D printer, as shown in Figure 16-3. Place the device so that none of the motherboard's edges are touching any metal pieces (such as nuts) or the surface the 3D printer is resting on. An ideal location is where the motherboard is 1/2" or so above the surface. Mark a small line or some points so you'll know where to attach the Arduino Mega after removing the motherboard.

■ **Note** One of the technical editors, Tony Buser, had this to say about inserting the motherboard into the Mega: "Be careful; it's very easy to bend the pins. It's a good idea to slowly push it in a bit at a time and not at an angle. If they do bend out of alignment, very carefully push them back straight."

Figure 16-3. *Finding the proper location for motherboard and Mega*

■ **Note** If the threaded tension rod inserted between the two sides sticks out too far, you'll need to trim it so that the Arduino Mega can be properly mounted using all four corner holes. When the motherboard is placed back on the Arduino Mega, you want to make certain that no part of it is touching the metal threaded rod or the nut.

Remove the motherboard and place the Mega against the side of the 3D printer and mark where to drill four pilot holes, as shown in Figure 16-4.

Figure 16-4. Use the Mega to mark the location of the pilot holes.

Next, use three nylon spacers (1/2" or 1" depending on length of wood screw you choose to use) and three #4 x 3/4" wood screws seen in Figure 16-5 to attach the Arduino.

■ **Note** You can use a fourth screw (and spacer) in the lower-right corner but you will have to file down the head on the wood screws as it won't fit between the headers on the Arduino.

Figure 16-5. Use #4 screws and nylon spacers to attach the Mega.

Now carefully push the motherboard onto the Arduino Mega. If you didn't use a fourth screw in the lower right-corner of the Mega, place a spacer underneath it to provide support as you insert the motherboard; you can remove the spacer when done. Figure 16-6 shows the motherboard inserted over the Arduino Mega.

Figure 16-6. *Motherboard added to the Mega*

Attach the X-Axis Stepper Motor Driver

Now it's time to add the first of four stepper motor drivers. This one will control the X-axis motor and will be mounted on the inside of the 3D printer just behind the motherboard and Mega, as shown in Figure 16-7.

Figure 16-7. *The X-axis stepper motor driver mounted under the table*

Carefully tip your 3D printer to expose the inside of the Lower Structural Side where the Arduino Mega and motherboard are mounted. Mark and drill three pilot holes (you'll likely find that the mounting hole closest to the rear tension rod makes it difficult to use but you can try; we found that using just three screws is sufficient to hold the motor driver properly).

Use three #4 screws and three nylon spacers to mount the X-axis stepper motor driver as shown in Figure 16-8.

Figure 16-8. *The X-axis stepper motor driver mounted on the inside of Lower Structural Side*

Carefully raise the 3D printer back up to its upright position. Next, you'll mount two more stepper motor drivers for the Y and Z axes.

Attach the Y-Axis and Z-Axis Stepper Motor Drivers

You've probably noticed that there is one final plywood piece that you cut and drilled that still hasn't been mounted: the Machine Back (Part O). You'll be mounting two additional stepper motor drivers to it, but you'll first need to attach the Machine Back to the 3D printer. You can use two 1-1/4" machine screws and barrel nuts to attach Part O to the left and right Upper Structural Sides or, as we've done in Figure 16-9, you can use a hinge (or two) on one side and a single machine screw and barrel nut on the other side to allow Part O to swing out, exposing the electronics components that will be mounted on it.

Figure 16-9. *Using a hinge on the Machine Back for easier access to electronics.*

Figure 16-10 shows Part O with the hinge attached and the Motor Back swung out to expose the inside where two stepper motor drivers will be attached.

Figure 16-10. The Machine Back swings out for access to stepper motor drivers.

If you choose to mount the Machine Back (Part O) with a hinge, you can begin attaching the Y-axis and Z-axis stepper motor drivers to it. If you choose to use machine screws, you'll need to mount the stepper motor drivers to the Machine Back before attaching it to the 3D printer frame.

Figure 16-11 shows the first stepper motor driver attached. It's best to use four screws, one per corner. Remember to pre-drill a pilot hole to make screwing in the wood screws easier.

Figure 16-11. *The first stepper motor driver attached to the Machine Back.*

Use four #4 wood screws to attach the second stepper motor driver to Part O. You can mount them side-by-side, as shown in Figure 16-12, or vertically.

Figure 16-12. The Y-axis and Z-axis stepper motor drivers mounted to the Machine Back

Attach the Extruder Stepper Motor Driver

Now it's time to mount the Extruder's stepper motor driver. This will be attached to the front of the Z-Axis Rail Support. Mark three locations to drill pilot holes and mount the stepper driver as demonstrated in Figure 16-13.

Figure 16-13. *Extruder stepper motor driver attached to Z-Axis Rail Support*

Because of the way you'll have to attach the stepper motor driver, you'll only be able to attach it with three screws. Make certain that the board is not touching any of the machine screws or nuts being used to hold the Strong-Tie brackets to the Z-Axis Rail Support.

Attach the Extruder Controller

The final task for this chapter is to attach the Extruder Controller just above the Extruder stepper motor driver. The Extruder Controller will also be attached using only three wood screws (with nylon spacers behind the board).

Hold the board in place and drill three pilot holes before attaching the Extruder Controller. When done, it should be mounted just above the Extruder stepper motor driver, as shown in Figure 16-14.

Figure 16-14. Extruder Controller mounted to the Z-Axis Rail Support

Summary

Now that all the circuit boards are attached, it's time to add all the wires. In the next chapter, you'll be adding a variety of wires and cables to connect all the various components together. You'll then connect everything to a power supply that will provide the voltage required to power the drivers, turn the motors, and allow that Extruder to heat up and print some plastic!

■■■

Wiring Part I

Now that you have all the electronics mounted, it's time to start wiring things up. The wiring process will be explained over two chapters. This chapter focuses on connecting the four-stepper motor drivers to the motherboard, along with a few other connections.

There is no soldering required in this chapter, but you will need a good pair of wire cutters and a wire stripper. Clear yourself a good large area to work, and go slow – the connections you'll make are not difficult, but you don't want to rush things and cut or damage any wires.

Required Parts Summary

For Chapter 17, you will be using the following components:

- Data cable, minimum three feet in length, (multi-color recommended) minimum of six-wire strands per cable

- Qty-8, six-wire connectors (these come with the stepper motor drivers from Makerbot.com)

- Qty-1, RS-485 cable (a standard Ethernet pass-through cable will work), minimum two-three feet in length

Connect X-Axis Motor Driver to Motherboard

The method used to connect the X-axis motor driver to the motherboard will also be used to connect the Y-axis and Z-axis motor drivers to the motherboard. The only difference will be in the length of wire needed.

Figure 17-1 shows a ribbon cable obtained for wiring up the motor drivers. You'll need a minimum of six strands (this one has 26, and is typical of a cable used to connect a computer hard drive to a motherboard).

Figure 17-1. *A mutli-colored ribbon cable is useful for wiring the stepper motor drivers.*

Use a sharp blade and cut six strands away from your ribbon cable; after cutting a few inches, you'll be able to pull the cable apart easily. For the X-axis motor to be connected to the motherboard, cut about 12 inches of cable. Figure 17-2 shows the cut ribbon of cable and the two connectors that will be needed.

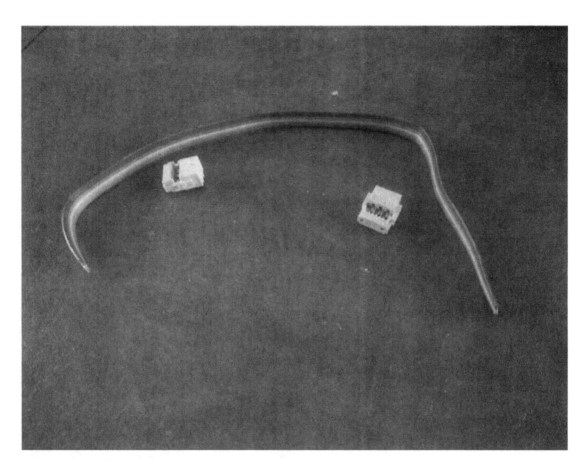

Figure 17-2. X-axis motor driver cable and connectors

Insert one end of the ribbon into the small connector, as shown in Figure 17-3.

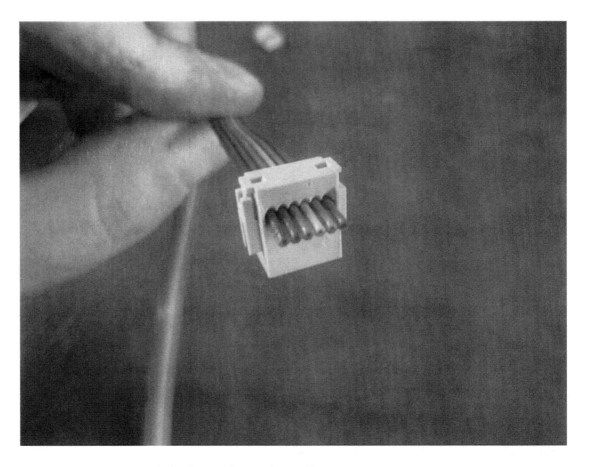

Figure 17-3. *Insert one end of ribbon cable into the small connector.*

Use a pair of pliers to squeeze down on the top and bottom of the connector, as shown in Figure 17-4. This will close the connector on the wire, and small metal teeth inside will bite into the wire. You can also use a vise to apply the pressure, but be careful not to crush the connector with too much force. You will be able to look at the connector and visibly tell when it has been properly closed or clamped down onto the wire.

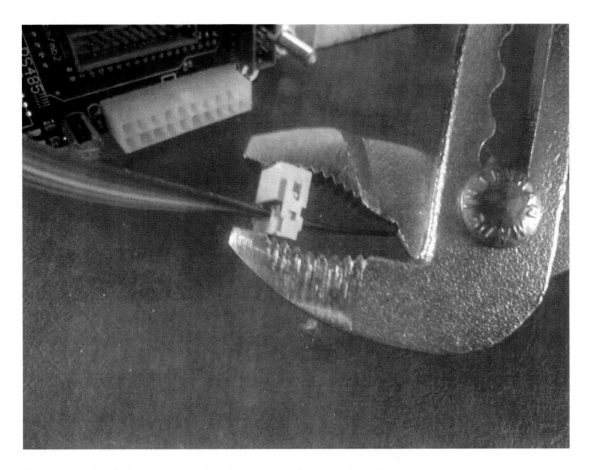

Figure 17-4. Pinch the connector with pliers to press down on the cable.

Place a second connector onto the ribbon, but do not close the connector with pliers yet. You must also take care to insert the connector so that it mirrors the orientation of the first connector, as shown in Figure 17-5.

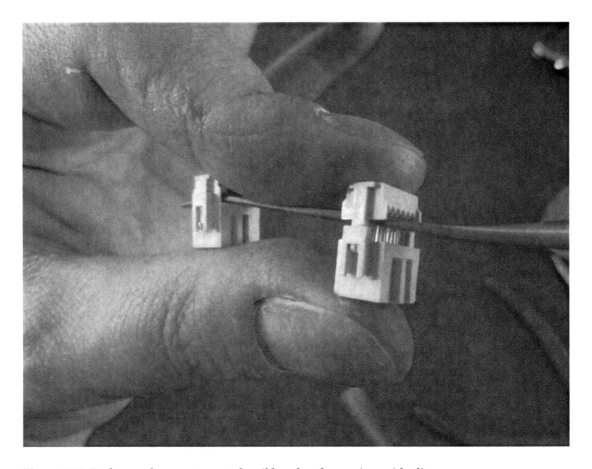

Figure 17-5. Push second connector onto the ribbon, but do no crimp with pliers.

Plug the first connector into the X-axis motor driver, as shown in Figure 17-6. The connector can only be pushed onto the connector one way.

Figure 17-6. *Push the first connector into the X-axis motor driver as shown.*

Wrap the cable around to the motherboard and determine a good location to cut the ribbon – ideally where the other connector will be pressed into the blue plug on the motherboard labeled X-axis. You can see the X-axis label in Figure 17-7.

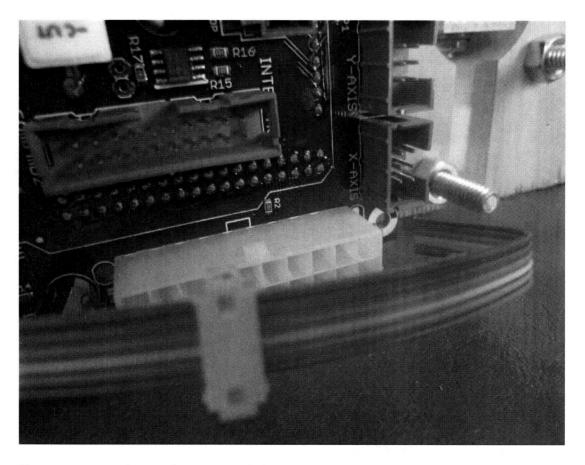

Figure 17-7. Crimp the second connector and plug into the X-axis port on motherboard.

Move the second connector towards the end of the ribbon and then use the pliers to close the connector. Plug in the second connector to the motherboard, as seen in Figure 17-8.

Figure 17-8. X-axis motor driver connected to motherboard with six-wire cable

Connect Y- and Z-Axis Motor Drivers to Motherboard

Next you'll connect the Y-axis and Z-axis motor drivers to the motherboard using the same process used for the X-axis. This time, however, you'll need longer ribbon cables, and you'll need to route them to keep them away from moving parts. You'll need approximately two and a half feet of cable for each motor.

Put one connector on the end of each cable and use a pair of pliers to close (crimp) it. Then place a second connector onto each ribbon, but do not crimp the second connectors. Figure 17-9 shows the Y-axis and Z-axis motor drivers, each with a cable plugged in. Note that the second connector on each cable that can move freely on the ribbon. (Notice also in Figure 17-9 that we've written Y-axis below the motor driver on the left and Z-axis below the motor driver on the right – you can reverse this, but just remember which is which.)

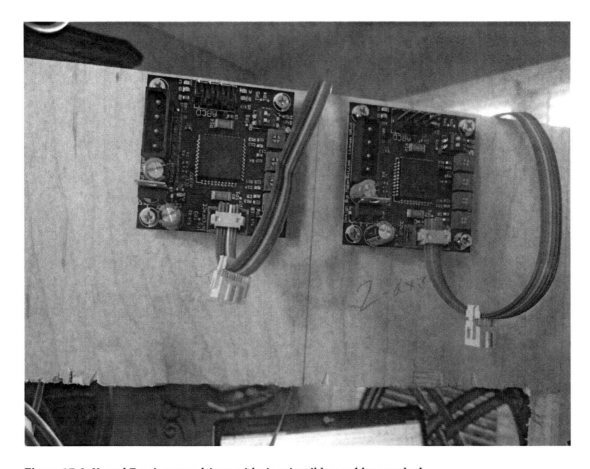

Figure 17-9. *Y- and Z-axis motor drivers with six-wire ribbon cables attached*

The Y-axis motor will move the Y- and Z-axis assemblies left and right on the Y-axis (Strong Tie) rails, and you don't want these ribbon cables interfering with that movement. Use a plastic tie to secure the wires to the side of the Machine Back, as shown in Figure 17-10. This will keep the ribbons out of the way and move them toward the side where the motherboard is mounted. Don't tighten the tie down much; leave a large opening, as you'll be using this opening later to route more cables.

Figure 17-10. *Use a plastic tie to pull the ribbons to the side, away from the motor.*

After the two ribbon cables are pulled to the right and secured with the tie, drop the ribbons down to the motherboard. Leave a little bit of slack in the cable. Don't pull them too tight, as you want a little flexibility and movement in the cables.

Determine which of the motor drivers will control the Y-axis and which will control the Z-axis (we recommend writing this in pencil on the Machine Back, just below each motor driver). You will once again move the second connector on each cable down toward the motherboard and crimp it with a pair of pliers before inserting into the motherboard.

One port is labeled Y-axis and the other Z-axis, so plug in their respective ribbon cables coming from the stepper motor drivers at the top of the machine. Figure 17-11 shows these two cables crimped and inserted into the motherboard.

Figure 17-11. Y- and Z-axis motor drivers are now connected to the motherboard.

Connect the Thermocouple Wire

Your next step is to connect the thick thermocouple wire to the Extruder Controller. Although the wire is a bit long, you can choose to leave the extra bit of wire looped and secured with a tie. But if you wish to shorten the wire to reduce wire clutter, you can cut the wire and re-do the ends with some shrink tubing. Just be careful when doing this; the outer sheath is more of a cloth-like coating that will fray and make a mess. The two wires inside are colored red and yellow, and you need to be careful to keep the colors separate and identifiable. Use red shrink tubing and yellow shrink tubing if possible to keep the two wires color coded and clean.

Because the thermocouple wire is a bit heavy, you'll want to secure it so it won't move as the Z- and Y-axis assemblies move during a printing process. To do this, simply use a plastic tie to secure part of the thermocouple wire to one of the bolts behind the Z-axis motor mount, as shown in Figure 17-12.

Figure 17-12. *Secure the thermocouple wire to a bolt with a tie.*

After securing the thermocouple wire, attach the red and yellow ends to the Extruder Controller, as shown in Figure 17-13. Insert the red wire into the screw terminal labeled T- (Tee-minus) and use a small slot screwdriver to tighten down the screw to hold it in place. The yellow wire goes into the screw terminal labeled T+ (Tee-plus); secure it in place as well.

313

Figure 17-13. Secure the thermocouple wire ends to the Extruder Controller.

Connect the Power Resistor Wires

Locate the two wires that are connected to the two power resistors that were bolted to the side of the Extruder's heater core. These two wires will now be attached to the Extruder Controller..

You'll connect these two wires to the screw terminals labeled HEATER (there are two screw terminals under the word HEATER). It doesn't matter which wire goes into which screw terminal.

Figure 17-14 shows these two wires secured to the Extruder Controller. If you look closely, you can just make out HEATER behind the two wires.

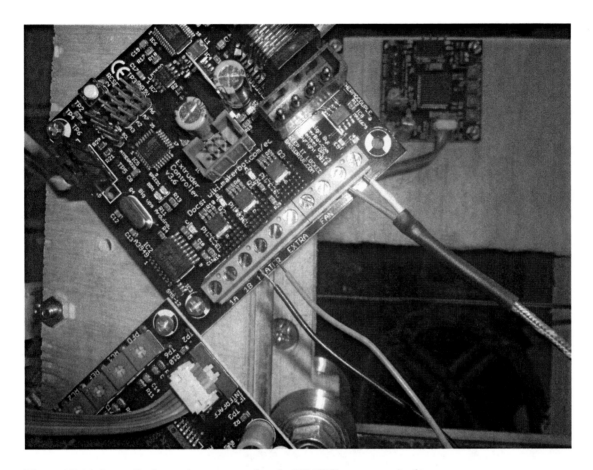

Figure 17-14. Power Resistor wires connected to the HEATER screw terminals

Connect Extruder Motor Driver and Controller

The last bit of wiring you'll do in this chapter involves connecting the Extruder motor driver and the Extruder controller to the motherboard. The motor driver will connect to the motherboard using the familiar six-wire ribbon cable process you've already done for the X-, Y-, and Z-axis motor drivers. The Extruder Controller will attach to the motherboard using the RS-485 cable (identical to an RJ-45 Ethernet cable commonly found in any computer store) and requires no special tools.

First, start by raising the Z-axis by rotating the motor shaft coupling under the Z-axis motor mount at the top of the machine. Raise it until the lead screw is almost flush with the bottom of the Z-axis Nut Mount (Part N). Figure 17-15 shows the Z-axis raised.

Figure 17-15. Raise the Z-axis until the lead screw is almost flush with Part N.

Now cut approximately three feet of ribbon cable (six-wire cable) and crimping a connector to one end. Connect this to the Extruder motor driver, add a second connector (oriented identically to the first), but do not crimp it. Plug in the RS-485 cable to the Extruder Controller, as shown in Figure 17-16.

Figure 17-16. Extruder motor driver and controller with cables attached

Push the Y-axis assembly all the way to the right. You want it as far from the motherboard as possible so that the six-wire ribbon cable can be trimmed but still have the minimum length required to connect to the motherboard. Use another plastic tie to hold the Extruder motor driver ribbon cable and the RS-485 cable. You'll want to secure them to the bolt under the Z-axis motor mount, as shown in Figure 17-17. Do not tighten the plastic tie just yet.

Figure 17-17. Route the two cables through a tie just under the Z-axis motor mount.

Next push these two cables through the opening of the first tie (used back for routing the Y- and Z-axis cables down to the motherboard). Cut and crimp the second connector on the six-wire ribbon and plug it into the port labeled A-axis on the motherboard, as seen in Figure 17-18. Plug in the RS-485 cable into either of the two RS-485 ports, also shown in Figure 17-18.

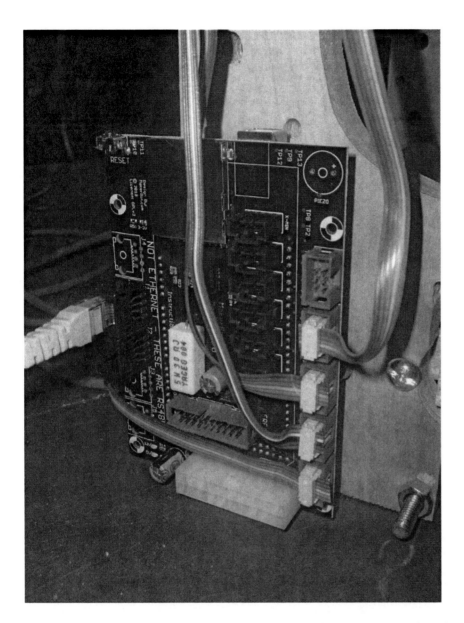

Figure 17-18. RS-485 and Extruder motor driver cables plugged into motherboard

Summary

You're a little over half done with the wiring portion of the machine. In Chapter 18, you'll continue with the wiring of the motors and then finish up by bringing in the power supply and wiring up all the components for power.

CHAPTER 18

■ ■ ■

Wiring Part II

There are a few more wiring tasks that must be completed before you get to the software. In this chapter, you'll wire up the motors to their respective motor controllers, connect the external power supply to all the circuit boards that require power, and add the endstops (also known as limit switches).

When you're done with this chapter, your machine will be complete. Your last task will be to learn about the software required to make it work.

Required Parts Summary

For Chapter 18, you will be using the following components:

- Qty- 6 to 8 Molex extensions (6" or longer)

- Qty- 3 or 4 Molex splitters (3 or 4 will do if you also buy extensions)

- Qty-3 Endstops (one cable per endstop is typically included but check before buying)

- Qty-8 #4-5/8" wood screws

- Qty-1 #6-32 machine screw, 1-1/2" length

- Qty-2 #6-32 nuts

- Qty-4 to 10 zip ties

Connect Motors to Motor Drivers

Each of the motors that you've attached has four wires that must be connected to their respective motor drivers. There are two ways to do this:

1. Use special Molex connectors (not covered here but a good option).

2. Solder the motors' wires to the leads on the motor drivers (this option is covered in this chapter).

Option 1 is probably the easiest, but it will require that you order some special Molex connectors and use a crimper tool to insert the wires into the connectors before attaching to a motor driver. You can purchase the special Molex connectors from Mouser Electronics at www.mouser.com; the Mouser part number is 538-09-52-4044 and you will need four of them. You will also need to purchase 16 of the pins that will be crimped to the individual wires before inserting into the Molex connectors; they are #538-08-70-0012.

If you choose to use this method, you'll also want to watch Patrick's wiring videos at www.buildyourtools.com for the proper techniques to crimp the wires as well as the order of the wires.

The method demonstrated in this chapter requires only a solder iron and some solder. As mentioned in Chapter 14, if you're not comfortable with soldering or lack the equipment, you can ask a friend or look online (Craigslist.com) for someone who would be willing to do the soldering for you.

There is an order for how the wires must connect to the motor drivers. If you look carefully at Figure 18-1, you'll see on each of the motor drivers a set of four metal pins labeled ABCD.

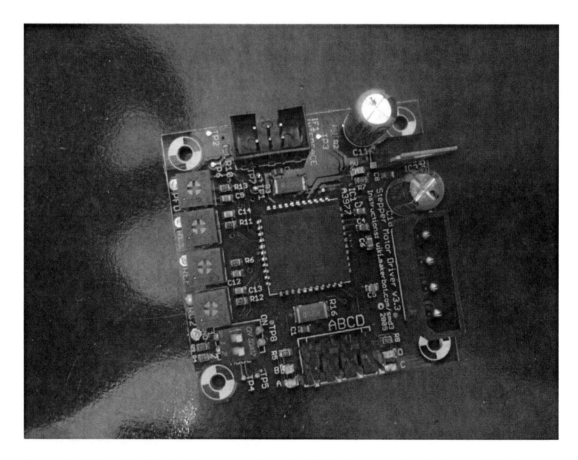

Figure 18-1. You will solder the four motor wires to the ABCD pins located at the bottom of the photo.

Again, the order of the wires is important. Look at Figure 18-2; we've written the letters associated with the wires on the back of one of the motors. Starting from the left (while looking at the back of the motor), the first wire will be soldered to A, the second wire from left will be soldered to B, the third wire from left will be soldered to C, and the final wire will be soldered to D.

Figure 18-2. Motor wires and their assigned pins on the motor drivers

If you look carefully at Figure 8-2, you'll see that this motor actually has six metal pins but only four of them have wires attached. If you number *all* of the pins, left to right, we are only using wires for pins 1, 3, 4, and 6. Pins 2 and 5 are not used.

▓ **Note** Most stepper motors use an identical wiring pattern, but you should consult the data sheet for the motors you have purchased to verify the function of each wire. Typically, however, there are two types of stepper motor configurations: 4-wire and 8-wire. (There are 6-wire motors, but these are not common). Both of these configurations are depicted as having two main coils in the motor. One coil will be wired to A+ and A- and the other coil will be wired to B+ and B- (A, B and C, D respectively). On a 4-wire motor, each coil has 2 wires each (the start and end of the wire). You want to keep the ends of each single coil of wire together and wire them to either AB or CD on a motor driver. The pinout of 1 and 3 is coil A+ and A- (shown as A and B on our electronics), and pins 4 and 6 is coil B+ and B- (shown as C and D on our electronics). The 8-wire stepping motor should be wired as bipolar parallel (consult the motor's documentation for the proper pairing) and the reader should consult the datasheet for which color wires are used.

You'll want to cut the wires from the motor to a length that will reach the motor's respective motor driver but also provide enough slack in the wire to allow full movement of the machine's moving parts. Before cutting the wires, experiment with different lengths by holding a point on a wire to the motor driver and then moving the various axes and table back and forth; make sure that the wire does not impeded any movement and make certain it doesn't interfere with any moving parts such as the lead screw or the table. After you've determined the proper length of the wires, cut them and then strip off about 1/4" to 1/2" of insulation from each of the wires' ends and solder them to their respective pins on the motor driver. In Figure 18-3, the first wire (for the Z-axis motor) has been soldered to pin A.

Figure 18-3. Solder the first wire to Pin A on the motor driver.

▧ **Note** You might find it easier to perform the soldering if you remove the motor drivers from the 3D printer frame and reattach after the soldering is completed.

Figure 18-4 shows all four pins with their respective wires soldered for both the Y-axis motor and the Z-axis motor. It's not pretty, but the wires will hold securely.

Figure 18-4. *Y-axis and Z-axis motors' wires soldered to their respective motor drivers*

Cut, strip, and solder the wires for both the X-axis motor and the Extruder motor to their respective motor drivers. You'll find that the X-axis motor wires and the Extruder motor wires can be cut extremely short because their motor drivers are mounted so close to the actual motors. Figure 18-5 shows the Extruder motor and its wires soldered to its motor driver.

Figure 18-5. Extruder motor with its wires soldered to the motor driver

Connect Power to Components

After soldering the motor wires to their motor drivers, your next task is to connect the power supply (that provides electrical power to the machine) to the various components that need power. These include the four motor drivers, the motherboard, and the Extruder controller.

The first thing you need is the external power supply. A standard PC power supply of the style found inside many desktop computers will work just fine. The power supply shown in Figure 18-6 is a 500W (watt) power supply but any power supply rated to supply 300W or more will work.

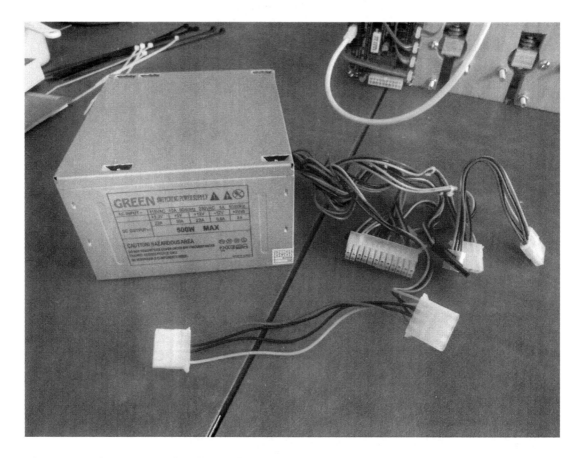

Figure 18-6. The power supply will provide power to the 3D printer's components.

You'll notice in Figure 18-6 that the power supply has quite a tangle of wires connected to it. The wires you are interested in have white connectors on their ends and are often referred to as Molex connectors (but Molex connectors come in various sizes so this is more of a general term). The first thing you'll want to do is find the larger connector like the one shown in Figure 18-7.

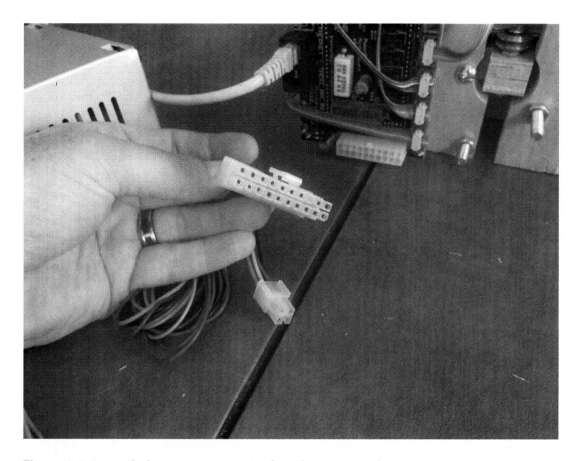

Figure 18-7. *Locate the large connector coming from the power supply.*

Plug it into the motherboard, as shown in Figure 18-8. There is only one way you can insert it, so don't worry about attaching it incorrectly.

Figure 18-8. *Attach the connector to the motherboard.*

Now locate the smaller white Molex connectors shown in Figure 18-9. Stretch them out to get a good idea of the length of the cables.

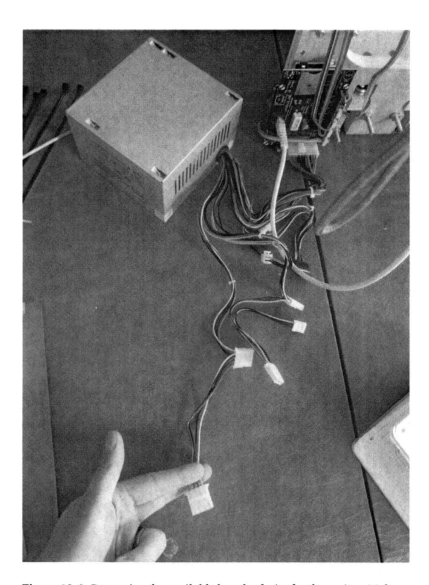

Figure 18-9. *Determine the available length of wire for the various Molex connectors.*

You're going to want as much length as possible and will use Molex extensions and/or splitters to extend the reach of the wires so they can be plugged into the motor drivers and Extruder controller.

Figure 18-10 shows a typical Molex splitter. You can buy these in various lengths, but do try to buy the longest you can find. You'll likely need 7 or 8 of the shorter 6" extensions shown in Figure 18-10 but they do make them in 12" lengths. Buy the longer lengths if you can find them.

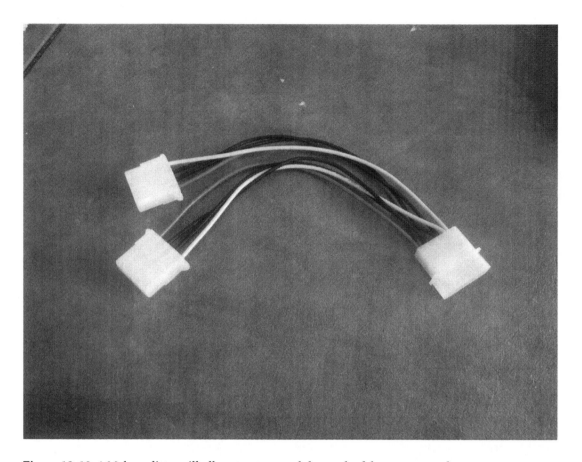

Figure 18-10. *A Molex splitter will allow you to extend the reach of the power supply.*

To use a Molex splitter, insert one of the male ends coming from the power supply into the female end of a splitter, as shown in Figure 18-11.

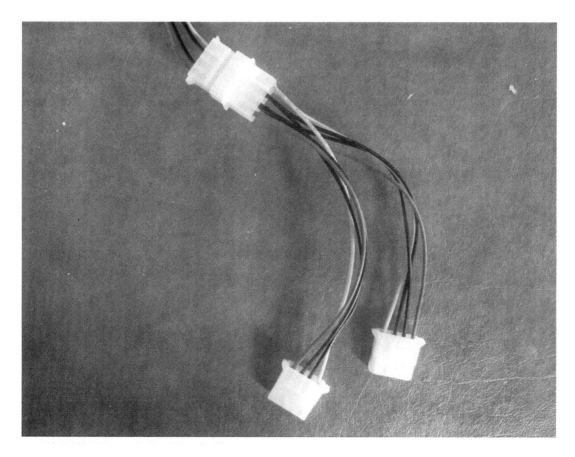

Figure 18-11. *A Molex extender connected to the power supply*

You now have two free male ends that can have splitters attached as well; this will allow you to daisy-chain more splitters so you can reach the motor drivers and Extruder controller. As with previous wiring of components, you'll want to use zip ties to pull the various wires out of the way of moving parts. And be certain to use enough Molex extenders to allow for slack and full movement of the lead screw, table, and other moving assemblies.

Figure 18-12 shows a final splitter reaching the Z-axis motor driver. Note that one free male end is left. You can cut the four wires back near the female end of the splitter to reduce wire clutter.

Figure 18-12. You can cut the free male Molex connector to reduce wire clutter.

When you reach the motor drivers or the Extruder controller, simply plug in the Molex connector to the board. It can only fit one place and it can only be inserted one way, so don't worry about attaching it incorrectly but you may have to push hard to get it in. Figure 18-13 shows the Molex connector inserted into the motor driver mounted under the table.

Figure 18-13. *Molex connector plugged into a motor driver.*

Figure 18-14 shows just how much wire clutter can start to appear as you use these Molex splitters/extenders. Don't skimp on them; it's better to have too many than too few, and you can always use zip ties to secure them to the frame once you've wired everything up for power.

Once all components have received power, try to find ways to route the power wires so that they are out of the way of moving parts. You may find alternative ways to get power to components by adding one or two Molex splitters and taking the wires in a different direction back to the power supply.

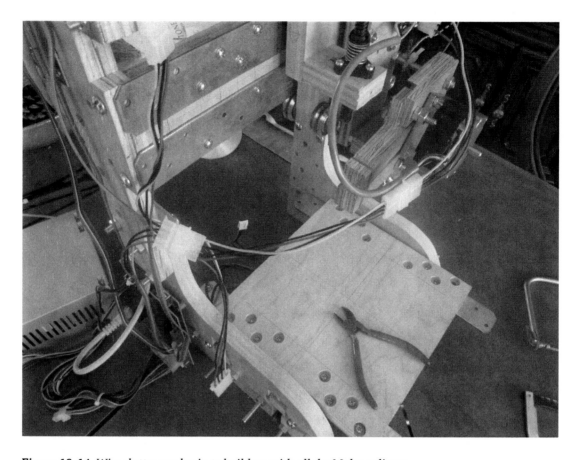

Figure 18-14. *Wire clutter can begin to build up with all the Molex splitters.*

When you are satisfied with the power wiring, you can also use zip ties to secure the unused wires from the power supply and then cut them short to reduce wire clutter. This is shown in Figure 18-15.

Figure 18-15. Use zip tie to secure unused wire and reduce clutter.

■ **Note** With a soldering iron, you can cut the various Molex wires and add simple wire extensions instead of using Molex splitters or Molex extensions. Doing so will require a bit more time and care, but it will also reduce wire clutter immensely. We chose to use Molex splitters because they are easy to find and inexpensive to purchase. If you don't mind the wire bundles, they are an easy method for providing power. But if wire clutter drives you crazy, you may want to investigate simply cutting the wires to a Molex connector and soldering in the needed lengths of wire (covered with electrical tape or shrink tubing) to reach a component instead of using splitters.

Figure 18-16 shows the 3D printer wired up for power. All that's left is to add the endstops.

Figure 18-16. All the components now have power.

Adding the Endstops

Your 3D printer will need three endstops, or limit switches, for a couple of reasons. The endstops prevent your machine from moving too far in one direction and will cut power to a motor if the machine attempts to move too far. But the main function of the endstops will be to allow your machine to self-calibrate before a printing job begins. We'll talk more about the endstops and how they are used in the next chapter, but for now you just need to install them. Figure 18-17 shows the three endstops and their cables.

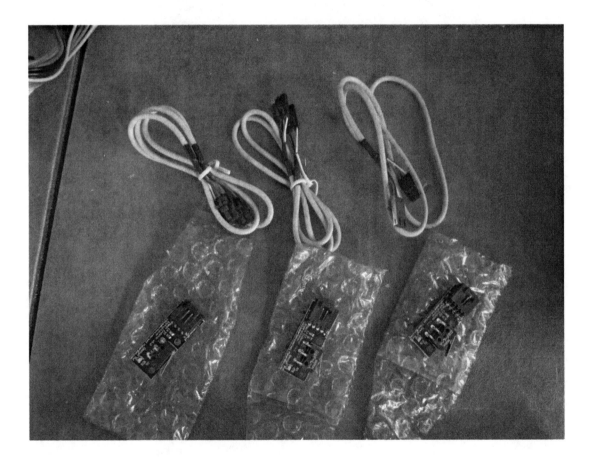

Figure 18-17. Three endstops, one per axis

We'll first attach the endstop to the Y-axis, as shown in Figure 18-18. This is the left side of the machine if you are looking at the machine from the front; the endstop is sitting on the top edge of the Upper Structural Side.

Figure 18-18. One endstop will be mounted on the Upper Structural Side's top edge.

Push the Y-axis assembly all the way to the left but stop just before the ZY Plate touches the Upper Structural Side. Place the endstop so that the metal pushbutton is facing the Y-axis motor mount. All of this is shown in Figure 18-19.

Figure 18-19. *Place the endstop so that it faces the Y-axis motor mount.*

Use a pencil and mark two points where the endstop will be screwed into the top edge of the Upper Structural Side; use two #4-5/8" wood screws to secure the endstop, as shown in Figure 18-20.

Figure 18-20. *Use two wood screws to secure the endstop.*

Use a pencil to mark where the endstop's metal pushbutton would touch the Y-axis motor mount if pushed to the left completely. Drill a pilot hole and then screw in another #4-5/8" wood screw, but not too far, as shown in Figure 18-21.

Figure 18-21. Add another wood screw that will press the endstop's pushbutton.

Determine the proper depth of the woodscrew by moving the Y-axis assembly to the left. You want the woodscrew in the Y-axis motor mount to press on the endstop's pushbutton just before the ZY Plate touches the Upper Structural Side. Figure 18-22 shows how the screw will push against the endstop's pushbutton.

343

Figure 18-22. *Set the depth of the screw to trigger the endstop's pushbutton.*

You'll next mount the table's endstop. To do this properly, push the table to the back of the machine as far as you can without risking the Strong-Tie's leaving the v-groove bearings. You'll want to mount the endstop in a location on the right-rear side of the machine, as shown in Figure 18-23 (yes, the endstop is upside down right now, but it's just leaning against the Lower Structural Side to find the best mounting location). Find a location where you can screw in the two #4-5/8" screws and use two 1/4" deep nylon spacers to allow the endstop's pushbutton to be over the table (and not the gap between the table's edge and the Lower Structural Side).

Figure 18-23. *The table's endstop is mounted at the rear and to the right.*

Drill two pilot holes and mount the endstop with the nylon spacers shown in Figure 18-24. Drill another pilot hole and place a single #4-5/8" wood screw so that it will press on the endstop's pushbutton just as the table reaches the maximum distance it can be pushed towards the rear of the machine; this is shown in Figure 18-24.

Figure 18-24. Add a wood screw to trigger the table's endstop pushbutton.

Finally, use the Z-axis motor couple to turn the lead screw until the end of the lead screw is completely flush with the underside of the Z-Axis Nut Mount (Part N). After doing this, the bottom edge of the Strong-Ties will just be visible, as shown in Figure 18-25. Insert a #6-32-1-1/2" machine screw into the Strong-Tie's hole (also shown in Figure 18-25) and secure it with a #6-32 nut so that it doesn't move.

Figure 18-25. *A machine screw will be used to trigger the final endstop.*

Drill two pilot holes and use #4-5/8" wood screws to secure the endstop, as shown in Figure 18-26. Add another #6-32 nut to the end of the #6 machine screw and turn it on the machine screw until it is in place where it will push against the endstop's pushbutton when the lead screw has reached its maximum height (flush with Part N.) (You can secure the nut in place with a hot glue gun or simply use a piece of duct tape to prevent it from turning on the machine screw.)

Figure 18-26. *The endstop's pushbutton will be pressed by a second #6 nut.*

After adding the endstops, it's time to connect them to the motherboard, but before you do that, we need to make a change to the 3D printer's naming conventions and explain why.

Axis Naming Conventions

Up to this point in the book, we've been referring to the table as the X axis, the left-to-right movement of the ZY Plate as the Y axis, and the up-down motion of the lead screw as the Z-axis. This was an early naming convention used by Patrick based on earlier designs of his CNC machines where a CNC machine's tabletop was called the X-axis and the left-to-right movement was called the Y-axis. It's not wrong, but it's not exactly right, either.

When it comes to the standards used in the 3D printing community, it turns out we've got our X and Y axes reversed. If you wish to communicate with other 3D printer users (such as Makerbot or RepRap owners) and print their shared designs with your own machine, you'll want to make certain you're talking the same language—and that means making a few simple changes to how this machine is wired up.

The first thing to do is switch the 6-wire data cables connecting the X- and Y-axis motor drivers to the motherboard. If you left enough slack in the data wires, you should be able to simply unplug them from the motherboard and switch their positions. Now the motor under the table is plugged into the Y-axis data port on the motherboard and one of the motor drivers mounted near the top of the machine (the one with its wires connected to the motor controlling left-to-right movement) is plugged into the X-axis data port.

All we can say is… sorry about that. (This late in the game, it was simply impossible to go back and rename components, change conventions in every chapter, etc.) When we discovered this issue, we simply chose to move forward knowing that in the end, all that would be required would be a few wiring exchanges.

So, now that you've exchanged the data cables for the X and Y axes, you can connect the cables for the endstops. Take one of the cables and connect it to the end-stop mounted just above the table (now called the Y-axis). Connect the other end of this cable to the motherboard where it's labeled "Y Min" (Y Minimum); this is shown in Figure 18-27.

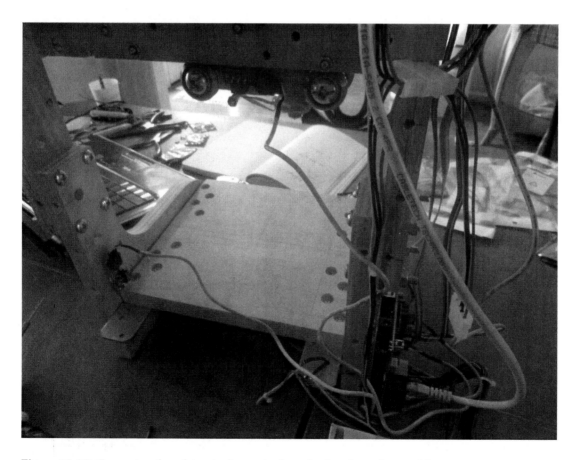

Figure 18-27. Connect each endstop to the motherboard using the endstop cables.

Connect the Z-axis endstop (the one mounted near Part N) to the motherboard where it's labeled "Z Max" (Z Maximum).

Finally, connect the X-axis endstop, the one screwed into the top edge of the left Upper Structural Side, to the motherboard where it's labeled "X Min" (X Minimum).

■ **Note** We'll explain this Minimum and Maximum stuff in Chapter 20. It's related to how the software will know where the Extruder is located at any given time.

Summary

Congratulations! The 3D printer is built! Now let's move quickly to the software so you can test your machine. Chapter 19 will show you everything you need to know to perform a test print with your new machine.

CHAPTER 19

■■■

The Software

You're almost done! In this chapter, you'll learn where to find the required software to make your 3D printer work, as well as how to install and use that software. There are also a couple of tasks that you'll perform to get the motherboard and Extruder controller ready to operate. We're close, so let's jump right in and get ready to print.

Required Hardware Summary

For Chapter 19, you will need the following components:

- A USB cable to connect your laptop or computer to the motherboard and Extruder controller

- A laptop or computer with an Internet connection

Download Required Software

You'll need several software packages to drive your 3D printer. ReplicatorG is the key bit of software. That's the program that takes design files and converts them into instructions to the machine you've just built. ReplicatorG depends upon several other packages. The following is the complete list of what you'll be downloading:

- ReplicatorG

- Java, required by ReplicatorG

- Python, also required by ReplicatorG

- Configuration files that define your 3D printer to the ReplicatorG software

Ready? Let's get to it.

ReplicatorG

Your first task will be to download an application called ReplicatorG. You can find it by visiting `www.replicat.org` and clicking on the Download link, as shown in Figure 19-1.

Figure 19-1. *Downloading ReplicatorG*

You'll be taken to a page where you must choose the version of ReplicatorG that matches your operating system. Click on the Windows, Mac, or Linux link, as shown in Figure 19-2, and save the installation file to your computer. (For the rest of the chapter, we'll be using Windows versions of all software.)

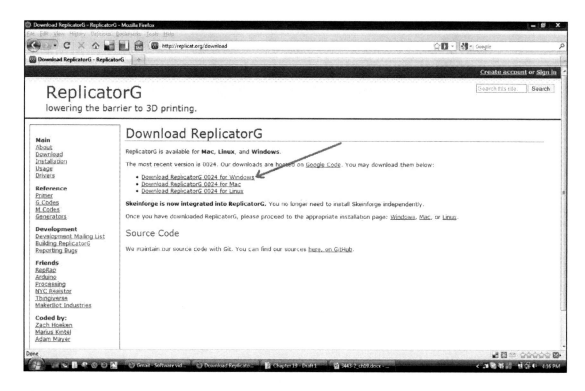

Figure 19-2. *Click one of the three links to download a version of ReplicatorG.*

■ **Note** It will make things slightly easier later in the chapter if you save all downloaded files into a single folder. We created a new folder on our Windows Vista desktop and called it "WhiteAnt 3DP," but you can name the folder anything you like.

Java

ReplicatorG will also require Java to be installed on your Windows computer. Point your web browser to http://java.com and click the big Free Java Download button, as shown in Figure 19-3. A test will be performed to see if you have the latest version installed. If you do, a message will tell you so; otherwise, the latest version will automatically install to your computer.

Figure 19-3. Install the latest version of Java on your computer.

Python

You'll next install the latest version of Python, required by the SkeinForge software that you will use to send 3D models to the ReplicatorG software for printing. Point your web browser to www.python.org and click the Download Python Now link, which is indicated in Figure 19-4.

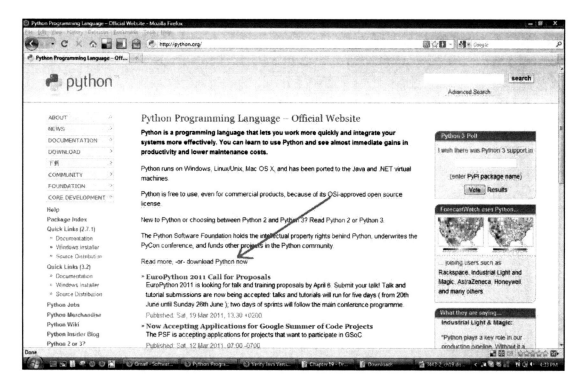

Figure 19-4. *Click the link to select a version of Python to install.*

We selected Python version 2.71 and clicked the Windows Installer version, as shown in Figure 19-5. After the Python file finishes downloading, double-click the file and follow the onscreen instructions.

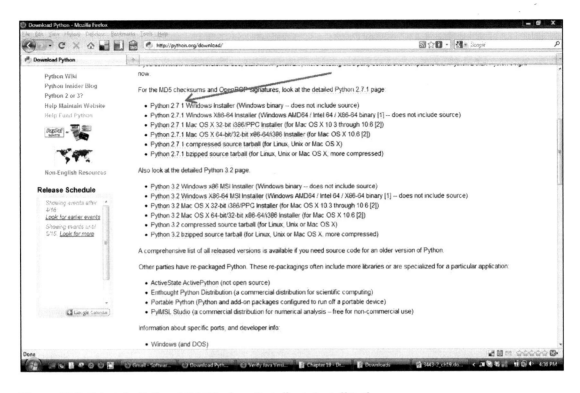

Figure 19-5. Select the Python 2.7.1 Windows Installer to install Python.

Configuration Files

Finally, you'll need to download two special configuration files that we'll open and examine later. Point your web browser to www.buildyourcnc.com and click on the CNC Machines tab, then click on the WhiteAnt 3D Printer/CNC link, as shown in Figure 19-6. Then right-click on both the links indicated and select Save Links As to save them to the 3D printer folder you created on your computer.

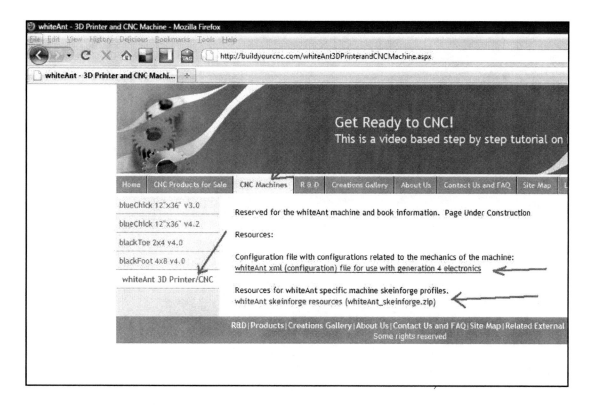

Figure 19-6. *Save both files to your computer.*

Add or Update Firmware to Motherboard

After you've downloaded the required software, it's time to configure the motherboard with its version of software called firmware. You'll do this by connecting the Mega to your computer with a USB cable. Note that you may have to unplug the motherboard from the Mega for this step. Figure 19-7 shows the USB cable plugged into the Mega.

Figure 19-7. *USB cable plugged into Mega*

Windows Vista and Windows 7 laptops and computers should automatically detect the Mega and install the correct driver. You should receive an alert message letting you know what COM port number was assigned.

▓ **Note** If you don't see the alert, you can check the Device Driver applet to get the COM port number. Click Start, right-click on Computer, and select Properties. When the Properties window opens, select Device Driver. The Device Driver will open and you will have to expand the Ports (COM&LPT) tree to see which COM port was assigned. If there are multiple ones, unplug the USB cable to the Mega and watch which one disappears. Then plug it back in and write down the COM port number you see appear again.

Now it's time to install the ReplicatorG software. Open the folder where you are storing all the previously downloaded files and double-click the ReplicatorG zip file. You will want to extract these files into the same folder. Figure 19-8 shows the ReplicatorG folder that holds the application's files.

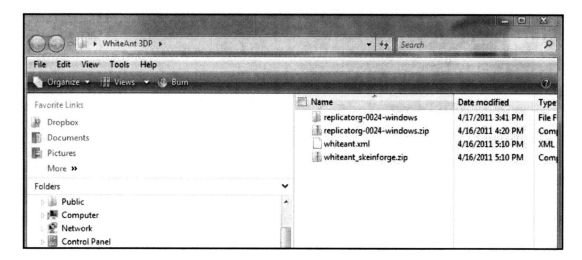

Figure 19-8. *Extracted ReplicatorG files and folder*

Next you'll need to move the whiteant.xml file you downloaded earlier into its proper folder. Cut and paste the file into the subfolder named machines. Figure 19-9 shows that the whiteant.xml file has been placed in the machines subfolder of the ReplicatorG folder.

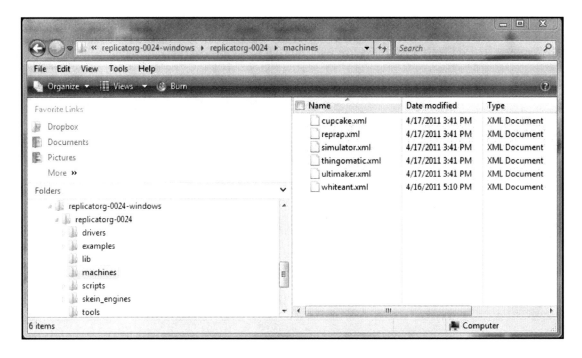

Figure 19-9. *Move the whiteant.xml file into the machines folder.*

If you disconnected your motherboard from the Mega, go ahead and attach the motherboard to the Mega now. Make certain the power supply is turned off, but you can leave the USB cable connected between the Mega and the computer.

Install Motherboard Firmware

Open the ReplicatorG folder and double-click the ReplicatorG.exe file indicated in Figure 19-10.

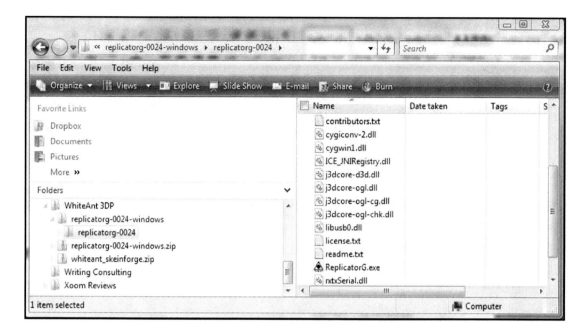

Figure 19-10. *Run the program by double-clicking the ReplicatorG.exe file.*

When ReplicatorG opens, click on the Machine menu, select Drivers, and then click on the Whiteant selection, as shown in Figure 19-11.

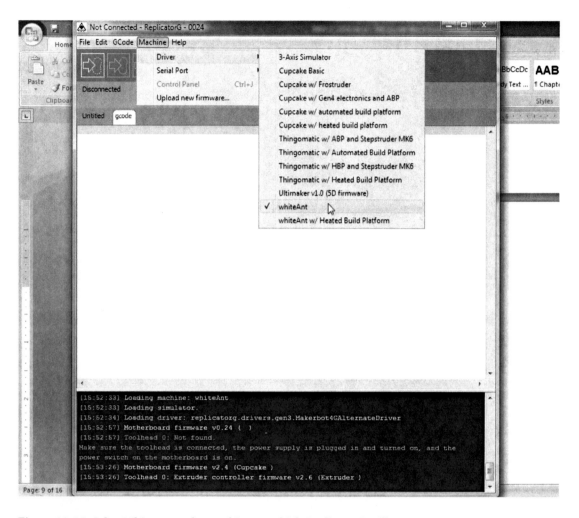

Figure 19-11. Select Whiteant as the machine on which ReplicatorG will operate.

Next click on the Machine menu again, but this time select Serial Port and then select the COM port number that was assigned earlier when you plugged the Mega into your computer, as shown in Figure 19-12. (Again, you may have to consult the Device Driver applet to find this number; see the Note in the previous section.)

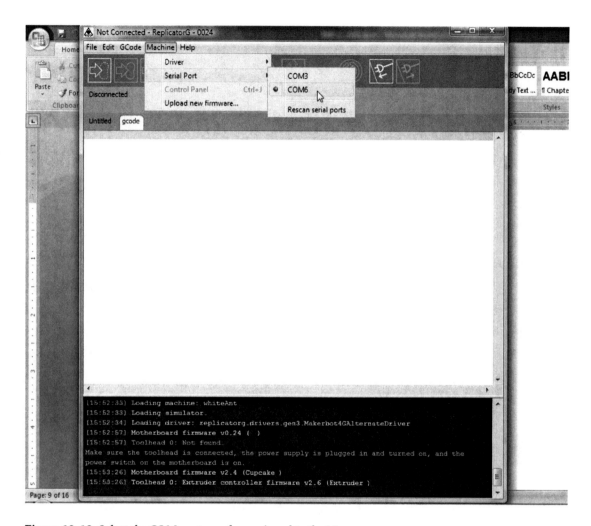

Figure 19-12. *Select the COM port number assigned to the Mega.*

Turn on the power supply. Lights on the motherboard (as well as all the motor drivers and Extruder controller) will light up. Click the Connect button indicated in Figure 19-13 and, if the connection is successful, you will see a message on a green background indicating that the Machine Whiteant is ready.

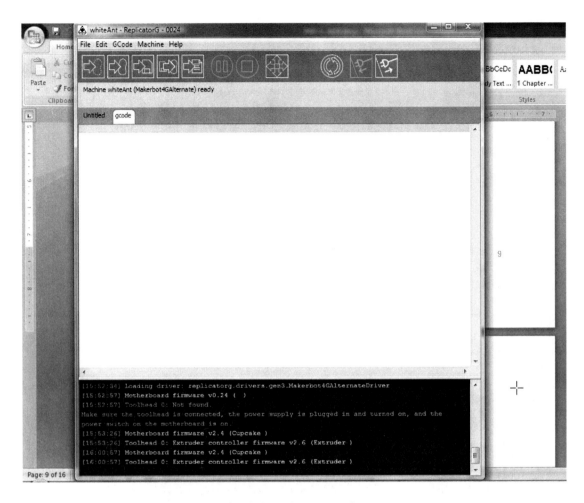

Figure 19-13. *Connect to the 3D printer by clicking the Connect button.*

After the connection is made, you will now need to upload the firmware to the motherboard. Click on the Machine menu and select the Upload New Firmware option shown in Figure 19-14.

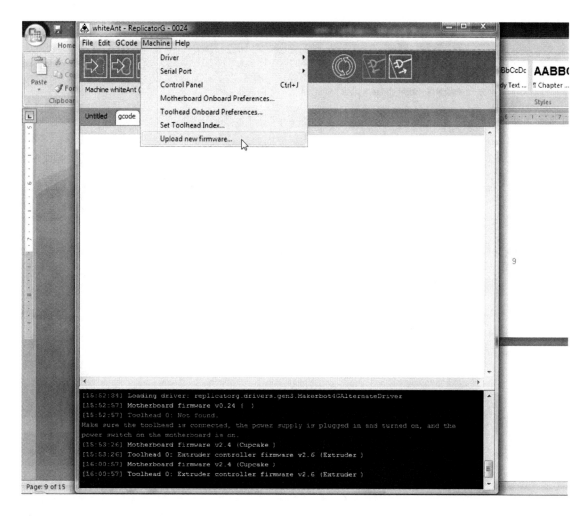

Figure 19-14. Upload the firmware to the motherboard.

Select the MakerBot Motherboard v2.X (Gen4) option in the window that appears, as shown in Figure 19-15, and click Next.

Figure 19-15. Select the proper firmware for the motherboard.

The firmware version window will open. Select v2.81, as shown in Figure 19-16, and click the Next button.

Figure 19-16. Select the firmware version.

On the next window, select the COM port number for communicating to the motherboard/Mega and click the Next button, as shown in Figure 19-17.

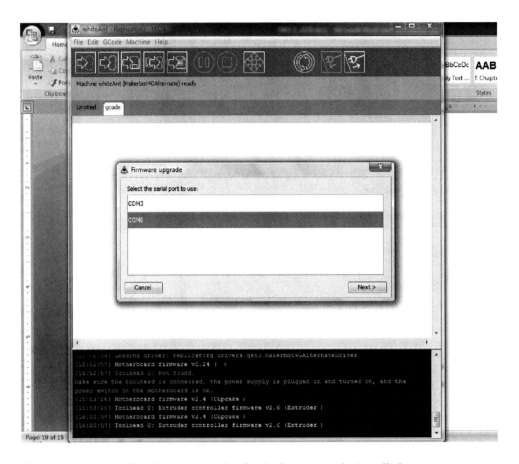

Figure 19-17. *Select the COM port number for the firmware to be installed.*

Now it's time to upload the firmware. Read the instructions on the screen carefully. In some instances, you will have to click the Upload button shown in Figure 19-18 at the same time that you press the Reset button on the motherboard. (The Reset button is on the top left edge of the motherboard if you are looking at it from the side of the 3D printer; it's a small black button.)

Tap the Upload button and, if you get an error message telling you it was unable to install, try again by pressing the Reset and Upload buttons together. Finally, if that doesn't work, try holding down the Reset button and then releasing it at the same time you press the Upload button.

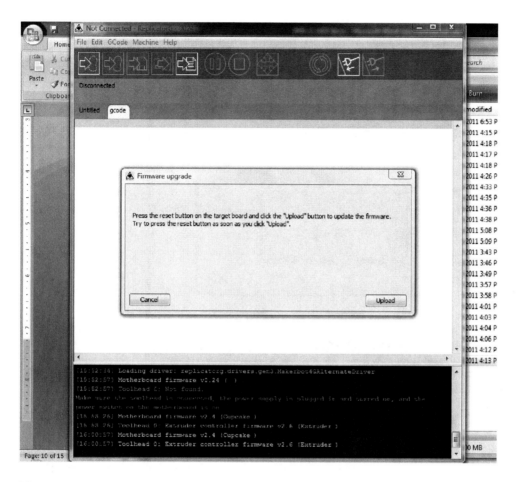

Figure 19-18. Install the firmware by tapping the Upload button.

When the firmware completes installing, you will see a message like the one shown in Figure 19-19.

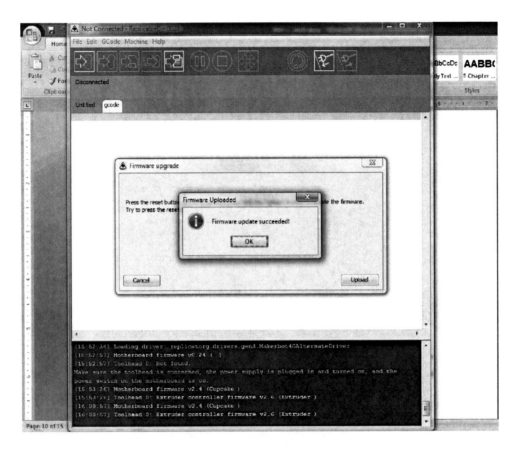

Figure 19-19. *The firmware was installed successfully.*

Install Extruder Controller Firmware

You'll also need to install firmware on the Extruder Controller. This is an almost identical procedure as the previous firmware installation to the motherboard. The difference is that you must unplug the USB cable from the motherboard and plug it into the USB port on the Extruder Controller. One you've done that, click on the Machine menu and select Upload New Firmware. A new window will appear. Scroll down the list and select Extruder Controller v3.X (Gen4) and then click Next, as shown in Figure 19-20.

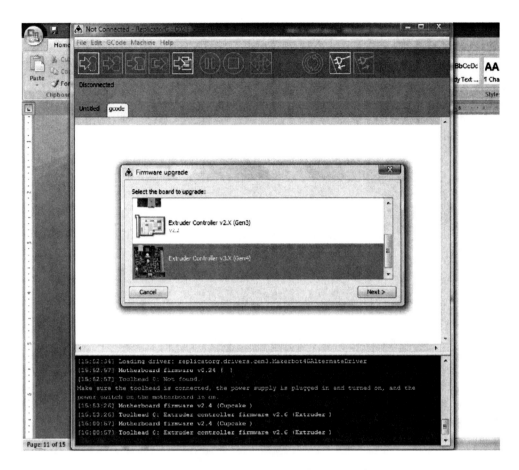

Figure 19-20. Select the firmware version for the Extruder Controller.

Select firmware version 2.81, as shown in Figure 19-21, and click Next.

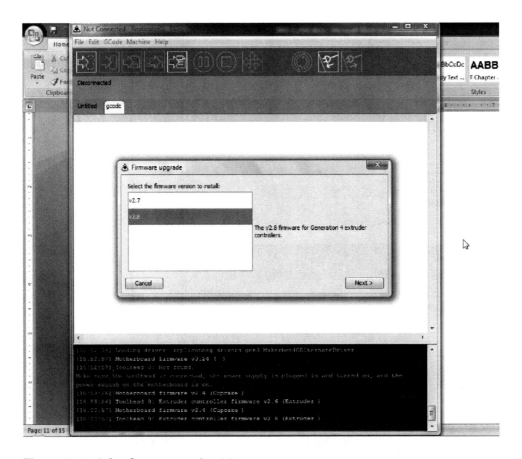

Figure 19-21. *Select firmware version 2.81.*

Select the COM port number for the Extruder Controller, as shown in Figure 19-22, and click Next. (The COM port number will be the new number that appears, but you can also verify it by opening the Device Driver applet and unplugging and replugging in the Extruder Controller to see what new port number appears in the Port list – see the Note earlier in chapter.)

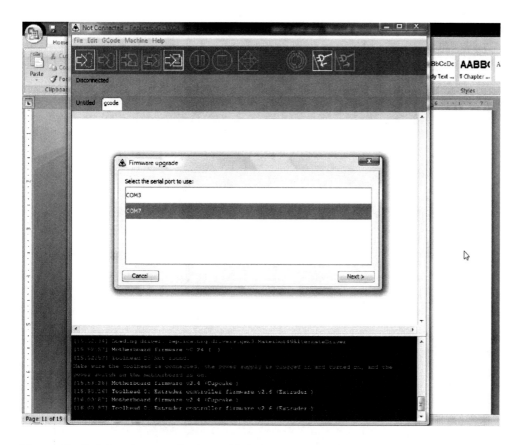

Figure 19-22. *Select the Extruder Controller's COM port number.*

Tap the Upload button shown in Figure 19-23 and wait for a confirmation message to tell you that the firmware was installed successfully.

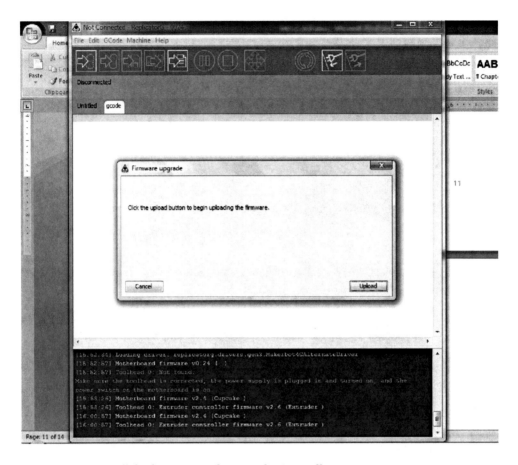

Figure 19-23. Install the firmware to the Extruder Controller.

Remove the USB plug from the Extruder Controller and replug it into the motherboard. Tap the Connect button once again on the ReplicatorG program and establish a connection with your 3D printer.

Summary

Now that you've got the software all installed, it's time to put all the moving parts through their paces with some simple tests, configure a few settings that control speeds and feed rates, and then… print something!

CHAPTER 20

■ ■ ■

Testing and Printing

Your 3D printer is built, you've downloaded the required software, and you've successfully connected the printer to your computer. All that's left is to configure the printer with some custom settings and you'll be ready to perform your first 3D print job!

Remember to check the book's web site, www.buildyourtools.com, for possible updates to this chapter; as with all software, there are likely to be updates, patches, and new versions of the various applications you're using. We'll do our best to keep you informed on the latest software information as well as provide assistance for properly installing and configuring it should that be necessary.

So, without further ado, let's get this software configured properly and get printing!

Configure the 3D Printer

First, open ReplicatorG and open the Control Panel. If you've got the ReplicatorG software running, you can open the Control Panel from the Machine menu or simply click the Control Panel button (shown in Figure 20-1) on the ReplicatorG toolbar.

Figure 20-1. *The Control Panel button on the Replicator G toolbar*

Make sure that the proper settings are specified in the control panel. First, set the Motor Speed (RPM) to 1.98. You may also need to experiment with the Extrude Duration setting to test your Extruder and determine if it is working properly. The Extrude Duration controls the length of time the Extruder will push the plastic filament through the barrel when the Forward button is pressed. Start with ten (10) seconds for the amount of time for this; you can change it if you find the Extruder is pushing too much or too little plastic into the barrel. Both settings can be seen in Figure 20-2.

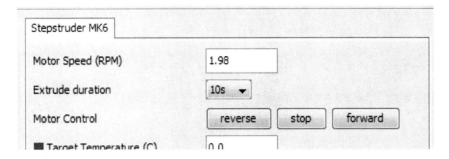

Figure 20-2. Set the Motor Speed and Extrude Duration.

Next, set the Extruder temperature and test the thermocouple. Begin by setting the target temperature (in Figure 20-3) to 100 C.

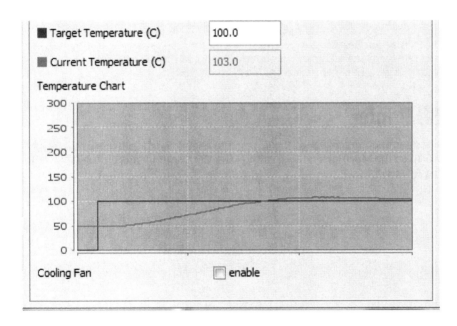

Figure 20-3. Set the target temperature and the current temperature will rise to match.

The control panel will show the current temperature and your target temperature. In the graph at the bottom of the window shown in Figure 20-3, the current temperature is in red and the target temperature is in blue.

When you change the target temperature, the blue line will immediately jump to that temperature. However, the red line (the current temperature) will more slowly change to your target temperature. If the target temperature is higher than the current temperature, the current temperature will attempt to match the target temperature. Note that increasing or decreasing the temperature can take anywhere from one minute to fifteen minutes or more.

Let the current temperature maintain at around 100 degrees for a few minutes to determine if everything is functioning properly. You will see minor fluctuations above and below the target temperature; this is normal so don't worry about it.

If everything seems fine, go ahead and enter 205 for the target temperature (shown in Figure 20-4). This is the temperature in Celsius to melt the plastic filament.

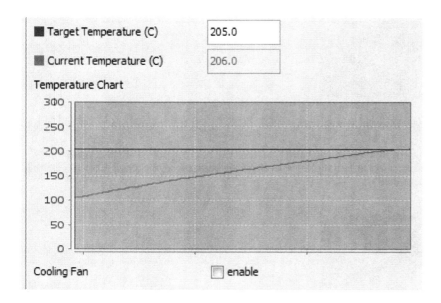

Figure 20-4. Set the target temperature to 205 degrees Celsius.

Once a temperature of 205 degrees Celsius is reached, insert some filament (also called PLA) into the barrel of the Extruder (the red PTFE tube), as shown in Figure 20-5.

▦ **Note** The filament can be purchased from a variety of sources (consult the book's web site for a complete list) but you can order a starting amount of 1 pound (lb) of 3mm silver PLA from Ultimachine `http://ultimachine.com/content/pla-3mm-silver-1lb`. Of course, you can order whatever color you like, but the silver shows up well in photos and video.

Figure 20-5. Insert the filament into the feed cyliner.

Secure the hinge mechanism made of Parts P and Q so that the bearing presses firmly against the PLA. Secure the end of the hinge mechanism tightly with a rubber band using the small grooves cut into Parts P and Q, as shown in Figure 20-6.

Figure 20-6. Use a rubber band to hold the filament tightly between bearing and serrated hub.

Now you'll test the flow of the PLA. Continue to tap the Forward button to begin pushing the PLA into the barrel. Check the consistency of the PLA as it streams out of the nozzle. If the PLA seems a bit drippy, decrease the target temperature. If the PLA is too stiff, or the stepper motor is having a difficult time pushing the PLA (you will definitely know when this happens as the motor will make a skipping sound), increase the target temperature.

Filament should begin to flow out of the nozzle end as demonstrated in Figure 20-7.

Figure 20-7. The filament will melt and extrude from the nozzle.

Checking the Axes for Proper Movement

Now that you have the Extruder working properly, you should confirm that the X, Y, and Z axes all move properly. You'll do this via the Jog controls on the left side of the Control Panel, as shown in Figure 20-8.

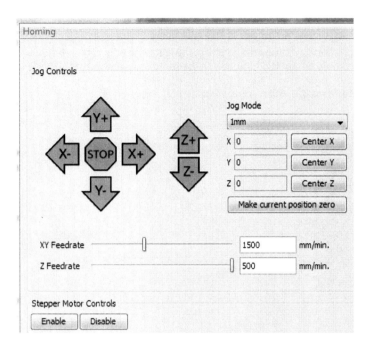

Figure 20-8. Test the axes controls using the Jog Controls section of the Control Panel.

First, set the Jog Mode to 1mm. If the jog mode is set to a higher amount, you run the risk of overshooting the axis travel if the driver is set to the incorrect stepping mode. For instance, if the driver is set to full step (not 1/8 microstepping), the jog mode set to 10mm, and the WhiteAnt configuration is used, then the mechanism being moved (Table, Extruder, or ZY Plate) will move 80mm, not 10mm. That's a big difference. If 1mm is set, a similar situation would only move the axis 8mm. Either way, make sure the mechanism that will be moved is pretty much at the midpoint of its corresponding axis by manually adjusting the mechanism. (Push or pull the table, for example. For the X and Y axes that use belts, gently push on either part to position it so that test movements will occur from a midpoint. For the Z axis, manually turn the collar until the lead screw is centered near the anti-backlash nut.)

Next, adjust the XY and Z feedrates shown in Figure 20-9. These are the rates at which the mechanisms for each axis (Table, Extruder, ZY Plate) will move in units of velocity (millimeters per minute). The numbers you will use are fast for a small machine, so be careful. The X and Y feedrates should be set to 1500 mm/min. The Z-Axis federate should be set to 500, or lower.

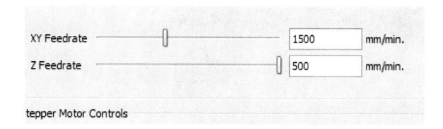

Figure 20-9. *Configure the feedrates for all three axes.*

To move a mechanism (or "jog" them), just tap and release that mechanism's respective axis letter (X+, X-, Y+, Y-, Z+, Z-) as shown in Figure 20-10. If the movement seems correct and moving at the expected distance (based on the estimated jog rate of 1mm per tap) for each press of the button, then the axes are configured correctly. As you are moving the axes around, remember the location of the Stop button. You will want to press the Stop button if either the X or Y axis gets too close to an edge, if the Z axis lead screw threatens to exit the anti-backlash nut, or if the Extruder gets too close to the table.

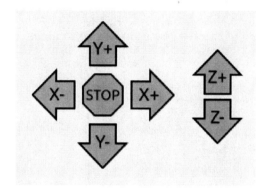

Figure 20-10. *Jog the three axes using the + and – buttons.*

You may find that an axis is moving in the wrong direction. Looking at the front of the machine, the X-axis (moving left or right) should move to the right when the X+ button is pressed and to the left when the X- button is pressed. The Y-axis should move towards you when the Y+ button is pressed (seems counter intuitive) and away from you when Y- is pressed. The Z-axis will move down as the Z- is pressed and up as the Z+ button is pressed. If any axis is moving in a direction opposite to what's described here, that axis needs to be inverted. To invert an axis, click on Machine ➤ Motherboard Onboard Preferences, as shown in Figure 20-11.

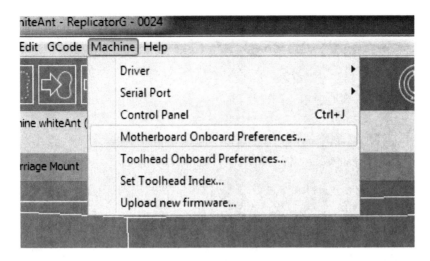

Figure 20-11. Invert an axis using the Motherboard Onboard Preferences option.

Place a check mark (or remove the check mark) on the axis that needs to be inverted, as demonstrated in Figure 20-12. You will notice that the "A" axis is checked (that controls the Extruder). We noticed that the stepping motor was actually pulling the PLA out of the PTFE tube, rather than pushing it into the tube.

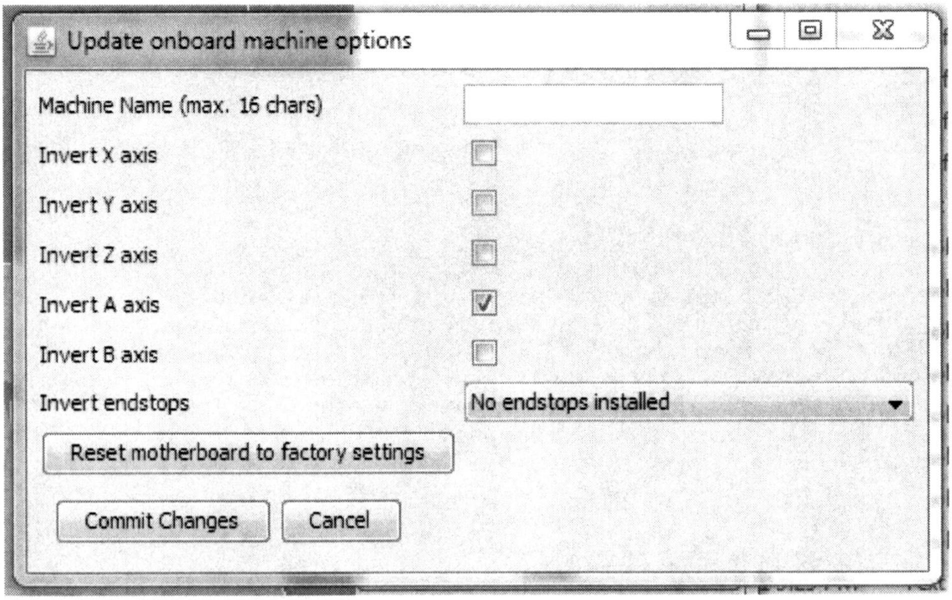

Figure 20-12. The checkboxes for the axes

Press the Commit Changes button and your changes will be made and the axis will be inverted. Test the axis again to confirm that the axis is traveling in the correct direction.

In summary, test each axis for the proper direction of movement, invert when necessary, and remember to use the Stop button if you must!

Homing the Machine

Now you will "home" the machine by finding and setting the default starting location for each of the three axes of movement (X, Y, and Z). Double-check the connection of the endstops (limit switches) by pressing their levers. The red LED should light up as you can see in Figure 20-13.

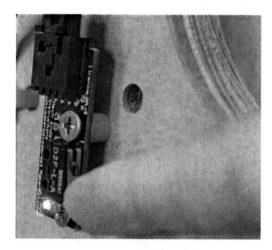

Figure 20-13. Test each endstop by pressing the button and looking for the LED to light.

Go to the Homing menu shown in Figure 20-14 and select an axis to home.

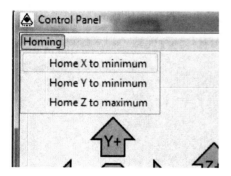

Figure 20-14. The Homing menu allows you to home each axis separately.

You will notice that the X and Y show minimum and the Z shows maximum. This is because the X and Y axes will home at the start of their axes (near the front left corner of the table) and the Z will home at the top and not the surface of the table top. As an axis homes (moves toward its limit switch), keep the mouse over the Stop button—just in case you see that part of your machine may be getting close to the limit of its movement. Each mechanism (Table, Extruder, ZY Plate) will move quickly towards its respective endstop and then stop immediately when the moving mechanism triggers a limit switch.

When you home the Z-axis, you will also need to determine the Z-axis height (the distance from its maximum raised position when the endstop is pressed to the flat surface of the tabletop). You will need to run a Gcode set of instructions to determine this height. On ReplicatorG's menu bar, click File ➤ Scripts ➤ calibration ➤ Thing-O-Matic calibration.gcode, as shown in Figure 20-15.

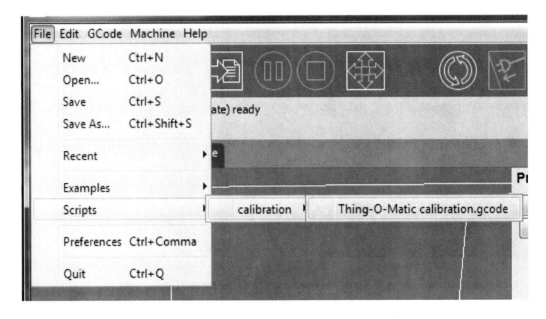

Figure 20-15. Run a special bit of code to determine the Z-axis height.

When the script opens, press the Build button shown in Figure 20-16 on the toolbar.

Figure 20-16. The Build button will prepare the script for calculating the Z-axis height.

A message will appear like the one in Figure 20-17 telling you to jog the z-axis, moving the Extruder down and towards the table.

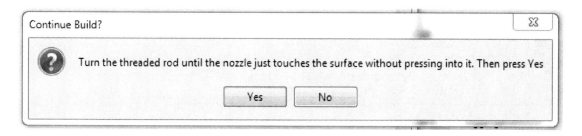

Figure 20-17. *Lower the Z-axis and Extruder only when told to do so.*

Jog the Z-axis down a few times and then use the Z-axis collar to manually turn the lead screw until the Extruder nozzle is just a hair above the table. Click the Yes button when the Extruder's nozzle tip is as close as possible to the tabletop without touching it, as shown in Figure 20-18. The Z-axis will then start to move up towards the endstop.

Figure 20-18. *The nozzle's tip should almost touch the table top.*

Another message will tell you to open the Control Panel (see Figure 20-19).

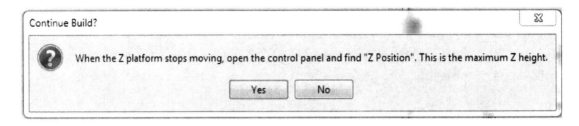

Figure 20-19. When the Z-axis moves to the top, return to the Control Panel.

The number in the Z-axis box (seen in Figure 20-20) will show the height from where the Z-axis was positioned (almost touching the tabletop) to the endstop switch. Write this number down in a convenient location. You will enter this number into a special file later.

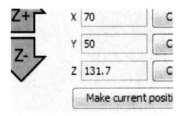

Figure 20-20. Write down the Z-axis height for later use.

Prepare Skeinforge

Skeinforge is a program that slices a three-dimensional model (created by you or someone else) and produces a Gcode file (a special file that tells your 3D printer where to move) that will be executed on the machine.

You'll first need to prepare Skeinforge by selecting the Skeinforge Gcode generator that will be used. Do that by clicking on GCode ➤ Choose GCode Generator ➤ Skeinforge (35), as shown in Figure 20-21.

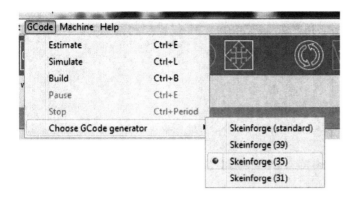

Figure 20-21. Select Skeinforge (35) as the Gcode Generator.

Next you will add the special profiles specific to the WhiteAnt 3D printer that you downloaded in Chapter 19. If you didn't download the files in Chapter 19, you can visit http://buildyourcnc.com/ whiteAnt3DPrinterandCNCMachine.aspx and click on the WhiteAnt-specific machine skeinforge profiles. You will download a file named whiteAnt_skeinforge.zip your computer. Extract this file (right-click the .zip file and click on Extract, or use the extract tool of your preference) and all of the contents will be stored in a folder named whiteAnt that you see in Figure 20-22.

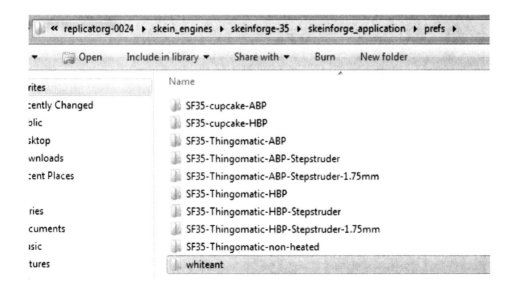

Figure 20-22. Extract the WhiteAnt profiles to your computer.

Copy the WhiteAnt folder to the `replicatorG--024\skein_engines\skeinforge-35\skeinforge-application\prefs` folder. You need to modify one of the files inside the whiteAnt folder to tell it the value you recorded for the Z-axis height. Start Notepad and click File ➤ Open and browse to `replicatorG-0024\skein_engines\skeinforge-35\skeinforge-application\prefs\whiteAnt\alterations` and select `Start.gcode`, as shown in Figure 20-23.

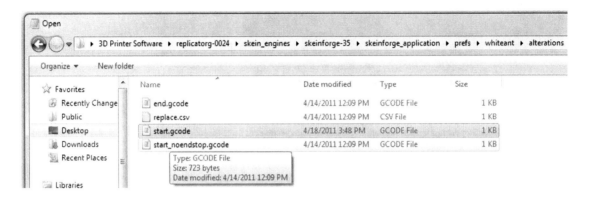

Figure 20-23. *Open the start.gcode file in Notepad.*

You will notice a single, never-ending line in the `start.gcode` file. Click on the Edit menu and select Find, as shown in Figure 20-24.

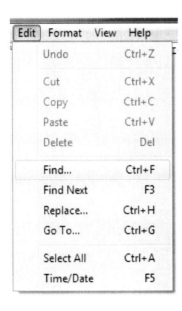

Figure 20-24. *Use the Find feature in the Edit menu.*

In the Find what: text box, enter the value g92, as shown in Figure 20-25.

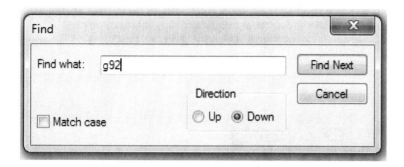

Figure 20-25. Search the file for g92.

Behind the g92 text is the Z100 value, shown in Figure 20-26.

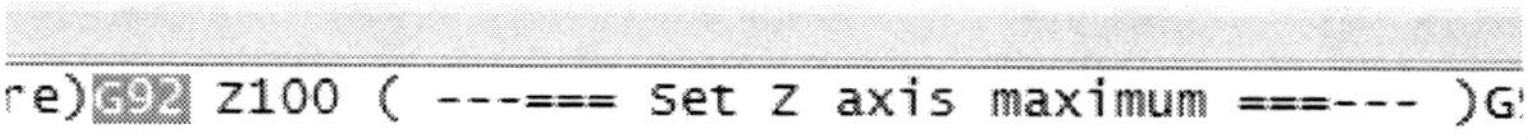

```
re) g92 Z100 ( ---=== Set Z axis maximum ===--- )G
```

Figure 20-26. Find the Z100 value in the start.gcode file.

Change the 100 to the value you recorded earlier for the Z-axis height, as shown in Figure 20-27. (Don't enter the value shown in Figure 20-27 as this value is what we recorded for our machine and may be too high a value for your machine. If you enter a value that's too high, the Extruder nozzle will impact the tabletop and possibly damage the nozzle tip.)

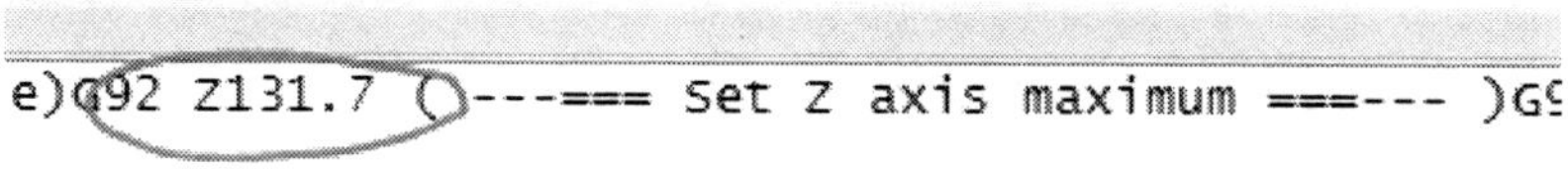

```
e) g92 Z131.7 ()---=== Set Z axis maximum ===--- )G
```

Figure 20-27. Change the Z100 value to the Z-axis height value you recorded earlier.

▨ **Note** If Python was installed, you are ready to print. Otherwise, double-click the python .msi file that was downloaded in Chapter 19 and install Python by following the Installation wizard.

You are now ready to print!

Time to Print

Before you can print, however, you're going to need a 3D model. A great place to get things to print is at www.thingyverse.com. The first "thing" you print will help you understand the calibration of the machine. It's called the Calibration Cube and it can be found at www.thingiverse.com/thing:5573, as shown in Figure 20-28.

Figure 20-28. You will print a small cube to test your 3D printer.

Scroll to the bottom of the page and download the 20mm-box.stl file shown in Figure 20-29. An .stl file is a watertight 3D model made in a CAD program, a special application used to design three-dimensional objects (among other things).

 **20mm-box.stl**
2 kb / 129 downloads

download

Figure 20-29. Download the 20mm-box.stl file.

Once this file has been downloaded, you can begin the printing process. Start ReplicatorG and open the file by clicking File ➤ Open, as shown in Figure 20-30.

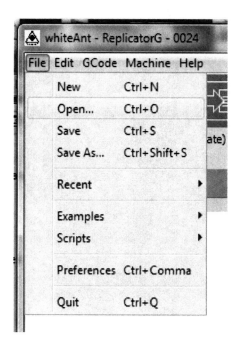

Figure 20-30. Open .stl files in ReplicatorG.

Navigate to the folder where you downloaded the 20mm-box.stl file and double-click the file, as shown in Figure 20-31.

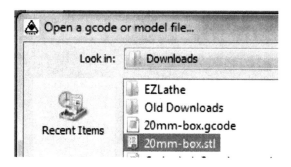

Figure 20-31. Find and open the Calibration Cube .stl file.

You'll see a model resembling the "thing" that will be printed (see Figure 20-32). You can use the mouse to rotate this model to get a better view, but make sure that you are in View mode. If you are in Move mode, clicking and dragging the mouse will move the object. There are many actions you can perform on this box or other models, but that's best tried when you have more experience.

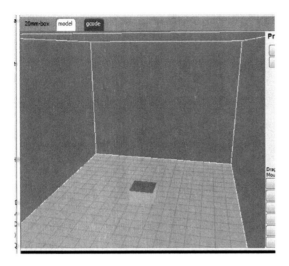

Figure 20-32. *View the cube and use the mouse to rotate it around.*

Because the 3D printer prints in layers, the model will need to be sliced and its Gcode created. Click the Generate Gcode button shown in Figure 20-33.

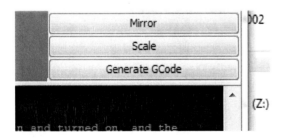

Figure 20-33. *Generate Gcode so the 3D printer will know how to print the cube.*

After clicking generate Gcode, the "Choose a skeinforge profile" dialog box will appear, as shown in Figure 20-34.

Figure 20-34. Select the proper Skeinforge profile before printing.

Select the WhiteAnt option and click the Generate button. (If you don't see WhiteAnt, then the whiteAnt folder was not copied into the correct folder in the previous section. Review the previous section and double-check the location of the WhiteAnt folder.)

A status dialog will appear with progress bars to show the progress of the Gcode being generated (see Figure 20-35). This can take anywhere from a minute to quite a while depending on the complexity of the 3D model you wish to print.

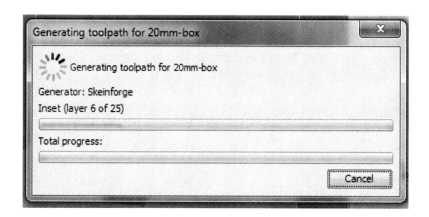

Figure 20-35. The Gcode is generated for the selected 3D model.

When the Gcode has finished being generated, go to the Control Panel, enter the target temperature and wait for it to be reached (if you haven't already done so), and then press the Build button shown in Figure 20-36 and watch the action.

Figure 20-36. *The Build button starts the printing process.*

The machine will home itself and pause in that position until the software is confident that the Extruder is hot enough to get started.

Figures 20-37 through 20-42 are a series of photos showing the printing process from start to finish, including measuring the cube for accuracy.

Figure 20-37. *The printing process begins.*

Figure 20-38. *The first layer completed*

Figure 20-39. Layers are printed on each other and the cube is taking shape.

Figure 20-40. Almost finished…

Figure 20-41. Finished!

Figure 20-42. Close to 20mm—not bad!

whiteAnt Logo

To commemorate your success in building your whiteAnt 3D printer, Patrick has created a special piece—the whiteAnt logo in plastic—for you to print and apply to your machine, as shown in Figure 20-43. It can be found at `http://buildyourcnc.com/whiteAnt3DPrinterandCNCMachine.aspx`.

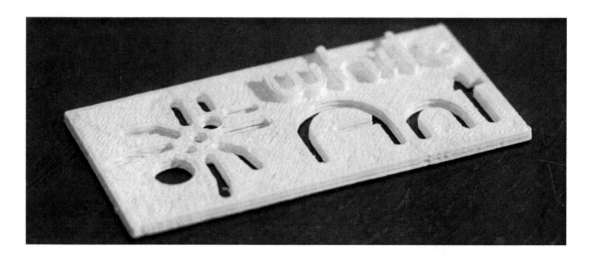

Figure 20-43. The whiteAnt logo for your handmade 3D printer

Visit the link and click on the resources section. The file is in the `.stl` format, so just download the model from the site, open it in replicatorG, click the Generate Gcode button, select whiteAnt as the skeinforge profile, and start printing by pressing the build button. Be sure to upload a picture of your final 3D printer, complete with whiteAnt logo to the `www.buildyourtools.com` forum and let us see your machine!

Summary

There's not much else to say here. You've got a 3D printer and the 3D printing world is wide open to you! Where do you go now? Well, if you want to create your own 3D models, you'll need to spend some time learning to use a good CAD program. And you'll definitely want to tune in to discussion forums related to 3D printing. We're including a list of 3D printing web sites—companies that sell 3D printers, companies that sell supplies, web discussion forums, and more.

Have fun printing in plastic!

■ ■ ■

CHAPTER 21

Addendum

During the more than five months it took to put this book together, two unexpected events happened. The first was that some of the earlier electronics we had planned to use were declared obsolete, and were no longer being made available for sale; fortunately for us, this happened well before we reached the electronics chapters, and we were able to identify the newest electronics (called Gen4) and that's what you'll find in this book.

The second event was the discovery that if the Extruder (see Chapter 14) was not attached tightly with the hose clamp, the melting plastic inside could slowly force the Extruder to slide out of the clamp. A decision was made to offer a secondary solution to attaching the Extruder, but by the time this issue had been discovered, we were close to completing the book.

We didn't want to offer this secondary solution only online at www.buildyourtools.com, because we were concerned some readers might not check the book's website to read about changes or modifications made to the machine after they had purchased the book. So we've decided to include the second method for attaching the Extruder here. It's going to be an abbreviated chapter, with a fast walkthrough of the steps involved. Questions related to this method can be posted on the www.buildyourtools.com forum.

Required Parts Summary

For Chapter 21, you will need the following components:

- The extra mounting parts that come with the Makerbot Extruder Kit
- Qty-4 #4x5/8" (or #4x1/2") wood screws
- PDF building instructions for Part S – see www.buildyourtools.com
- Qty-3 3" x ¼" machine screws
- Qty-2 2-1/2" x ¼" machine screws

Prepare Extruder Mounting Base

Your first step will be to modify the Extruder so that it can be bolted to the metal mounting base. Figure 21-1 shows the components required for this step.

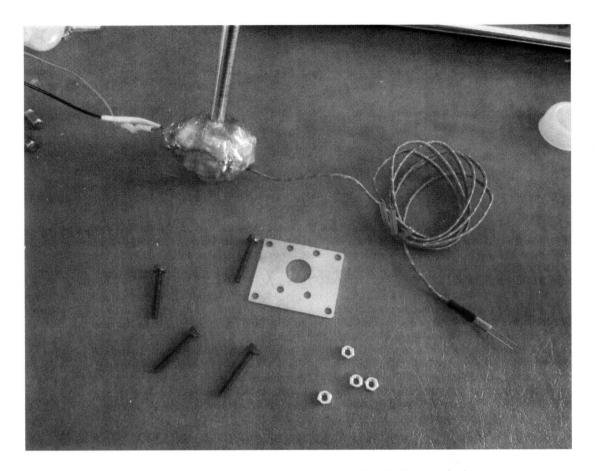

Figure 21-1. *The mounting plate and other hardware are included with the Extruder kit.*

Start by inserting the four Allen screws into the mounting plate and securing them with the four nuts, as shown in Figure 21-2. Do not tighten the nuts against the mounting plate; instead, leave a quarter inch of space for now.

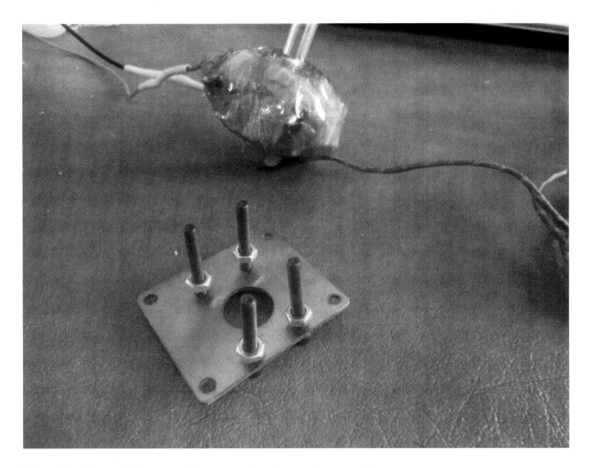

Figure 21-2. Insert Allen screws into mounting plate and secure with nuts.

Use a sharp blade to cut away a square on top of the Extruder. You will be cutting away the Kapton tape and the ceramic tape below it to expose the four screw holes shown in Figure 21-3.

■ **Note** Take your time with this and cut away a small square at first, and then enlarge little by little until you find the screw holes. If you'd rather avoid cutting away this much of the Kapton and ceramic tape, you can try to cut small Xs in the four corners and just peel back the tape to find the holes.

401

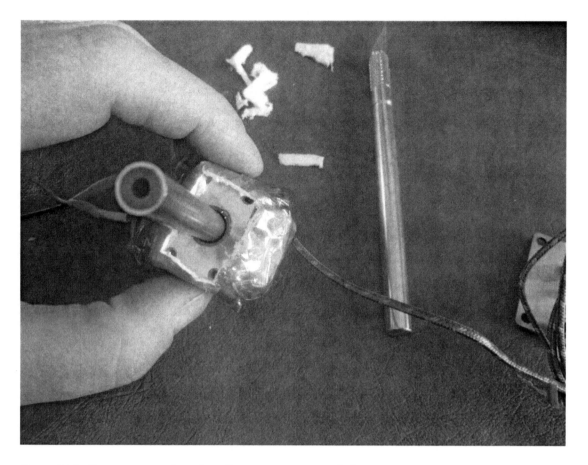

Figure 21-3. Cut away a small portion of tape to expose screw holes.

Insert a small piece of ceramic tape over the hole, but trim it so that it does not cover the four exposed screw holes, as shown in Figure 21-4.

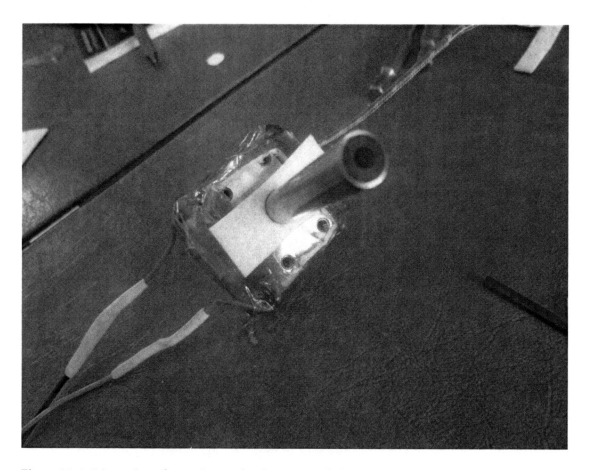

Figure 21-4. Trim a piece of ceramic tape that leaves screw holes exposed.

Cover the new strip of ceramic tape with more Kapton tape to hold it in place while avoiding covering the screw holes. After the Kapton tape, place the heat sink over the feed tube, as shown in Figure 21-5.

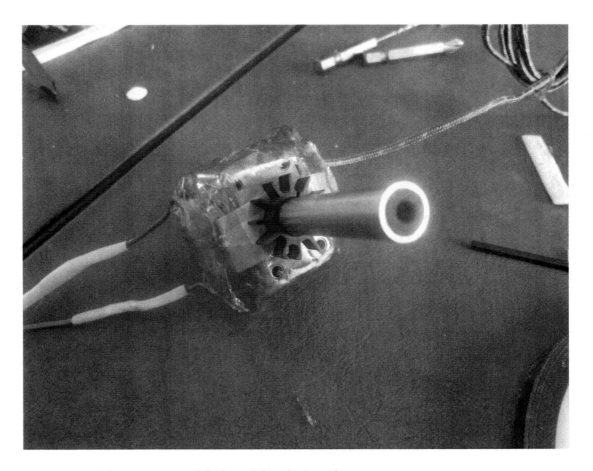

Figure 21-5. Add Kapton tape and the heat sink to the Extruder.

Next screw, in the four Allen screws to the top of the Extruder heater core, as shown in Figure 21-6.

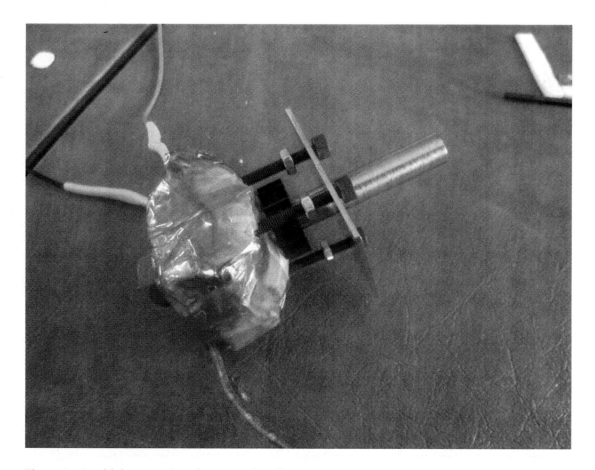

Figure 21-6. *Add the mounting plate using the Allen screws.*

Use an Allen wrench to screw the Allen screws completely into the heater core until they stop. Then use a small wrench and tighten the nuts on the Allen screws against the mounting base, as shown in Figure 21-7.

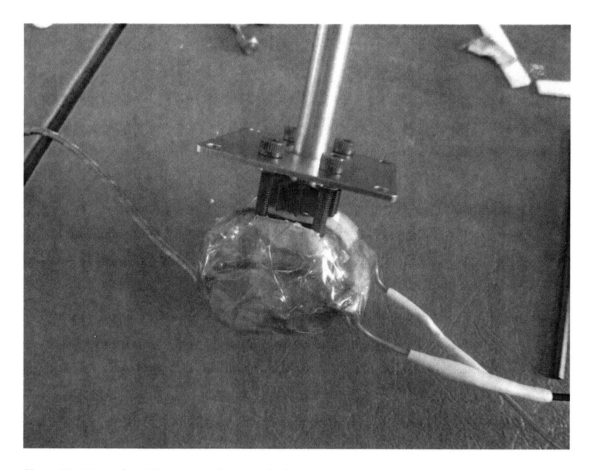

Figure 21-7. Extruder with mounting base attached

Attach Extruder to Filament Feed Mechanism

Before you attach the Extruder, you will need to make a slight modification to Part Q, the Extruder Bearing Hinge 2. You will need to cut off the small notch; Figure 21-8 shows the modified part on the right along with the original part with the notch on the left.

Figure 21-8. Cut the notch off Part Q, seen on the left.

Refer back to Chapter 15 for the hardware required to attach Part P to part Q. You will also need to add the motor as described in Chapter 15. After installing the motor, instead of using the hose clamp and zip tie to secure the Extruder, you will now use the new Part S shown in Figure 21-9.

Figure 21-9. Part S will be temporarily bolted on to Part Q.

Insert two 2-1/2" machine screws through Part Q, as shown in Figure 21-9. Add Part S so that the hole is up against Part Q and secure with two ¼" nuts, as shown in Figure 21-10.

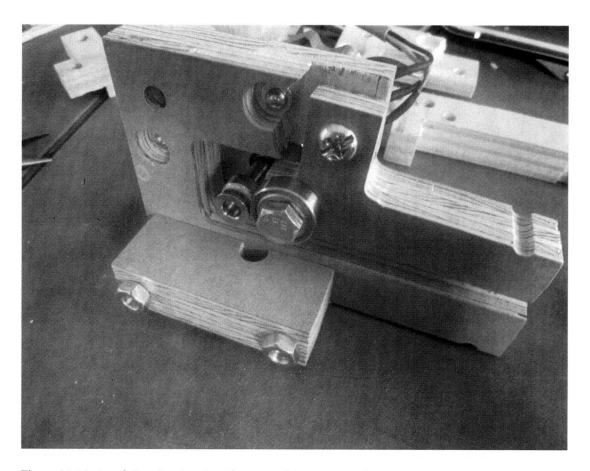

Figure 21-10. Attach Part S to Part Q with two machine screws and nuts.

Insert the Extruder's feed tube into the hole on Part S so that the thermocouple wire and the two power resistor wires are not pointing left or right, as shown in Figure 21-11. (They should be pointing toward you or away from you.)

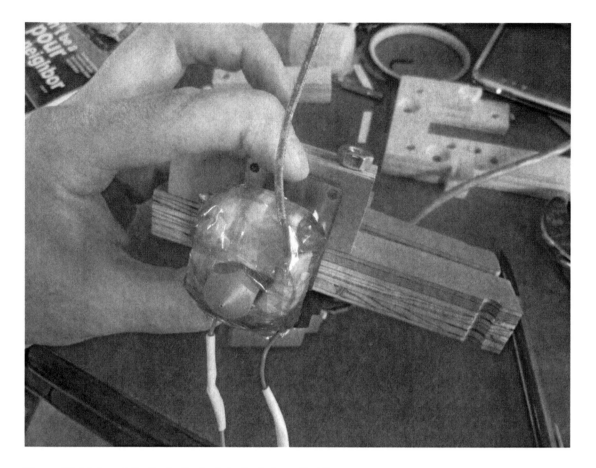

Figure 21-11. Insert the feed cylinder into the hole on Part S.

Look carefully at Figure 21-11 and you'll notice that the empty hole in the upper-right corner, if drilled, would cause the wood screw to impact the 2-1/2" bolt holding Part S to Part Q. If this is the case, flip the Extruder around and you should find that the empty hole is not in line with the 2-1/2" machine screw. Mark all four holes with a pencil and drill pilot holes, as shown in Figure 21-12.

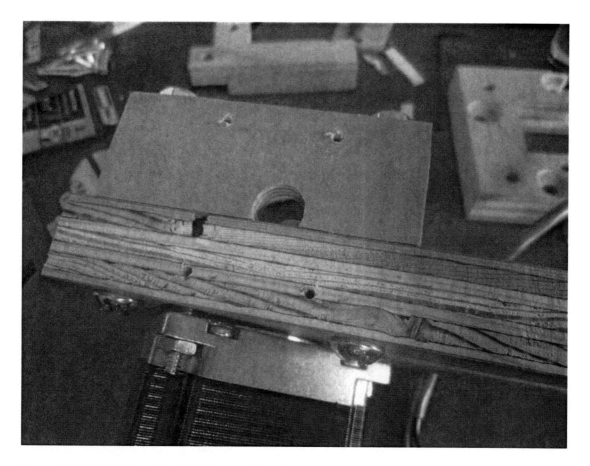

Figure 21-12. Mark four pilot holes for attaching the mounting plate to Parts S and Q.

Use four #4-5/8" (or #4-1/2") wood screws to attach the mounting plate to Part S and Part Q, as shown in Figure 21-13.

***Figure 21-13.** Use wood screws to attach the mounting base to Part S and Part Q.*

Next, remove the two 2-1/2" machine screws you used to attach Part S to Part Q; they were temporary, and will be replaced by three 3" machine screws from the Z-axis Rail Support.

Modify Z-Axis Rail to Hold Extruder Mechanism

If you attempt to attach the Extruder Mechanism (consisting of Parts P, Q, and S plus Extruder and motor), you may find that the three machine screws seen in Figure 21-14 are not long enough to allow for a nut to be added.

Figure 21-14. You will need three 3" machine screws to attach the Extruder Mechanism.

If the machine screws are not long enough, you will need to detach the anti-backlash nut from Part N and pull out the Z-axis Rail Support from the v-groove bearings. After removing this piece, you will need to remove the two Srong-Tie rails and replace the three bolts with three 3" machine screws, as shown in Figure 21-15. Also, add a single nut to the bottom two machine screws and two nuts to the top machine screw (also shown in Figure 21-15). You might also try to remove the nuts from the existing three machine screws to see if that provides you enough length for the tips of the machine screws to be exposed for the nuts to be attached.

Figure 21-15. Three longer machine screws plus nuts will hold Extruder Mechanism.

Now carefully put the Extruder Mechanism onto the three machine screws, as shown in Figure 21-16, and secure them with a single nut each.

■ **Note** You will push the Extruder Mechanism until Part S is touching the Z-axis Rail Support, as shown in Figure 21-16.

Figure 21-16. *Extruder Mechanism bolted onto Z-axis Rail Support*

Your 3D printer is now to the point where you can return to Chapter 16 and begin installing the electronics.

APPENDIX A

■ ■ ■

Hardware List

This appendix provides a list of all the hardware we used in this book. We've included the items from all the chapters and tried to combine, for example, the three #6-32 1-1/4" screws from Chapter 12 with the twelve #6-32 1-1/4" screws from Chapter 13 so that you'll see a total of 15 #6 screws in the list. (This is just an example – the actual count may be higher.)

For a more up-to-date list of hardware, we're going to point you to an online spreadsheet. If we find any errors related to the hardware (such as too few of a certain kind of washer or a missing screw of length 1-1/4"), we'll fix it in the spreadsheet. You'll also find in the spreadsheet a list of sources for many of the items required for your 3D printer. The spreadsheet can be found at:

http://buildyourcnc.com/whiteAnt3DPrinterandCNCMachine.aspx

If you believe you've found an error related to the list of required hardware, please post a comment over at the book's forum located at www.buildyourtools.com, and we'll check it out. Definitely be sure to download the spreadsheet before you actually begin the build, as the spreadsheet will be the most up-to-date parts list that we keep in sync with the most up-to-date set of blueprints on our website.

One last thing: you may choose to buy some hardware, such as nuts and machine screws, in larger quantities (boxes of 100, for example) to reduce the overall price per item. In some instances, you may discover you can substitute a part you already have for a different part used in the book's instructions (a 1-1/2" machine screw, for example, in place of a 1-1/4"). We encourage you to make such substitutions if you determine the change will not affect the overall functionality of the printer.

Table A-1 lists all of hardware at the time this book was printed.

Table A-1. *Hardware in this book*

#	Hardware
3	2-1/2" machine screws, 1/4" diameter
64	1/4" nuts
6	Strong-tie metal brackets
7	#6-32 machine screws, 1" length
25	#6-32 nuts

Continued

#	Hardware
4	#6 nylon spacers, ½" length
25	#8-32 x 1" machine screws
45	#8-32 nuts
3	3" machine screws, 1/4" diameter
4	2-1/4" machine screws, 3/8" diameter
4	3/8" nut
8	Small red washer for 3/8" diameter bolts
8	3/8" washer (1" diameter)
8	3/8" V-groove bearings, 1-1/4" diameter
14	1-1/2" machine screws, ¼" diameter
11	Barrel nut, 1/4" x 7/16"
16	#8-32 x 3/4" machine screws
1	4140 Alloy steel precision Acme threaded rod, length 11", 3/8"-10 ,1/5" Travel/turn, 2 Start
15	#6-32 machine screws, 1-1/4" length
18	#6 washers
1	Anti-backlash nut, 3/8-10, 2 Start
2	Bearings 3/8" (inner diameter) x 7/8" (outer diameter)
1	Collar 3/8"
1	Motor couple (3/8" to lead screw and 1/4" to motor)
4	3/16" V-groove bearings
4	#10 machine screws, 1-1/2" length

#	Hardware
8	#10 washers
8	#10 nuts
8	2" machine screws, 1/4" diameter
4	NEMA 23 stepper motors (with wires already attached)
4	4" x 1/4" machine screws
4	3-1/2" x 1/4" machine screws
6	Bearings (1/4" inner diameter)
2	Belt pulleys
2	Belts
1	Motor collar
1	Motor mating piece
2	Threaded rod, 13" length x 1/4" diameter
4	#8-32 Machine screws, 1-1/4" length
2	Metal brackets (aka, "mending plates," Home Depot part# 339-482)
8	#8-32 washers
1	Mark-5 extruder kit from MakerBot
1	Ceramic tape, 9"
1	Kapton tape
1	Thermocouple
2	•0-guage stranded wire, 12" (preferably in two colors)
n/a	Shrink tubing
1	5/16" bearing

Continued

#	Hardware
1	5/16" x 1" hex head bolt
1	5/16" nut
1	Tube clamp (approx 1-1/2" diameter)
1	Zip tie
1	Serrated collar
1	Heat sink for feed cylinder on extruder
1	Arduino mega
1	MakerBot motherboard (book using v2.4)
4	Stepper motor drivers (book using v3.3)
1	Extruder controller (book using v3.5)
30	Nylon spacers, 1/4" long x 1/4" outer diameter x .14" inner diameter
24	#4 x ¾" flat head Phillips wood screw
3' minimum	Data cable, minimum 3' length, (multi-color recommended), minimum of six wire strands per cable
8	6-wire connectors (these come with the stepper motor drivers from Makerbot.com)
1	RS-485 cable (a standard Ethernet pass-through cable will work), 2-3' length minimum

APPENDIX B

∎∎∎

Converting to a CNC Machine

If you've got your 3D printer working properly, you might be interested to know that it can be converted from printing plastic (using the Extruder) to cutting, drilling, or milling – the same functionality provided by a standard CNC machine. You will be limited to using a handheld rotary tool, such as a Dremel 200 or 300 series or their newest cordless versions (www.dremel.com), but for cutting, drilling, and milling soft metals, wood, and plastic, you'll find your 3D printer can easily serve as a mini-CNC machine.

To make this happen, you'll need to cut a few additional pieces of plywood to make a special holder for the rotary tool. Visit www.buildyourtools.com and look for the PDF building plans for whiteAnt rev1.3-Dremel Bottom Mount (WA-160-S).pdf and whiteAnt rev1.3-Dremel Top Mount (WA-150-S).pdf. These are the extra PDF building instructions that will provide for the mounting of a rotary tool, and you can find complete instructions for putting it all together on the website as well. Figure B-1 shows a drawing of how the conversion will look with the rotary tool swapped out for the Extruder.

Figure B-1. *The 3D printer converted to use a rotary tool*

Resources

This appendix provides a list of resources related to 3D printing. This is by no means a comprehensive list – new websites and organizations related to this technology are appearing constantly.

Please always check the book's forum at www.buildyourtools.com for new resources related to 3D printers, including new sources for electronics, filament, and other items related to maintaining your printer.

BuildYourCNC.com Website Resources:

- Bearings: http://buildyourcnc.com/bearingsproducts.aspx

- Electronics (Patrick's version of the Gen4 electronics will be available shortly): http://buildyourcnc.com/electronicscombo.aspx

- Shaft Couplings: http://buildyourcnc.com/couplings.aspx

- Mechanicals (will include the timing belts and drive pulleys soon): http://buildyourcnc.com/CNCMachineMechanicalParts.aspx

CNC variation of whiteAnt:

- Very important wiring videos: http://buildyourcnc.com/CNCElectronicsandWiring.aspx

- Dremel tool and accessories: www.dremel.com/Pages/default.aspx

- Dremel mounts based on the Dremel 300 series: www.dremel.com/en-us/Tools/Pages/ToolDetail.aspx?pid=300+Series

Hardware

- MakerGear ((`http://makergear.com`): Makes and sells lots of useful hardware and kits for DIY 3D printing projects

- Ultimachine (`http://ultimachine.com`): A great source of plastics and other 3D printing electronics and hardware

- MakerBot (`www.makerbot.com`): sells the Thing-O-Matic, a popular 3DP kit, along with electronics, filament, upgrades for your machine, and more. (Much of the electronics used in the whiteAnt in this book was purchased from MakerBot.)

- RepRap (`www.reprap.org`): An open source, DIY 3D printer website that provides instructions for building the RepRap 3D printer

- McMaster-Carr (`www.mcmaster.com`): A good resource for machine screws, motor collars, nuts and bolts, and other hardware

Software

- `http://tinkercad.com`: Very easy-to-use, simple, but powerful web-based 3D modeling

- `http://sketchup.google.com`: Easy modeling (requires STL plugin `www.guitar-list.com/download-software/convert-sketchup-skp-files-dxf-or-stl`)

- `www.openscad.org/ore`: Advanced modeling

- `www.blender.org`: Very advanced modeling

- `http://meshlab.sourceforge.net`: Advanced model cleanup and modification tool

- `www.pleasantsoftware.com/developer/pleasant3d/index.shtml`: ESSENTIAL software if you use OSX

- `http://meshmixer.com`: Makes it "easy" to mix and mash up models in interesting ways

- `http://my3dscanner.com`: Take pictures of things and have them turned into 3D objects (requires skill with meshlab and/or blender)

- `http://cloudscad.com`: Under development; my website that will one day allow people to write and share openscad object

Content

- `www.thingiverse.com`: Really *the* source for 3D printable objects

- `http://reprap.org/wiki/The_RepRap_Object_Library`: Hopefully one day have a better selecting, but pales in comparison to thingiverse

Other Resources

- `http://tonybuser.com`: Musings and creations from tech editor, Tony Buser.
- `http://3dprinterforum.org/`
- `http://reprap.org/wiki/Mailing_Lists`

Index

lead wires and extension wires soldered to, 252–254

screwing nozzle into, 242

wrapping with Kapton tape, 265

HEATER screw terminals, 314

High Density Overlay (HDO), 36

hinges

Extruder Bearing 1, 63–65

attaching, 268–270

Part P, 135–139

Extruder Bearing 2, 65–67

attaching, 268–270

Part Q, 139–144

holes, counterbore, 20–26

homing, printer, 383–386

Homing menu, Control Panel, 383

hose clamp, for attaching Extruder to filament feeding mechanism, 278–280

HRS12 version, Simpson Strong-Tie, 90

I

Incra rulers, 19, 31–32

ink jet printers, 1

Instructables web site, 240

instructions for building 3D printers, 4–5

J

Java, required software, 353–354

jigsaw. *See* bandsaw

Jog controls, Control Panel, 379–380

K

Kapton tape

modifying Extruder to bolt to metal mounting base, 401–404

wrapping ceramic tape with, 263–264

wrapping heater core assembly with, 265

wrapping thermocouple with, 257

Kelly, Darrell, 4, 256

Kelly, James Floyd, 4

L

labeling parts, 33–34, 37

laser printers, 1

layering method, printing, 2

lead screws, Z-Axis, 190, 197

leads, power resistor, soldering wires between, 250–254

limit switches (endstops), 383

connecting cables, 349

wiring, 339–348

logos, whiteAnt, 396–397

CPSIA information can be obtained at www.ICGtesting.com
Printed in the USA
244392LV00003B/75/P

9 781430 234432